WE ARE
NOT HERE
TO BE
BYSTANDERS

WE ARE NOT HERE TO BE BYSTANDERS

A Memoir of LOVE *and* RESISTANCE

LINDA SARSOUR

37INK

SIMON & SCHUSTER

New York   London   Toronto   Sydney   New Delhi

37INK

SIMON &
SCHUSTER

An Imprint of Simon & Schuster, Inc.
1230 Avenue of the Americas
New York, NY 10020

First 37Ink/Simon & Schuster hardcover edition March 2020

37Ink /SIMON & SCHUSTER and colophon are trademarks of Simon & Schuster, Inc.

For information about special discounts for bulk purchases, please contact Simon &
Schuster Special Sales at 1-866-506-1949 or business@simonandschuster.com.

The Simon & Schuster Speakers Bureau can bring authors to your live event. For
more information or to book an event, contact the Simon & Schuster Speakers
Bureau at 1-866-248-3049 or visit our website at www.simonspeakers.com.

Interior design by Jill Putorti

Manufactured in the United States of America

10 9 8 7 6 5 4 3 2

Library of Congress Cataloging-in-Publication Data has been applied for.

ISBN 978-1-9821-0516-7
ISBN 978-1-9821-0518-1 (ebook)

*For Basemah Atweh
and those who fight with
every breath, as she did.*

*For my family, my reason,
the ones who have my back
and hold my heart, always.*

What are the tyrannies you swallow day by day and attempt to make your own, until you will sicken and die of them, still in silence? . . . The fact that we are here and that I speak these words is an attempt to break that silence and bridge some of those differences between us, for it is not difference which immobilizes us, but silence. And there are so many silences to be broken.

—Audre Lorde,
author and revolutionary feminist

Contents

Foreword Purpose and Grace, by Harry Belafonte   xi

Introduction What Is Your Jihad?   1

Part One
Homegirl

One   The Choice I Made   13

Two   El Bireh to Brooklyn   21

Three   Broken Windows   36

Four   Sitty Halima's Wish   50

Five   Everything Changed   59

Six   Our Sons Are Not Terrorists   68

Seven   Basemah, Beloved   80

Part Two
Intersectionality

Eight   Breath and Memory   93

Nine   Lessons in Activism   101

Ten   The Pit Stop   110

Eleven   A Tale of Two Mosques   118

CONTENTS

Twelve   Love Letter   127

Thirteen   Rakers and Spies   136

Fourteen   Your Fight Is My Fight   147

Part Three
The Sisterhood

Fifteen   Social Justice Voltron   157

Sixteen   Nine Days in April   167

Seventeen   Road Warriors   178

Eighteen   Silence Will Not Protect You   190

Nineteen   The Women Who Marched   197

Twenty   Stand with the Dreamers   214

Twenty-One   We Are Not Here to Be Bystanders   223

Epilogue   Love Is Not Done   233

Acknowledgments   241

Notes   245

Purpose and Grace

by Harry Belafonte

As my good friend Martin once said, "We've got some difficult days ahead, but it really doesn't matter with me now, because I've been to the mountaintop . . . I've seen the Promised Land. I may not get there with you. But I want you to know tonight, that we, as a people, will get to the Promised Land."

That quote, spoken by Dr. King less than twenty-four hours before he was assassinated, resonates with me deeply as I contemplate my affection for Linda Sarsour. I have been aware of this tremendous young woman for several years now. I find her to be bold and brilliant and unexpected—a combination of qualities that inspire me. When Linda first crossed my threshold, brought into my midst by Carmen Perez, who runs my social justice organization the Gathering for Justice, I was immediately drawn to her. Quite the spitfire she was, unapologetic and strong. I saw in her a burning fire, and she drew me in. I watched her and her comrades shift the ground and make waves and stop the machine. I delighted in their tenacity, their bold vision for Black and brown liberation, and their radical approach to movement work.

I am no stranger to movement work. It is grueling and gut-wrenching and absolutely necessary. I was twenty-five years old when I met Martin and the folks of the Student Nonviolent Coordinating Committee, or SNCC. Martin was twenty-two. There was an undeniable urgency to his message, and his principles of nonviolence fueled the work. While we may not have made it to the Promised Land, my peers and I, my brothers and sisters in liberation can rest easy knowing that the future is in the hands of leaders like Linda Sarsour. I have often said to Linda that she embodies the principle and purpose of another great Muslim leader, brother Malcolm X, who said, "If you're not ready to die for it, put the word 'freedom' out of your vocabulary."

And that's another thing about movement work—the sacrifice, the personal assaults, the violence. It wasn't that long ago we lost Martin and Malcolm and Bobby. We lost so many more to assassins' bullets, to lynching. When I read the vitriol and vilification directed at Linda and her sisters of the Women's March, I recognize the despair, the isolation, the fear. I also recognize the strength it takes to rise each new day and face an uncertain and dangerous world. We cannot allow the forces of oppression and evil to divide our precious movement. And we cannot sit idly by while these forces try to rewrite our history and co-opt our narratives of peace and justice and equity. We have to celebrate women like Linda and her comrades now, and not allow the ravages of time to silence our sung praises.

I may not make it to the Promised Land with you, but we will get there. I know this because I know Linda Sarsour and I have witnessed her passion, commitment, and determination. This generation of activists and organizers, they're getting it right. They are building the beloved community with radical intention. And that's all I could hope for our world. How wonderful that you all have the opportunity to read this fine book, and to experience Linda's grace. We are all richer for it.

February 21, 2019
New York City

WE ARE
NOT HERE
TO BE
BYSTANDERS

What Is Your Jihad?

In one of my favorite stories from the Hadith, a man asks the beloved Prophet Muhammad: "What is the best form of jihad?" I have always loved the Prophet's answer: "A word of truth in front of a tyrant ruler or leader, that is the best form of jihad." For me, this call to peaceful yet courageous action expresses our highest human responsibility—to care for one another by showing up and speaking out for the voiceless among us. It's a call that I believe is especially crucial in these times.

I shared this story when I gave a keynote address at the Islamic Society of North America's fifty-fourth annual convention in Chicago in July 2017. After recounting for the audience the words of our beloved Prophet (may peace be upon him), I went on to observe that in standing against oppression in our communities, "we are struggling against tyrants and rulers not only abroad in the Middle East or on the other side of the world, but here in these United States of America, where you have fascists and white supremacists and Islamophobes reigning in the White House."

As a Palestinian American woman addressing a hotel ballroom full of fellow Muslims, all of whom understood the context and meaning of the story I told, I wasn't trying to be provocative. Standing at that podium, I could sense that my words were resonating, that I was giving the right message to the right people at the right time. The feeling in that room was galvanizing. Speaking truth to power? *Yes.*

I flew home to Brooklyn the next morning, looking forward to a short hiking trip in Cold Spring, New York, that I planned to take with my three teenage children and my nephew. The following Tuesday was July 4, and I observed our country's birthday with my extended family, sharing a meal together just like countless other families across America. I finally fell into bed past midnight, putting my cell on *do not disturb* because texts from a group chat about a local political campaign I was working on kept pinging my phone. *I'll catch up in the morning*, I thought.

Five hours later I opened my eyes, blinking against the sunlight streaming into my room. The house was quiet, my kids still asleep. I would need to wake them soon, as they all had places to be that morning. I reached for my phone to check the time, and my heart stopped. More than a hundred text messages awaited me, and my WhatsApp and Facebook feeds were blowing up, too. I knew at once that something bad had happened. I feared one of our elders had died.

I started scrolling through the text messages:

"Sister Linda, are you okay?"

"Do you need anything?"

"We love you, Linda, stay strong."

"We got you, Sister Linda. We're proud of you."

Now I knew that I was the source of everyone's concern, but I still didn't have any idea why. So I did the next logical thing—took myself to Twitter to see what was going on. That's when I got the shock of my life. There was my picture right at the top of the trending topics screen. Emblazoned across my face was a caption that claimed I had called for a holy war against the president of the United States.

I tried to stand, but my knees buckled. It was as if I'd been punched in the gut. Sitting on the edge of my bed, my face in my hands, I tried to absorb the lunacy of that Twitter topic. My head was still spinning as I roused my kids and saw them out of the house. After they left, I crawled back into bed, wondering if I should have told them what was unfolding. Social media–savvy teens that they were, they'd find out for themselves soon enough. Maybe I should have reassured them first. As I lay there pondering what to do next, the thought that my children might be going through their day worried about my safety was almost the worst part. "I have a 33. caliber pill that'll help ya sleep you nasty beasty" was typical of the comments rolling up my timeline. Most were infinitely more violent than that, and viciously profane.

My mind kept circling the possibility that I was now a danger to my family. Even walking down the street beside my children could put them in harm's way—and all because a notorious right-wing media outlet had taken references to jihad from my speech the previous weekend and posted them out of context. Onstage, I could be fiery and confrontational, but the clips of me on Twitter had been edited and spliced with the specific intent to inflame Islamophobes, to fan the stereotype of Muslims as terrorists. Indeed, the usual alt-right suspects were out in force, as so-called true patriots posted threats on social media to rape my daughters, hang me for treason, and assassinate me on sight. LINDA SARSOUR CALLS FOR "JIHAD" AGAINST TRUMP ADMINISTRATION, blared the conservative mouthpiece Breitbart News. Even the president's older son poured oil on the flame: "Who in the @DNC will denounce this activist and democrat leader calling for Jihad again [*sic*] Trump?" he tweeted, ensuring that every major news outlet in the country would soon enter the fray.

———

As the executive director of the Arab American Association of New York, I'd joined with three powerful women to cochair the hugely successful Women's March for human rights the previous January. Since then, I'd become used to people accusing me of being anti-Semitic, saying I want to impose sharia law on America and that I am a terror-ist sympathizer. As you read this book, you'll come to understand that none of this is true, and yet deep-pocketed conservatives have spent millions trying to defame and discredit me. I take their efforts as evi-dence that my social justice activism is working. As author and feminist bell hooks observed, "Sometimes people try to destroy you, precisely because they recognize your power—not because they don't see it, but because they see it and they don't want it to exist."[1]

I wasn't about to fold and go away just because some right-wing extremists didn't like me or felt threatened by my effectiveness as an organizer. But this tweetstorm over my use of the word *jihad* was a new level of hell. Perhaps the most maddening aspect of the whole uproar was that every single one of those vile comments on Twit-ter completely misconstrued the meaning of the Arabic word, which translates simply as "struggle" or "to strive." While the concept of jihad has lately been co-opted to refer to the military defense of Islam, in fact, for most Muslims the word denotes a deeply spiritual and nonviolent desire to live one's faith and become a more loving person in the eyes of God.

At some point, I forced myself to get dressed and began returning phone calls, assuring people that I was weathering the storm. Though I was profoundly shaken, I was determined to present a public demeanor of fortitude. I now had an important decision to make. I could do noth-ing, stay away from social media for a couple of weeks and let the frenzy run its course; I could put out a carefully worded statement, essentially apologizing for using a word many people outside the Muslim faith found controversial; or I could double down.

I doubled down.

"Buckle up," I told family and friends, "because it's going to be jihad, jihad, jihad with me for the next few days."

Many people tried to convince me to walk the middle ground by crafting a conciliatory press release. "We just want you to be safe," they said. "You have to be careful, Sister Linda. You know how crazy some people are." I loved them for having my back, but at the same time, I couldn't help thinking: *Look how scared our people are.* Don't get me wrong. I was scared, too, especially after I discovered I'd been doxed, with my home address and my parents' home address posted online. But I also truly believe that the minute we allow fear to govern our actions, we have lost. And so, when a reporter from the *Washington Post* reached out to me the next morning, I told him I wanted to write an op-ed explaining my position.

"Go ahead and send us something," he encouraged me. I got to work right away, enlisting the help of my friend Deepa Iyer, to come up with a coherent draft. As we worked on my editorial over the next couple of days, a shaft of light broke through: A BuzzFeed News reporter named Chris Geidner had found the original tape of my speech. He took it upon himself to transcribe the entire recording, and posted a screenshot of it on Twitter. "Hey you people scare-sharing Linda Sarsour's speech, read this transcription, which I just made because you all are trash misquoting her,"[2] he tweeted. In a matter of hours, the transcript of my speech went viral, and soon there were as many people applauding what I'd said as there were criticizing me.

Amid this unexpected groundswell of support, my editorial ran the following Sunday under the headline ISLAMOPHOBES ARE ATTACKING ME BECAUSE I'M THEIR WORST NIGHTMARE. "In my speech . . . I sent not a call to violence, but a call to speak truth to power and to commit to the struggle for racial and economic justice," I wrote. "My statements were clear, and my activism track record is even clearer: My work has always been rooted in nonviolence as espoused by the Rev. Martin Luther King Jr."[3]

I went on to explain how Muslims understand the word *jihad*, pointing out that every person alive engages in jihad every single day; whether reaching for harmony in a relationship or success in a particular endeavor, the nature of being human is "to strive." And what was my jihad? My commitment to fighting for the rights of all marginalized people and against the Muslim and refugee bans being called for by the current president. "My views are not unique or special, and many activists around the country express them as well," I pointed out. "Indeed, those targeting me have an even broader agenda: to silence and discredit racial-justice activists altogether because we are awakening the masses."[4]

In the days after my op-ed appeared, an extraordinary thing happened. Media outlets everywhere ran stories on the true meaning of *jihad*. They interviewed Muslim academics and spiritual leaders who defended our right to interpret the idea as the beloved Prophet Muhammad had framed it—as a quest for human dignity and global peace. And then all across social media, Muslims began freely claiming the word. Using the hashtags #WhatIsYourJihad? and #MyJihad, people shared the most beautiful expressions of the concept.

"What's #YourJihad? Maybe it's working for an America for All. Maybe it's just loving your kids," one mother posted.

"#MyJihad is not letting Islamophobes or terrorists hijack its meaning," an Islamic scholar added.

Even non-Muslims were joining the chorus. As one man who called himself Jihadi Jew wrote: "#MyJihad is to live today as if I am a new creation, to shake off the heaviness of all the days that have gone before, to ignore the scary specter of all the days to come, to simply be in the present because yesterday is now already a dream and tomorrow another world entirely."

Scrolling through all the responses, I felt elated and vindicated. In refusing to back down, I'd taken one for the team. And in the end it was worth every threat, every vitriolic message, and every stomachache to see people all over the country, and indeed the globe, embracing a word that had been so misunderstood and maligned. At the height of the firestorm, the malevolence and hatred people spewed at me on social media had astounded me, but it had led to a national conversation in which Muslims fearlessly and vocally proclaimed a core tenet of our faith. In the end, the call to love had won.

Why am I telling you this story? Because it helps to explain why I decided to write this book. More than a memoir of my three-plus decades on this earth, my narrative is a social justice manifesto, a rallying cry for every one of us to step forward and serve our country, embracing its rich diversity with open arms, insisting that our leaders respect the rights of *all* its citizens while behaving morally in the world. In this book, and in my life, I strive to follow the guidance that the beloved Prophet Muhammad laid out for us—to speak up for my people and for all people, to confront injustice in all its forms, and to challenge the dangerous misperceptions about who we are. In following this path, I refuse to be intimidated. I will not allow myself to be controlled by other people's fear of what they don't understand.

For the sake of my own mental health, I try not to engage with all the hate and venom that comes at me, but sometimes I simply have to jump in to affirm that I am not ashamed or afraid to be who I am—unapologetically Muslim American, unapologetically Palestinian American, and unapologetically from Brooklyn, New York. There are people who hate what I represent. I shatter every stereotype they have of Muslim women, whom they seem to believe should be submissive and subservient, unseen and unheard. I am seen everywhere and I make my voice a megaphone, speaking up for my people to those who would vilify and dehumanize us. I will not sit by and allow my people, your people, anyone's people to be vilified and dehumanized, because when hate goes uncontested for too long, atrocities happen, as the history of this very country has shown. And so I will keep organizing, building power, and speaking out against injustice, because that is my right and my charge, and because, in the face of hate, it is the ultimate expression of love.

When it comes to resisting oppression in our world, and especially in this political moment, women have a powerful role to play. Already we have begun to step forward in droves: when millions of us turned out to the Women's March on the day after the new president's inauguration in January 2017—the largest protest against tyranny, injustice, and patriarchy that the nation had ever seen—we demonstrated that we can be an unstoppable force for good. Since then, women and other marginalized people have electrified the political sphere, with more of us running for office than ever before, and brand-new organizational structures, including reimagined approaches to campaign financing, being put in place to support the cause.

Now more than ever, we must resist the temptation to hide our light, bide our time, to make ourselves appear less formidable than we are. If you ever ask yourself, *Should I not share the position I hold on this lightning-rod issue? Should I shrink myself in certain rooms where my voice is not welcomed? Should I appear less Palestinian, less Latina, less Black today?* Always, the answer is no. We must never negotiate away or compromise our principles and values. Instead we must bring all our complex identities to the table, transforming those spaces in which any part of who we are is not welcomed, because our country's future—and the world our children will inherit—depends on our courage and commitment now.

I want everyone who reads this book to walk away understanding that the path to change lies in building coalitions across marginalized communities—not just among Muslims, but also women, immigrants and the undocumented, Black Lives Matter advocates, supporters of LGBTQ rights, people with disabilities, the elderly, poor people, everyone struggling for equal treatment under the law. We must recognize that unity is not uniformity. Rather, it is the key to our very survival. If we are able to bring all oppressed communities together inside one tent, and bring all of our allies with us into that tent, our collective will vastly outnumber the opposition.

Once we grasp that we are not actually outnumbered, we will no longer be out-organized by those who seek to divide us by provoking tribal animosities. Instead, we will join together to become this nation's unshakable moral compass. Let us therefore stand shoulder to shoulder and keep our voices loud, remembering always that fear is a choice—and so is freedom. We are the majority, and we must become the conscience of this country, its true north, knowing that when we resist injustice against any of us, we advance the cause of justice for all of us.

Look around you, my sisters and brothers. We are each other's greatest hope, the beating heart of a nation. *We* are what democracy looks like.

Part One

Homegirl

*The passion to change the world flickers in you like a flame,
and if you let that light go out, you will be robbing the world of
your greatest gift. Your task today is not to know what the future
holds; your task is to vow to protect that flame.*

—Valarie Kaur,
founder of the Revolutionary Love Project

Chapter 1

The Choice I Made

My name is Linda. I'm from Brooklyn. Don't mess with Brooklyn."

You only have to hear me talk to know I'm a Brooklyn homegirl born and raised. Still, I get a secret thrill when I introduce myself that way, confident that the other essential part of who I am, an American Muslim woman, is already known. It's visible in the way I present myself, in the garments I wear out in the world. There is the *before* in my life as an activist and there is the *after*, and the day that I put on my first hijab was the beginning of my after.

I had just turned nineteen. It was a chilly Saturday morning in April 1999. One of my mother's friends had just returned from Mecca, where she had performed the hajj, a pilgrimage that all Muslims who are able are required to undertake at least once in their lifetimes. Every year, Muslim women make the annual trip to Islam's holiest city for the religious experience, but truth be told, a lot of them also go for the shopping. My mother's friend, whom we called Um Sharif (meaning "mother of Sharif") as a sign of respect, was no exception. When the devotional rituals were done, some of the world's most exquisite abayas and modest dresses could be found in the shops in and around Mecca. And so a few days after Um Sharif returned home to Brooklyn, she visited my mother lugging an overstuffed suitcase. She set the case down in the middle of our living room floor and unzipped it. A riot of color spilled everywhere.

"You get to pick whatever you want," Um Sharif announced to my mother.

Yumma immediately called all her daughters to gather around, including me. Already married for more than a year and living with my husband in Bay Ridge, Brooklyn, I happened to be at my parents' house in neighboring Sunset Park that morning. The oldest of seven—five girls followed by two boys—I was several months pregnant with my first child, and was in college studying to become a high school English teacher. My sisters, Lena, Heeba, Hanady, and Hela, who ranged in age from sixteen to twelve, all still lived at home, along with our brothers, DJ, almost nine, and Mo, who at almost eight was the youngest. That I was with them at the house when Um Sharif arrived was no surprise. I stopped by to see my family most days. Yumma, my sisters, and I crowded around the open suitcase, talking eagerly as we riffled through the piles of beautifully sewn garments, luxuriously woven scarves, velvety sticks of black kohl, and assorted hijabs, the traditional Muslim woman's head covering.

"Ooooh, Heeba, that would look so good on you," Um Sharif cooed encouragingly as my fifteen-year-old sister held a long ocean-blue abaya with gauzy sleeves against her jeans and faded yellow T-shirt. Heeba struck a pose in front of the full-length hall mirror, turning this way and that, considering. Yumma was at her shoulder, one hand tracing the brightly colored embroidery that adorned the sleeve.

"Just beautiful," she agreed.

No one noticed me as I picked up a black two-piece hijab and slipped it over my dark, shoulder-length hair. I smoothed wayward strands under the headband and walked over to the mirror, standing on tiptoe behind my mother and sister to see myself. "What do you think?" I asked them. Everyone turned my way, and the voices around me hushed one by one. My mother and Heeba moved aside to allow me an unobstructed view of myself. Yumma reached out and adjusted the soft black cloth gently, then touched my cheek. "It suits you, *habibti*," she whispered, as if loath to disturb the unexpected reverence of the moment.

I could tell she sensed the emotion welling up inside her oldest daughter. My sisters, watching me silently, recognized it, too, because gazing into the gilt-edged mirror, I felt as if I was truly seeing myself for the first time. A young Muslim woman stared back at me, her chin lifted high, dark kohl-lined eyes alive with interest, and something more. For the first time in my nineteen years, I appeared to the world as exactly what I was, unapologetically Muslim. I remember placing a palm over the mound of my belly and thinking simply: *This is it*. Three small words, yet they held a lifetime of searching.

Before I offered the world a visible sign, no one ever guessed what I was. When people saw me, with my light skin and straight black hair, and heard my heavy Brooklyn accent, they assumed I was Puerto Rican, or Dominican, or maybe Italian. My name didn't help. It wasn't like I was called Fatima Muhammad, which might have clued people in that I was Muslim. Linda Sarsour could have been anything.

When I told the kids at my public school that my family was from Palestine, the response was always the same.

"Palestine? Where's that?" they'd ask, brows wrinkling.

"It's all the way on the other side of the world, in a place called the Middle East," I would explain in a patient and reasonable voice, though inside I was churning with frustration and just wanted to disappear. "It's right near Syria and Jordan." I would continue, "It's the Holy Land, where Jesus was born." I was always trying to add more explanations, always trying to prove my national and cultural origins.

One day in eighth grade, our social studies teacher divided the class into groups to do research projects on different countries. My group was assigned Australia, and we planned to do a poster board with maps and facts about that continent. There were four of us at our table: me;

an African American boy named Jalal, who was the class joker; a Haitian American girl named Chantal, who was one of my best friends; and a kid named Carlos, whom I didn't know very well. He had coppery brown skin and shiny black hair, and he'd joined our class just that year.

"Hey, Carlos," I said as I positioned tracing paper over a page in an atlas and began to draw the outline of Australia. "Where's your family from?" I was just trying to make friendly conversation.

"My mom's Puerto Rican and my dad's Dominican," he said.

Jalal piped up. "Hey, Linda, where's *your* family from?"

"We're from Palestine," I said, bracing for what I knew came next.

"Palestine?" Jalal said. "What's that?"

I went into my usual explanation—the Middle East, the Holy Land, where Jesus walked, the whole nine. Jalal, Chantal, and Carlos were looking at me in a curious way. I knew without asking that none of them had ever heard of my family's homeland before I said its name. Then Jalal, who had a lively, bubbly personality, jumped up from his chair and stood in front of a huge map of the world that hung on the wall right next to our table. He peered at the map, his fingers traveling over mountains and oceans and coming to rest over the Middle East.

"Where's Palestine at?" he said. He stabbed the map with his fingers. "I see Syria," he said, now in full-on jokester mode. "I see Jordan and Israel, but I don't see no Palestine here. Where do you see Palestine?"

He was right. Palestine was *not* on the map.

I sighed and went back to tracing the coastline of Australia.

But Jalal wouldn't let it go.

"Hey, Linda, I don't see no Palestine on this map. You sure you're really from there? How come I never heard of it?"

"You know, there was a war, and a lot of problems happened there," I mumbled, a sinking feeling in my midsection. And then I just decided I was not going to go down this road again. Not today. Jalal clearly didn't understand how deep this went for me, how much his teasing interrogation hurt. I knew he wasn't trying to be mean. He just thought he was being funny. He was even chuckling, trying out comedic voices as he kept repeating, "Where you see Palestine at? I don't see no Palestine. Why they leave your country off this map, Linda?" His playful questions filled me with shame. I was embarrassed that I couldn't show I was from Palestine, or that such a place even existed.

If you're Black in America, you visibly belong to a particular group. Granted, being Black in this country comes with great risk, but you can claim your culture with pride, and no one questions you. But me, I was so ambiguous I felt almost invisible. Maybe if my parents hadn't grounded me so firmly in my Palestinian identity, if I hadn't spent summers with my grandparents and cousins back in their hometown of El Bireh in the West Bank, it wouldn't have bothered me so much that no one outside my Muslim community really understood where we were from. At thirteen years old, I knew our whole story, but how do you take someone, especially a middle school kid, down a path of military occupation to explain why he's never heard of your country? How do you tell an eighth grader that the reason he never read about your homeland in the school's history books is because your people's land was stolen in a war in 1948, the year your father was born, the same year Israel declared independence and expelled 750,000 Palestinians from their homes, barring them from returning?

"I don't know, Jalal," I said finally. "Why don't you go ask the teacher?"

Something flickered across Jalal's face, as if he was starting to catch on that I didn't find any of this amusing. I hunched over the table and began to color in my map of Australia with hard, furious crayon strokes. Chantal moved beside me to help me color. Jalal now seemed lost in studying the red-inked borders of the Middle East on the wall map next to us. From the corner of my eye, I caught Carlos watching me, his face scrunched into a frown. I wondered if he thought I was lying. Why did that make me feel so shattered?

———

"Linda, you look beautiful in this, but are you sure?"

My mother and I stood admiring my reflection in the hall mirror, me in my brand-new hijab. "Yumma, I'm sure," I said.

"But I want you to really think about it," she insisted. "It's not a good idea to start wearing the hijab and then take it off. People will think it was forced on you, and that maybe you decided to push back and stop wearing it. Everyone knows you have a strong mind. You don't want people gossiping and making up stories about you."

I took Yumma's hands in mine, feeling tender at her concern. "I'm going to wear it home today and go from there," I told her, but I already knew this wasn't a light dalliance for me. Still, I understood my mother, who had begun wearing a hijab herself just ten years before. It had been her choice, made at a time when her faith was growing deeper, and her attendance at mosque on Friday afternoons was becoming more regular. My father never expressed an opinion on the matter; Yaba would never have forced the decision on Yumma in any way. Whatever my mother wanted for herself had always been fine with him. Now my mother wanted to be sure that my own decision to start wearing a hijab was my choice alone, and that I was making it freely, without pressure from anyone. Yumma need not have worried about me. I hadn't known it consciously until this moment, but now I realized that I'd made the decision to one day wear a hijab the morning in eighth grade when Jalal asked me about Palestine.

That Saturday, I wore my hijab out onto the street for the first time, feeling a quiet excitement that everyone who saw me now knew exactly what I was, who I was, and could guess the broad outlines of my story. From that day forward, I have continued to wear a hijab in public, everything from plain black, gray, or navy blue slip-ons, to the leopard-print head coverings that were my signature for a while, to the simple, brightly colored hijabs for which I am recognized today.

Of course, it makes all the difference that I was able to *choose* this outward expression of my culture and my faith. I believe deeply that for a Muslim woman, the hijab should be a personal choice. Some of us veil ourselves in observance of the principles of modesty set down in the Qur'an, and as a statement of our devotion to God. Others wear hijabs as a way to publicly declare our cultural identity, in solidarity with our countries of origin and all those who follow Islam. Still others go bare-headed, preferring to express our faith and Muslim identity in ways that are not defined by clothing.

None of my four sisters covers her hair, and that doesn't make them any more or less Muslim than I am. Yet many people in this country have the idea that the hijab is a sign of my oppression. They argue that I'm covering my body because of some sort of patriarchal instruction; that somehow I'm not at liberty to choose this on my own. This notion that a hijab symbolizes Muslim women's submission is embedded in Western feminism. Committed opponents of hijabs are often intensely well intentioned, yet their insistence on telling me what is and isn't acceptable for me to wear strips me of my self-determination, in much the same way that Muslim dictatorships rob women of the right to freely choose.

In Iran, for example, ruling ayatollahs decree women must cover their hair, and those who don't comply are punished. One woman who dared to remove her hijab in public protest was sentenced to two years in prison and eighteen years of probation.[1] But then in France we have the other extreme, with officials deciding that Muslim women who cover their hair have been forced to do so. They assume these women have no agency in the matter, and that's a form of oppressive thinking, too. I'm caught in the middle, outraged by Islamic dictatorships that force the hijab on women, yet also outraged at supposedly liberal societies like France, which forbids women to wear hijabs at public schools or in public-sector jobs, and allows workplaces to ban headscarves as well.

The way I see it, whether we decide to wear a bikini or a burkini—a long-sleeved bathing suit—at the beach all women should have sovereignty over our bodies. So I was clear-eyed as I assured Yumma that I didn't put on a hijab because someone else wanted me to do so. My husband and the rest of my family really didn't mind one way or the other, nor had anyone else tried to compel me. Instead, surrounded by my mother and sisters on an ordinary Saturday in my native Brooklyn, I freely chose. All my life I had yearned for a visible identity in the world, and that morning, seeing my reflection in the hallway mirror, I had found it at last. That was the day I began to feel whole.

Chapter 2

El Bireh to Brooklyn

On the morning I was born, my father was overjoyed, but my mother was worried. Yumma had wished for a boy, because her own mother back in El Bireh, on the West Bank of Palestine, had planted the idea that a wife's first duty was to give her husband a son. My grandmother, Sitty Sarah, reminded her newly married daughter that Arab men dream of the day they will be called Abu ("father of") followed by the name of their boy child. So when news reached Palestine that I was a girl, Sitty Sarah called at once, urging Yumma to waste no time in trying again. "Men will take another wife if the first one doesn't give them a boy," she warned. Yumma trusted that even though Allah allowed a man up to four wives, my father was not of that mind-set. And yet Sitty Sarah's words weighed on her, complicating her excitement at my birth.

My mother knew better than to voice her unease, because Yaba was so clearly euphoric at my arrival. From that day on, he introduced himself as Abu Linda. Even when a son was born, ten years and four more daughters later, our father still answered proudly to my name. And when he bought and opened his own bodega in a predominantly Black and Latinx section of Brooklyn when I was four, he announced the store would be called Linda Sarsour's Spanish & American Food Center. Over Turkish coffee on the front steps of our house, his friends tried to persuade him to wait until he had a boy and could put his son's name on the bright new yellow-and-red awning, but Yaba didn't see their reasoning. "Why should I wait?" he said. "Linda is everything to me. Why shouldn't I celebrate her as I would a boy?" Indeed, for the next thirty-five years, that bodega at the corner of Troy Avenue and Montgomery Street in Crown Heights would continue to bear my name.

When my mother tells this story now, Yaba's response surprises no one. My father always went his own way. The third of four boys born to a taxi driver and his wife in the village of El Bireh, he took his first breath just four months after Israel seized Palestinian lands and declared independence in the 1948 Arab-Israeli war. The West Bank, then under the control of Jordan, lay an hour north of the bitterly contested city of Jerusalem, which had been split into East and West, segregating Arabs and Jews. Perhaps because Palestinians were deep in mourning at the loss of their homeland, my father was given the name Nidal, which means "to struggle and fight in defense." And yet my father was a cheerful soul. Tall for his age and gangly, with a thick shock of black hair, he had an irrepressible sense of humor. Even the constant military skirmishes, with Israeli security forces pushing against the borders of the land now designated as Palestine, were no match for Yaba's booming laugh and tenacious optimism.

By the time Nidal was sixteen, young Arab men were being actively recruited by Jordan to help defend the West Bank. Yaba believed in the cause, but as the old saying goes, he was a lover, not a fighter—he wanted nothing to do with being a soldier. And so when his older brother Naji, who at the time was working in Kuwait, wrote to say he had a job for Nidal, my father stuffed a few clothes into a bag and boarded a bus to join his brother. It didn't go according to plan. Nidal disliked the job in a Laundromat that his brother had found for him, which barely paid enough to subsist on, and after two years he decided to go home. The journey back to El Bireh took him through Amman, the capital of Jordan. The year was 1966, and Nidal had just turned eighteen, the exact age at which young men were being conscripted into the Jordanian army. Jordan's military was bolstering its ranks in preparation for the coming war with Israel. Ironically, Yaba had gone to Kuwait to avoid having to serve in the army, but now he was summarily drafted and prevented from returning home.

The Six-Day War with Israel erupted a year later. By the time it ended, Israel had seized Gaza from Egypt and the West Bank from Jordan and, in violation of international law, began constructing settlements on the newly occupied land. Travel between Jordan and the West Bank was now restricted, requiring a raft of permissions and documents, and so Nidal stayed on in Amman after the war. He found a room with some other young men and talked his way into a job as a taxi driver, even though he didn't yet have an official license.

A few years later, my father, now in his midtwenties and getting by on his own in the capital, picked up a familiar-looking man. It was his older brother Nabeel.

"Nidal?" Nabeel said, grabbing Yaba's shoulder in disbelief. "Is that you?"

My father turned and hugged his brother happily, and demanded to be caught up on all the family news. He learned that Nabeel had married a Jordanian woman and now lived in Amman himself. Their younger brother Mohammad had also married. His wife was an American woman of Palestinian descent, and Mohammad had moved with her to New York City, where he was now an American citizen. Their oldest brother, Naji, was back in El Bireh with their parents. He, too, had found a wife, and he was the father of two sons. And then my uncle's face grew somber. "Our mother misses you, Nidal. Her heart has been broken with you gone for so long." And there was even worse news: their father was slowly sinking into a fog of dementia, and if Nidal didn't return soon, he might well not remember his third son.

My father took his brother's words to heart and applied for permission to visit the West Bank. He stayed there a month, reconnecting with his mother and father, who beamed with happiness to have him home. However, all the joy of being back with his parents didn't deter him from packing his bag again and traveling to the other side of the world when his brother Mohammad proposed that Nidal join him in America.

It was the midseventies: immigration to the United States from Arab countries was easier then. America didn't hate us yet. And as far as anyone in Palestine knew, America was the land of the free, where young men like my father could make a good life. Yaba's papers came through in 1976. He kissed his mother on both cheeks, hugged his father hard, and boarded a flight to New York, where a job working alongside his brother in a Brooklyn bodega was waiting for him.

———

My mother joined my father in Brooklyn three years later. Her own journey to America began the day her parents informed her they'd received inquiries about her from the family of a young Palestinian man who lived in the United States, and asked if she would meet him and see whether she liked him well enough to marry.

My grandparents were eager to have their second daughter, Maha, make a good match, especially one that might offer her a safer life in America. If they could get their younger daughter away from the persistent threat of war, then it might be worth it to send her so far away. As it was, they'd had to pull Maha out of high school when she was sixteen. A bright student, my mother wanted nothing more than to graduate, but her parents judged it too dangerous to let her continue. With regular protests happening in the streets, the chances of her getting arrested were too great. Often, students were simply traveling home from school and they'd get swept up and arrested with the crowd. Their parents would have to pay three thousand shekels, roughly the equivalent of $1,000, to get them released. My grandparents didn't have that kind of money. They were humble shepherds with six children, four boys younger than Maha and a girl older than my mother, who had married a Palestinian exile whose original village of

Lifta had been seized by Israelis during the war of 1948. Life had been a continuous struggle for my mother's family. Now, with an American expressing interest in marrying their second daughter, they hoped for a betrothal.

My father's mother, Sitty Halima, was the one who'd identified Maha as a possible wife for Nidal. Their two families often socialized at weddings and other communal gatherings. The village was small enough that Maha knew Yaba's brothers, but she'd never met the third son, as he'd been away in Jordan, and then Brooklyn, for most of her life. Nidal was eleven years older than Maha, who had just turned nineteen, but because her parents thought he might be a good husband, she agreed to meet him.

On my father's next trip home—travel to the West Bank was far easier to arrange from America than it was from Jordan—Sitty Sarah invited him to tea. Nidal and his parents would sit with Maha and her parents, and everyone would try to get a sense of whether a marriage between the two young people would work. On the afternoon of the tea, my mother arrived home from her job as a pill counter at a local pharmacy and bounded into the living room. Wearing a cropped khaki jacket and skinny jeans, she had let down her thick, glossy black hair, which fell long and loose around her shoulders.

Her mother gasped when she saw her. "Maha, you go and put on a dress right now," Sitty Sarah scolded. "You are meeting the man who might be your future husband. He can give you a prosperous life in America. You need to make a good impression."

My mother only laughed. "The American should see the real me," she countered. "I'm going to meet him in these jeans and if he wants to marry me, then what I'm wearing won't matter."

Maybe my grandmother felt relieved when Yaba walked in wearing bell-bottom pants with a big-buckled leather belt and a wide-collared floral shirt, the style in America in the seventies. In any case, my mother was right about one thing: my father didn't care one bit about the clothes she wore. Even though Maha was coy and reserved as they sipped their tea, her beauty hit Nidal like a lightning bolt, and he made no effort to hide how enthralled he was. My parents are both like that to this day: my dad's every emotion is plainly visible, while my mom is more inscrutable, and reveals herself slowly.

By the end of the afternoon, my father knew he'd found his bride. Since Yumma was agreeable, a dowry was given, and the two of them were married a week later in a wedding celebration with family and friends at one of El Bireh's many banquet halls.

Days later my father flew home to Brooklyn and began the process of sponsoring his new wife. She arrived in Brooklyn in early 1979, and they moved into a house he'd found for them in Sunset Park, home to one of the largest communities of Palestinian immigrants in New York. A year later, on March 19, 1980, I was born.

———————

My mother was pregnant almost every year for the next decade. By the time my youngest brother was born on May 15, 1991, our family had grown to nine. Yaba had never intended to have such a large brood, but my mother was determined to keep having children until she gave him a son. After the birth of their second daughter, Yaba announced, "Okay, this is good. We can stop now." But Yumma insisted on one more.

When a third and then a fourth daughter were born, Yaba declared, "We have four girls now. That is exactly enough. This is not Palestine, *habibti*. We live in an apartment, not on a farm."

"But we don't have a boy," Yumma said.

"I am content," my father told her. "I am rich beyond measure with my four daughters."

Of course, Yumma adored every one of her girls as much as Yaba did, but that didn't lessen her resolve to bring a son into the world. By the next year, my mother was once again expecting—another girl. Yumma sighed when Dr. Ahmad Jaber, the OB-GYN who delivered us all, asked what the child would be called. "I don't even know," she confessed. "I was so fixed on this one finally being a boy, I didn't even consider girls' names." And so Dr. Jaber chose my youngest sister's name. He called her Hela, which is "welcome" in Arabic. As he placed the infant in my mother's arms, he said gently, "Maha, we are going to welcome this child."

While my mother fretted about not bearing a son, my father was ecstatic every single time he brought her and the new baby home from the hospital. Seeing how excited and solicitous he was as he ushered them from the car, with the baby bag over one shoulder and a little red suitcase in his hand, our neighbors would swarm out of their houses, ready to welcome the long-awaited boy.

"No, no, no," Yaba would tell them happily, "we had another *arousa*"—another "little bride."

In a culture that venerates sons, Yaba's friends wondered what was wrong with him that he was so elated be the father of five little brides. Many years later, I would credit Yaba's beaming pride in his five daughters as my earliest instruction in feminism. I was already the executive director of the Arab American Association of New York and was actively working for the rights of Muslim women when it dawned on me that the equality of women had always been a given in our household. Even my mother, who kept having more children in the desire to give my father a son, relaxed into this truth as she witnessed Yaba's joy at the birth of each of his daughters, which was fully equal to his joy when, three years after the fifth girl, a son was born. A year later, right in the middle of my brother's one-year-old birthday celebration, another boy made his appearance.

I was eleven when my parents finally stopped having children. As the oldest, I was expected to set an example and help out with my siblings. And since my mother wasn't yet fluent in the language of her new country, she relied on me to translate for her with teachers, at the pediatrician's office, or when paying bills at the utility company. I was the one who made sure my sisters and brothers did their homework before going outside to play, and I filled out school forms and signed my mother's name on every permission slip or teacher's note they brought home from class.

To hear Yumma tell it, I was a natural in my take-charge role. I was the kind of child who loved nothing more than to please my parents, and besides, there were perks to being the oldest. When my mom went out to run errands, for example, that was my cue to wrangle my siblings to get the house cleaned up so Yumma wouldn't have to do it herself when she returned home. I'd tear a sheet of paper into pieces, and on each piece I'd write the name of a room—kitchen, bathroom, dining room, living room, hallway. I'd fold the pieces of paper into tiny balls and shuffle them in a bowl. Then I'd invite my siblings to pick from the bowl. Whatever room was written on the paper they chose was the one they'd have to clean. They were so seduced by the idea that we were playing a game, and jubilant when they avoided the hardest-to-clean kitchen and bathroom, that it was months before they realized I never had to choose a room. My mother watched me carry out this routine with amusement, until at last my sister Lena, who was two years younger than me, caught on.

"Hey, how come you don't have to clean any rooms?" she cried one afternoon.

"Someone has to be the organizer," I said archly.

Coming through the front door at that moment, her arms full of groceries, Yumma collapsed onto the freshly vacuumed brown leather couch, threw back her head, and laughed. None of us guessed that I had just declared my future.

Like most first-generation American children, I knew what it was to live in two worlds. From the time I was four, I would spend summers with my grandparents in the West Bank of Palestine, in the place my parents have never stopped calling "home." In El Bireh, my sisters, cousins, and I ran together in the streets, made friends with neighborhood children, rode horses into the hills, and helped Yumma's father, Grandpa Atif, pick fruit from his orchards. On weekends, we attended weddings.

The banquet hall in my grandparents' neighborhood had four floors, and most Saturdays there would be a wedding taking place on each of those floors. In a village where everyone knew everyone, families would go from one ceremony to the next, celebrating each union. Usually, we had stayed up late the night before for the prenuptial *sahra*, which was a joyful block party with lights strung from house to house along the street, and tables overflowing with sweets, stuffed grape leaves, olives, peanuts, and coolers full of drinks. Music blared from large speakers set up on the sidewalk, and men danced jubilantly in the street. At some point in the night, they'd belt out traditional songs, while someone followed along on the flute. Since both sets of my grandparents lived on the main road, these nighttime festivities happened right outside their houses, which meant that when we children tired of weaving in and out of the revelers, we could climb to the roof and watch the entertainments from up there. Many nights, we fell asleep under the stars.

My paternal grandfather, Ahmed, stayed inside on these evenings. He seldom left his home anymore, except to sit in his backyard dozing under a cloudless expanse of sky. It never occurred to me to question his isolation from the rest of us until an afternoon when two cousins and I were in the front yard playing and laughing loudly. Suddenly Seedy Ahmed came barreling out of the house, waving his cane and roaring at us as he chased us into the street. I was seven years old and so confused until one of my older cousins sat me down. "Linda, Seedy Ahmed has no idea who we are," he explained, tracing circles with his forefinger next to his head. "He thinks we're some neighborhood kids making too much noise during his afternoon nap."

Seedy Ahmed's dementia was just one of the sobering truths I would be asked to accept that summer. Another was that some of my cousins lived in a *mukhayyam*, or refugee camp, on the edge of town, where they shared a single room inside a box-shaped cinder-block house set down in a ravine below the sidewalk. Five minutes away stood soaring luxury homes belonging to exiles who had prospered in other countries and returned to build extravagant mansions in their old village. It was a stark and painful juxtaposition of wealth and poverty, a disparity that felt wrong to me even then.

Perhaps the most difficult lesson of that summer came on the day we visited one of my uncles in an Israeli prison. At twenty-four years old, my mother's younger brother had already been in jail for a year on the day I went with Sitty Sarah, Yumma, and his young wife to see him. My grandmother had been up before daybreak, cooking favorite family recipes, rolling grape leaves stuffed with minced lamb and vegetables, and making sweets to take to my uncle. The trip was an all-day excursion, with a long drive by car to the edge of a desert where we joined several other families for a bus ride through rocky terrain to the jail.

The prison itself was a low-slung building constructed of unpainted concrete blocks set against a gravelly hill. The scrubby desert stretched out around us as far as the eye could see. Inside the building, along a long, dimly lit corridor, groups of a dozen or more men were held in windowless cells fronted by chipped, green-painted iron bars. Visiting family members would stand at those bars, two at a time, and greet the prisoners, who were dressed in regular jeans and T-shirts. In addition to gifts of food wrapped in foil and wax paper, relatives would bring toiletries and changes of clothes for the men, and sometimes cigarettes and reading material.

Always a talkative child, I fell silent that day, taking in the drab and unfamiliar surroundings. I remember how my uncle and his wife laced their fingers through the iron bars and shared a kiss before letting go. On the way back home that evening, as the bus bumped along the desert highway, returning us to the place where we'd parked our car, I peppered my mother with questions.

"Why is Khalo in jail?" I asked her. "What did he do?"

Yumma explained that my uncle had been married for exactly three weeks when Israeli soldiers swept him up with about fifty other young Palestinian men whom they claimed had been involved in an uprising against the Jewish state. My uncle tried to tell them he'd simply been walking home to his new wife, but his explanation fell on deaf ears. He was found guilty in a military tribunal and incarcerated. The length of his sentence we did not know. This was not unusual. With the continued expansion of Jewish settlements on land seized from Palestinians in the West Bank, young Arab men were routinely arrested to thin the ranks of protestors and break the back of the resistance. These men could be held for years, released only when the Israeli civil authority decided to let them go. In my uncle's case, the jail sentence would last for another year.

"But why are so many people protesting?" I pressed my mother.

We were back in the car now, headed for El Bireh, and home. As pink and orange streaks washed the evening sky, and the refugee camp where my cousins lived came into view, my mother recounted the recent history of our people. She told me about the *nakba*, Arabic for "catastrophe." I had heard the word before; coincidentally my two brothers had been born one year apart on Nakba Day, May 15. But that car ride home was the first time I grasped the lasting consequence of the 1948 Arab-Israeli war that had led to Palestinians' somber observance of that date.

For my people, Israel's declaration of independence on May 14, 1948, had been the destruction of our homeland. By the next day, Nakba Day, three-quarters of a million Palestinians had been forced to abandon their homes and the lands their families had occupied for generations. Their mosques were razed to the ground, their houses demolished, their possessions taken, their cemeteries and olive groves destroyed. Hordes of exiled Palestinians poured into Jordan, Syria, Lebanon, and Egypt, and amassed on the West Bank of the Jordan River, becoming refugees overnight. Prohibited from returning home after the war, some seven million descendants of those refugees remain a displaced people seventy years later, the majority of them restricted to territories occupied and controlled by Israeli security forces.

In the most stark terms, the barrier to Palestinians' right of return has been a matter of numbers: Israel will continue to bar Arabs from reclaiming their original lands as long as the number of Arabs continues to exceed the number of Jews. With Israel's population standing at roughly eight million in 2018—a number that includes one and a half million resident Arabs—welcoming seven million more Arabs as citizens with full rights under the law would render Jews a democratic minority.[1] This prospect has stymied peace talks for decades and rendered the notion of a merged state—the "one-state solution" proposed by so many international observers—a nonstarter for Israel.

Of course, at seven years old, I could not fully comprehend the depth of the conflict that had fueled such agonizing cycles of intifadas and war in my parents' homeland. After that year, however, my summers in Palestine would never be quite as innocent and carefree as before. I now knew the story of my people. Their resistance was in my blood.

———————

Despite my family's turbulent history, when I look back on my childhood it seems like an immigrant fairy tale. My parents loved that in the melting pot that was Brooklyn they could embrace their old-country traditions while pursuing the American Dream. Surrounded by aunts, uncles, and cousins from El Bireh who had also settled in Sunset Park, our family gathered often for weddings, graduations, birthday celebrations, engagement parties, and fund-raisers for Palestine. Even though my parents weren't particularly religious, they were attentive to keeping their culture and faith alive in their seven children. On Saturday mornings they sent us to Islamic school, where we read the Qur'an, sang old Palestinian folk ballads, and mastered the quick, intricate footwork of dabka, a Palestinian folk dance. My sisters and I even formed an official dabka dance troupe, which for a while was in great demand as entertainment at social events.

In our close-knit community, my sisters were my best friends, and our Muslim neighbors were a big, boisterous village. A large Yemeni clan lived right next door, with one child for every one of ours, all roughly the same age. Across the street was another Palestinian family with seven kids, also in our age range, except they had five boys and two girls, the opposite of our family. Several Puerto Rican, Honduran, Guatemalan, Haitian, and Filipino families also lived on and around our block, and on hot summer afternoons, with the water hydrants spraying full blast, brown, Black, and beige kids swarmed the street, playing Wiffle ball or tag until our parents called for us to come inside for dinner. I imagine we looked and sounded like every nineties portrayal of the borough ever seen in a Spike Lee Joint.

In my particular Brooklyn story, I was the vigilant big sister whose job it was to look out for my younger siblings. I took this personal charge very seriously. If anyone came after my sisters or brothers, they'd have to go through me. I remember one afternoon when I was in seventh grade and was sitting at our dining table doing homework. Suddenly, I heard a commotion outside. I jumped up and ran to our front door, where my mother stood holding the broom she had been using to sweep the stoop. In front of her on the street was a Dominican girl I recognized from my sister Lena's fifth-grade class. Standing next to her was her mother and three men, one of whom I knew to be the girl's uncle. Their faces were familiar from the neighborhood.

"Where's Lena?" the woman was screaming. "You get her out here now!"

My mother frowned. "Lena? Why do you want her?"

"She said something to my daughter, so she better come out here and fight her right now!" the woman yelled.

Later, we would learn that this woman's daughter had been bullying Lena because she thought my sister had stolen her best friend. For weeks she had been pulling Lena's hair, shoving her in the hallway, and chasing her after school. That day, Lena had finally stood up for herself. "If you touch me one more time, you and I are gonna fight," my sister had told her. This was the provocation that had led to the girl and her mother now standing in front of our house, spoiling for a showdown. I watched as the woman advanced toward Yumma in an alarming way. She looked as if she might attack her, and I wasn't going to let that happen. I darted around my mom and bounded down the five steps of our

33

stoop, placing myself squarely in the woman's path. She let out a string of expletives and told me to get out of the way. I didn't move.

"Are you serious right now?" I asked her, my voice bold though my heart was trembling. "No way is my sister coming out here to fight anyone. We don't do that in our family. I don't know what your problem with my sister is, lady, but nobody is doing any fighting at our house or on our street today."

By this time a troop of about twenty kids who had been playing in the street had formed a semicircle around us. The moment felt dangerous.

"Linda, go inside," my mother commanded me in Arabic, her hand reaching for my shoulder. I knew she was afraid for me, but I also knew her English wasn't fluent enough to meet this woman's wrath.

"It's okay, Yumma," I responded. "Let me talk to the lady."

There I was at twelve years old, negotiating with a woman the same age as my mother, doing my best to defuse a tense situation. I knew I didn't dare back down.

"You can stand out here all day," I declared, "but my sister is not going to come down here and fight your daughter. It is not going to happen."

The truth is I was scared that the girl's mother or one of the men would strike me, but I stood my ground and set my jaw as I held the woman's gaze. I had already decided I would take their blows myself before I let them lay a hand on my mother. And they definitely weren't going to get a shot at my sister.

The woman glowered at me for a long moment, then seemed to loosen her stance. "Well, you better tell your sister if she ever threatens my daughter again, we're coming back for her," she warned. With that, she grabbed her daughter's hand, turned on her heel, and marched off down the street, the three men trailing her.

I exhaled, weak with relief that the woman had relented, even though I could hardly believe that she'd listened to a child. That was the day I understood I would stand up for other people, even when afraid.

I began to walk my sisters to and from school after that, to make sure the waters between the girl and Lena stayed calm. Fortunately, I can't recall another day in my childhood when I felt in such jeopardy. Mostly, our days unfolded amiably, the tone set by Yaba and Yumma's harmonious partnership. If my parents were stricter than the American parents we saw on television, it hardly mattered, because our family mirrored all the other immigrant and first-generation families in our neighborhood.

As my sisters and I moved into our teen years, our parents instituted the same ridiculously early curfews, observed the same prohibition on sleepovers with friends, and had similarly restrictive views on boys and dating as our immigrant neighbors. At home, my parents insisted we speak only Arabic because they wanted us to be fluent and able to converse easily with relatives in Palestine. Even in this we were like our neighbors; my best friend Rosa Rodriguez's Puerto Rican–born mother insisted she speak Spanish in her home, and my friend Chantal Jean-Baptiste conversed with her family in Haitian Creole. I never felt any different from my friends, whose parents, like mine, spoke with thick accents and slipped into mother languages that sounded as musical to my ear as my own.

The strange thing is, as idyllic as my childhood seems in memory, I came of age at a time when my neighborhood was crawling with gangs, with Sunset Park known throughout the borough as "Gunset Park." In my Brooklyn, however, neighbors looked out for each other and disciplined one another's children, and except for the afternoon when we faced down Lena's bully, I was never afraid.

Chapter 3

Broken Windows

Y aba came to a stop as the light turned red. Sitting next to him in the front seat of his enormous burgundy Chevy, I could pick out the redbrick building with its intricately carved stone facade two blocks away. From every direction, students streamed in through the tall wooden doors of the building. Watching them, I brooded over how it would look to pull up in this conspicuous twelve-passenger vehicle with its matching burgundy velvet curtains at the windows. Would it be better to jump out of the car now and walk the rest of the way? I mean, whose father drives them right up to the front door on the first day of ninth grade, and in such a ridiculous car? Definitely not cool in a place where kids stuffed bandannas in gang colors out of sight as they approached the school.

I already knew that John Jay High School was a notorious gang farm. All summer my friends had been telling me how tough the kids were. "Damn, girl, why you going *there*?" my neighbor Abdo had said. He was the oldest sibling in the large Yemeni family who lived next door. We were sitting on the concrete ledge that separated the front stoops of our houses, watching our little sisters play a game of hopscotch chalked on the sidewalk. Abdo frowned. "You know they call that place Jungle Jay, right? I'm telling you, Linda, watch your back."

Abdo would enter tenth grade at Midwood High School in the fall.

Midwood had been my first choice, too, but my parents had vetoed that plan.

"Midwood?" Yumma frowned when I'd presented her with my list of public high schools in preference order. "Never heard of it."

"It's near Flatbush?" I said helpfully. "Abdo goes there."

We were standing in my parents' bedroom. "Flatbush?" Yumma repeated doubtfully. She rummaged in a dresser drawer and located a dog-eared subway map. She laid it out on the bedspread and smoothed its wrinkles with her palms. Then she carefully counted the number of train stops to Midwood, which was over by Brooklyn College. My heart sank as I saw her notice that I'd have to switch train lines to get there. She lifted the map from the bed, folded it in half, and studied it some more.

"Too far," she announced finally.

John Jay, on the other hand, was my zoned public school, just a couple of stops away on the subway, and my friend Rosa from up the block would also be going there in the fall. It comforted Yumma to know that Rosa and I could travel together on the train. Never mind that Midwood offered a gifted and talented program, while John Jay had a secure berth on the city's worst-schools list. To my parents, none of this mattered. They simply wanted me, the test subject for all new child-rearing experiences, closer to home. As far as they were concerned, I could learn at any school if I just stayed out of trouble and applied myself.

Now, up ahead, I saw a tall, skinny girl with waist-length locs high-five a girl with a short 'fro. Instead of moving toward the school's entrance, they hoisted themselves onto the sidewalk railing, talking and laughing like they hadn't seen each other in a while. Another girl joined them. Her shiny mane of black hair caught the morning sun as she squinted in our direction, as if looking for someone.

"Hey, Yaba, I'll just get out here," I said quickly, grabbing my book bag from the floor as the traffic signal flashed to green. Not waiting for an answer, I pushed open the Chevy's heavy door and leaped down onto the sidewalk. I actually loved that car, which looked like a cross between those stretch limos celebrities ride in to red carpet events and a straight-up pimpmobile. With three rows of passenger seats plus a back row that folded down into a bed, it held our sprawling family comfortably on road trips to see my uncle Mohammad Almahbooba and our cousins in Boston, where they'd moved some years before. But today everything about that burgundy beast embarrassed me as it made its stately way toward my school, hulking over every other car on the road.

"See you later, Yaba!" I called as I slung my book bag over my shoulder and darted across the street ahead of our car. Yaba rolled down his window and yelled something to me in Arabic. I didn't catch what he said, but I raised one hand in acknowledgment without turning my head or breaking my stride.

Dodged that bullet, I thought.

In front of the school, a police car idled at the curb, the two officers inside sipping coffee and biting into fat bagels as they surveyed the arriving students. As far as I knew, there was a squad car stationed outside every high school in the city on the first day. I passed by them without a second thought.

Rosa was waiting for me inside the front door, just as we'd planned. She looked fly in her black jeans and red Converse high-tops, but she was distracted, hugging her cropped denim vest across her chest with tightly folded arms.

"'Sup, girl," I said, bouncing to a stop beside her, full of my own nervous energy. "You ready for this?"

She didn't answer. She was watching the scene in the large hall in front of us, which served as the cafeteria. I followed her gaze and saw the long lines of students, almost all of them Black or Latinx, filing through large metal detectors and putting their bags through X-ray machines like the ones at airports. Beyond the barrier, the kids were lining up against the wall as security monitors moved down the line, running wands up and down the students' clothes and book bags, then peering into their open mouths. Some kids got sent to a table where other monitors searched through their bags and made them turn their pockets inside out. Next to the table, a large, matronly-looking woman gestured for a Latina-looking girl to take down her topknot. The woman ran plastic-gloved hands through sections of the girl's hair and then, with a flick of her chin, moved her on. Next up was a Black girl with long microbraids. The woman investigated her braids by the handful as the girl gazed at the peeling gray paint on the ceiling and chewed gum nonchalantly. I touched my own hair, which I'd worn pulled back from my face in a half ponytail that day, not an insignificant decision for a fourteen-year-old girl on the first day of high school. I hoped I wouldn't get sent to that table, too.

The whole scene inside the cafeteria was organized pandemonium. Students yelled out to one another excitedly, their voices reverberating in the grand yet dilapidated chamber as the metal detector beeped, teachers' wands danced through the air, pocket change jingled into metal bowls, and the zipping of book bags made a soft percussive *swish*, punctuating everything.

Soon, I would learn that the girls with braids or locs or upswept dos were being searched for razor blades secreted in their hair. Apparently blades could also be smuggled into school hidden under tongues, so mouths had to be inspected, too. By the time I discovered all this, morning lineups had become as routine and unremarkable to me as they were to the girl chewing gum indifferently while a teacher searched her braids on that very first morning.

———

John Jay was a barred school: all the windows had padlocked iron screens or vertical bars, and students were regularly stopped and frisked by cops outside the school long before "stop and frisk" was an official New York Police Department policy. With an enrollment of more than three thousand students, the school was 90 percent Black and Latinx, and 10 percent everybody else—a cluster of Asian kids, a few white kids, and maybe ten or fifteen Arab kids in the entire school.

And yet, I never felt like an outsider at John Jay. Maybe because I spent a lot of time at my dad's grocery store in the predominantly African American and Caribbean neighborhood of Crown Heights, I'd always felt an affinity for Black people. And the Black kids at John Jay embraced me in return. I felt safe around them. If something bad was going down, I trusted they'd have my back. Maybe they saw I didn't really have any other group to belong to. At John Jay, no one cared that I worshiped as a Muslim. In fact, my family being from Palestine gave me a few extra cool points with some kids. It was the midnineties, and a whole new school of hip-hop artists were rapping about the struggles of people in Palestine. Although few of my schoolmates knew the details of that decades-long military occupation, what they did know was that, like Black people in America, Palestinians were an oppressed group.

Given that my social life outside my extended family fell mostly within school hours, I'd made a conscious decision not to let what I'd heard about John Jay on the outside cloud the way that I interacted with people inside. I knew that some of my friends were in gangs, but it never came up between us. At school, we were just regular teenagers doing class projects together, putting on plays in drama club, and staging fashion shows every spring. Eventually, as relationships deepened, I learned which friend was being raised by a single mother, whose family was getting by in a shelter, whose father was incarcerated, whose brother had been roughed up for no reason by a cop, whose cousin was strung out on drugs. But it took a long time for my friends to share these things, and even then, I didn't fully grasp how socially and economically precarious so many of my classmates' lives truly were. For some of them, gangs had become a surrogate family, an umbrella of safety in crime-ridden environments, a place to be and people to hang with outside of school, as well as a means of getting money in a poverty economy that showed them no other way.

Often, my schoolmates' involvement in gangs was even more nuanced. For example, some of them had been recruited back in middle school, when the hunger to belong runs deep. A lot of the kids also came from households where generations of the family belonged to gangs; their membership was essentially inherited. In other cases, parents weren't around; maybe they worked two or three jobs just to put food on the table, or maybe they were involved in criminal activity themselves.

With so many rival gangs inside my school—the Crips, the Bloods, the Latin Kings, the Papi Chulos, and others—John Jay could be a dangerous place. I would occasionally hear about a kid getting knifed in a stairwell, or someone getting a beatdown after school, yet I seldom witnessed actual violence. The minute I sensed a situation getting heated, I would move the hell away. However, there is one fight I remember vividly. It broke out right next to me in the cafeteria when I was in tenth grade.

At my school, lunch was an assigned period. To enter the cafeteria, you'd show your class program at the door. If you didn't have lunch marked on your program at that time, the teacher would turn you away. There were ways around this; the most common was to borrow another student's program so you could get in to have lunch with your friends or, more likely, your girlfriend or boyfriend. As many as 250 kids flowed through the cafeteria during each lunch period, so the lunch monitors didn't always pick up on who was or wasn't supposed to be there.

One day, I noticed a Guatemalan kid from my grade who I knew didn't have the same lunch period as me, yet there he was, marching over to the long picnic-style table where I was sitting with my friends Rosa and Samantha. From the look on Ricardo's face, I knew something bad was about to happen. Sure enough, he walked up to a Dominican kid named Mateo, who was eating lunch a couple of seats away from me, and he crumpled up a piece of paper and launched it at Mateo's head. The paper didn't do any damage, of course, but Mateo had been disrespected and he lunged across the table at Ricardo. Food trays clattered to the ground, with mac and cheese and chocolate milk spattering the boys as they wrestled and writhed around on the floor. The rest of us leaped from our seats, too, and formed a tight circle around them. Kids were cheering and chanting as two lunch monitors pushed through the crowd and stooped over, trying to pull Ricardo and Mateo apart. Samantha, who lived around the corner from Rosa and me, grabbed my arm and pulled me a little way back from the action.

"I heard Ricardo's pissed 'cause Mateo's been talking to his girl," she yelled above the racket. "I'm staying outta that mess."

That's how I knew this wasn't a gang fight, but that someone had caught feelings for someone else's girlfriend.

The next thing I knew, police officers were storming into the cafeteria with guns drawn. I remember thinking: *These are two fifteen-year-old boys upset over a girl. It's really not that serious.* But at the same time, I had no point of reference to help me realize that this sort of thing wasn't happening at high schools like Midwood. I actually thought that cops brandishing guns inside a public school building was normal.

Along with everyone else, I watched as the officers handcuffed those boys before holstering their weapons. They led Ricardo and Mateo away, and we didn't see them again for several days. I heard they were taken down to Central Booking and charged, but I don't know if they were held in custody for a few days or just got suspended from school. All I knew was that Ricardo and Mateo now had official police records, and all because of a stupid fight over a girl.

———

Years later, I would understand that the very presence of police officers in schools escalates the criminalization of students, and in particular students of color, with Black students three times more likely to be suspended or expelled for the same behaviors as white students.[1] I was a panelist at a social justice conference in New York City in 2005 when the light bulb finally came on. A young Black woman was talking about the "broken windows" approach to school discipline, which advocated aggressively policing minor offenses as a way to deter more serious crimes. The problem was, she pointed out, suspending students for minor infractions like being disruptive in class—or, as happened in one case, biting a Pop-Tart into the shape of a pistol and waving it around—had consequences far more devastating than the original behavior warranted. Numerous studies had shown that after a single suspension, a student became more likely to be held back a grade, to drop out of school, and, within a year, to become involved with the juvenile justice system.[2]

Belatedly, I would recognize that my school, like so many in poor Black and brown neighborhoods, was severely overpoliced. Every few days, it seemed, some kid was perp-walked out of the building, usually for a very minor offense—a scuffle in the hallway, a Swiss Army knife found in a backpack, arguing with a teacher, gang colors worn openly in defiance of school policy. Guidance counselors could have handled this sort of teenage acting-out far more effectively than armed police officers, but since we had only three counselors for more than three thousand students, cops with guns regularly trooped into our midst, slapping handcuffs on teenagers and guaranteeing them a one-way ticket on the school-to-prison pipeline.

As I left the conference that afternoon, I felt almost ashamed that it had taken me so many years to realize what I had witnessed day in, day out at my high school. As I delved deeper, I learned that even though Black children were just 15 percent of the nation's school population, they accounted for 31 percent of all school arrests and referrals to law enforcement.[3] While not a single study had ever shown that Black students misbehave at higher rates than white students, they were far more likely to be suspended and even arrested for reasons that amounted to little more than pissing off an adult—discretionary violations that fell under the general heading of "being disrespectful" or "insubordination" or "willful defiance."[4]

Erica Meiners, a professor of education and women's and gender studies at Northeastern Illinois University, observes that "broken windows" policing disproportionately targets communities of color because of the way Black and brown children are stereotyped in the culture at large. "Certain children in our culture get to be children, and others don't," she explains, citing research that shows Black children are less likely to be seen as innocent and more likely to be judged as "thuggish," "predatory," and several years older than their actual age, making them more likely to become subjects of overpolicing. Sadly, once a juvenile has a record of suspension or arrest, even for a minor nuisance offense, any subsequent infraction will be dealt with more harshly, resulting in that student being funneled directly into the juvenile justice system.[5]

Education analysts and social justice experts agree that the first step to breaking the cycle is to remove police officers from schools. Unfortunately, with the rise in school shootings since Columbine, this approach has often been met with stiff opposition. But even in those schools that choose to retain armed security officers, restorative justice programs can and must be adopted. Restorative practices focus on building strong relationships between teachers, school administrators, and students, creating an atmosphere of trust and the opportunity to resolve disciplinary issues through discussion and counseling. As Erica Meiners notes, "These are de-escalation strategies. We're shifting the question aimed at students from, 'What's wrong with you?' to 'What happened to you?' We're considering the 'why' behind some of the behaviors we see."[6]

At John Jay in the 1990s, there was no formal program of restorative justice, although one teacher, Mr. Harris, definitely tried to do his part. A math teacher and an assistant principal, he was known for taking groups of students under his wing. As an African American, he seemed to feel a responsibility to mentor the students of color who walked through the doors of the school. To be honest, most of the other teachers were just putting in time; they felt no investment in how their students turned out, but Mr. Harris was different. He really cared about us. He had the ability to make students feel as if they could do something special in the world. And even when you were no longer in his class, Mr. Harris never stopped checking in with you.

I was part of a group of girls that he met with regularly. In addition to Rosa, Samantha, and me, there was a girl named Cecily and another named Kenisha. Both Cecily and Kenisha commuted from East New York, which back then was called the "killing fields" of New York. "Hey, ladies, let me see your report cards," Mr. Harris would say, walking up to us in the hallway. If our grades weren't where he thought they should be, he'd pepper us with questions to get at why we might be having trouble in a particular class and offer suggestions for how we could do better. And at the start of every term he'd request to see our programs, scanning the courses we'd been given to make sure we were being properly challenged.

Mr. Harris also actively mentored the guys on our school football team, the new immigrant kids, the gay and trans kids, and students who'd been in trouble with the law. Really, he took an interest in anyone who would let him, and if you were smart, you let him. Mr. Harris made you feel super worthy. He saw our potential and expected us to live up to it, and he helped us navigate the peer pressure to fall in with a particular gang. Even though students weren't allowed to wear gang colors inside the school building, some of them would still signify by wearing colored rosary beads on their wrists or lacing up their sneakers with colored shoelaces. Mr. Harris was always on the lookout for such clues, and if he caught any of us signifying in that way, he'd take us aside. Honestly, we were all a little intimidated by the man, so we tried not to do anything to trigger "the talk." The last thing any of us wanted was to have Mr. Harris call us out for something.

Looking back, I see so clearly how Mr. Harris's no-nonsense guidance helped me and my friends get through high school unaffiliated with any gang. I realize now that if kids knew Mr. Harris was looking out for you, they wouldn't even try to recruit you. A lot of us might have gone down a bad path if it hadn't been for this one teacher. Instead, all "Mr. Harris's kids" ended up doing well in life, with most of us going to college and ending up in solid professions like law, medicine, social work, and education.

Mr. Harris was tall and clean-cut, and he wore a suit and tie to school every single day. He showed us how a professional, highly intelligent Black man carries himself. I think he especially wanted to be a role model for the young men on the football team, all of whom were Black, and most of whom came from difficult circumstances. They were always hanging around Mr. Harris, joshing with him, and asking his advice. Mr. Harris kept those young men out of trouble as much as he kept my group of girls on the straight and narrow. He's a big part of why I loved my high school, and why, when I graduated, I decided I wanted to be a high school teacher. But not just any kind of high school teacher—I wanted to be the kind of teacher *he* was, which, if you think about it, is a powerful form of community activism.

———

At John Jay, I began to recognize that my experience as a first-generation Palestinian American Muslim was inextricably interwoven with the everyday reality of my Black and brown brothers and sisters in this country. I would soon learn that my father had embraced this truth long before I ever gave it a conscious thought.

Yaba's very first job when he arrived in Brooklyn in 1976 was working the cash register at a bodega in Crown Heights, where he eventually bought his own store. Crown Heights in the eighties and nineties was home to African Americans, Caribbean and Central American immigrants, and Puerto Ricans, with a few Orthodox Jewish enclaves. They all came to Yaba's store. People called him Nick and stopped awhile to chat and bring him up to speed on their lives. Because of the bodega, I grew up in Crown Heights as much as in Sunset Park. I knew by sight the kids from the neighborhood who traipsed in and out of the store, and I dutifully wrote their parents' names in the marbled composition notebooks where my dad listed the credit he extended to regular customers until payday or less meager times. Orthodox Jews who forgot something for the Friday evening meal but weren't allowed to handle money after sundown on the Sabbath also got entered in those books—Yaba kept a section of kosher goods just for them. Behind the counter, those marbled notebooks were stacked in neat little towers, meticulous records from years past. Yaba never worried about when the ledgers would be squared. His customers paid what they could until they could pay in full, and Yaba trusted them with a simplicity that moved me, even as a young girl.

Starting when I was twelve, I used to work in my dad's bodega after school. My sisters and I, and later my brothers, ran the cash register for Yaba on different afternoons. My days were Tuesdays and Thursdays. My mom would pick me up from school in her red Lincoln Navigator and drive me the twenty-five or so minutes to Crown Heights. Seated on the high stool behind the counter, which was right next to the door, I'd greet familiar faces and ring up purchases in between doing my homework. When I was older, Yaba would sometimes take a break to sip Turkish coffee with his friends in other stores—many Arab men owned bodegas in Brooklyn in the nineties—or to chat with them at the counter in his own store.

I remember one afternoon when I was sitting behind the cash register, gazing out at the intersection of Troy Avenue and Montgomery Street, watching the kids from the public school across the way being rowdy at the bus stop. My dad was next to me behind the counter when a skinny African American boy with hair cropped so close to his head it was hardly more than a shadow entered the store and walked past us. He couldn't have been more than twelve. He went to the coolers toward the back where Yaba kept the sodas and the twenty-five-cent juices, which were popular with school kids. The boy picked up a quarter juice, then moved deeper into the store, where he picked up a twenty-five-cent Hostess lemon cake from a display rack. He looked around, making sure he was blocked from view by the store shelves, and then he tucked the juice box and cake into his pockets.

He didn't realize that Yaba was tracking his every move in the large circular mirror positioned in a high corner, which allowed a funhouse view of the four long aisles of the store. I looked at Yaba, who was sitting back on his stool, leaning against the shelves behind the counter, the ones holding cigarettes, pain relievers, first aid items, and school supplies. His arms were crossed and his expression was calm. I took my cue from him and stayed silent as the boy walked back to the front of the store, pushed open the glass door, and left. Yaba followed him outside.

From my perch behind the cash register, I saw my father walk up to the boy.

"Jerome," he said, "please give me what's in your pockets."

He called the boy by name. I should not have been surprised.

Jerome spun around, looking stricken. Like me, I don't think he'd realized that Yaba knew his name. "I—I—I don't have anything in my p-p-pockets," he stammered.

"Don't lie to me, son, I saw you put that quarter juice and quarter cake in your pocket. Now give them to me."

Looking caught and terrified, Jerome pulled out the stolen items and put them in my father's waiting palm.

"Why did you steal these things?" Yaba asked the child. He sounded disappointed, almost hurt. "I know your mother," he went on. "She didn't raise you to do something stupid like this. What do you think she would say if I told her what you did?"

"She's at work," Jerome mumbled, his voice so soft I barely caught the words, "and I didn't have any money."

Yaba sighed and looked up to the sky. "Stay right here," he finally told the boy. "You don't move."

My father came into the store and asked me to give him a small brown paper bag from under the counter. He dropped the quarter juice and the little cake into the bag and folded the top down securely, then went back outside and handed the bag to Jerome. He stooped down from his six-foot-two height so that he was at eye level with the boy. "The next time you are hungry and don't have any money, you don't steal what you want," he told him. "You come in here and you ask me and I will give it to you. Do you understand?"

Jerome nodded vigorously, his eyes filling up with tears. Yaba patted him on the shoulder and stood watching as he turned and ran off down the block, clutching the brown paper bag. Then my father walked back into his store and returned to his spot on the stool next to me. He crossed his arms, leaned his head back against the shelves, and said nothing more. It occurred to me that Yaba could have called the police on Jerome, and then he'd have had a record like the two boys at my school who had tussled over a girl. Though I didn't know anything about restorative justice in those days, I have often thought back to that afternoon in the bodega, wishing that more of the kids I grew up with had encountered men like my father and Mr. Harris at critical moments in their lives.

Chapter 4

Sitty Halima's Wish

Sitty Halima was dying. My paternal grandfather, Seedy Ahmed, had already passed away a few years before, leaving our grandmother to hold everything together in that two-story house that had once been filled with rambunctious boys. Now the cancer was everywhere in her body, and she was growing weaker. My father made preparations to go and be with her in Palestine. I begged to go with him, but he planned to stay for several weeks and didn't want me to miss that much school. I was inconsolable at the thought that I might not see Sitty Halima again in this life. She had always made me feel like her favorite. The fact that her other grandchildren felt the same way only confirmed her magic for me.

That evening, after Yaba left for the airport, I lay in my bed, staring up at the ceiling, wondering how my fiercely independent grandmother had managed alone as her body grew more frail, and whether she regretted her sons moving so far away. My heart ached at the thought of her rambling through the empty rooms of that house, where I had known so much laughter in my childhood.

The door opened and my mother came into my room. She sat on the edge of my bed and placed a palm on my forehead, as if checking to see if I had a fever.

"What's the matter, *habibti*?"

"Sitty Halima is so alone," I mumbled into my pillow. "We should all be there."

"She's not alone," Yumma assured me. "Allah sent her angels."

I lifted my head and looked at her questioningly.

"The family next door," she explained. "You remember them?"

I remembered them well. There were thirteen children, and I used to play with two of the younger siblings during my summers in El Bireh. I also remembered how their father, a large, strapping man, would lift my grandfather down the stairs when he asked to be taken to the backyard, where he would sit in the sun for hours. His neighbor would then carry Seedy Ahmed, still seated in his chair, back up the stairs to his room. It was a feat of pure strength because my grandfather was a big man himself.

Now that my grandmother was alone in the house, Yumma told me, the neighbors who had been my childhood playmates came over to help her scrub the floors, do laundry, and prepare meals. The middle son in the family was perhaps her staunchest support. He was nine years older than me, with a quiet, serious demeanor that had invited no inquisition from a girl who could strike up a conversation with anyone. I was endlessly curious about people's stories. As a little girl, I would walk up to strangers in restaurants, on the bus, in my father's store, and ask them questions. "Where did you get your blue hat?" "What are you eating?" "How old is your baby?" But the middle son of the family who lived next door to my grandma had had a solitary air about him that even I knew not to disturb.

This young man had become the rock on which Sitty Halima leaned. Yumma told me that he would do light tasks around the house, such as hanging picture frames—Sitty Halima's walls were covered with photographs of her American grandchildren—and on nights when there was a *sahra*, he would help my grandmother to her roof so that she could watch the festivities and share in the joy. Imagining Sitty Halima's tiny frame swaddled in a shawl and looking out over the dancing in the street, I felt a rush of gratitude for the solemn young man with whom I had never spoken.

What none of us knew was that Sitty Halima had plans for this young man. Soon after Yaba arrived in El Bireh, my grandmother sat my father down and told him about her neighbor's steadfast qualities, and suggested he would make a good husband for me. "It is my dying wish," she said, "that you will marry your daughter to this man. He has treated me like his own grandmother. He is compassionate and kind. I would like that kind of husband for my granddaughter."

Yaba waved off the suggestion. "Linda's much too young to be thinking about marriage," he said. "She's only fifteen."

Sitty Halima covered my father's sun-browned hand with her thin, wrinkled, blue-veined one and looked into his eyes. "Think about it, Nidal," she told him. "Promise me you will consider him. He is a good young man from a wonderful family. He would be a loyal husband for your Linda." Yaba nodded and kissed Sitty Halima's cheeks to appease her, but he immediately put the idea out of his mind, never mentioning a word of it to me upon his return to Brooklyn.

As it happened, I did get to see Sitty Halima again before she died. I had asked to spend that summer with her in El Bireh, and as soon as school let out, I boarded a plane to Palestine. My sister Hanady came with me: she was suffering from tonsillitis and needed her tonsils removed, a surgery that in Palestine would cost a fraction of what we might have to pay in the U.S. Since we did not have health insurance in America and paid cash for all medical care, it only made sense for her to have the operation in El Bireh.

By then, one of my aunts had moved in with Sitty Halima, and while she tended Hanady as she recovered from her tonsillectomy, I became my grandmother's shadow. I slept beside her in the night and watched grainy old wedding videos with her during the afternoon, listening to her stories about the people in the videos. And every morning, no matter how she was feeling when she opened her eyes, she rose from her bed and dressed herself in one of her beautiful embroidered dresses or velvet robes, tied a matching handkerchief around her hair, rouged her cheeks, and set about her day.

I spent hours in the kitchen with my grandmother that summer—she was determined that I should know how to cook traditional Palestinian dishes such as *galayet bandora*, a stew of tomatoes, garlic, and onions, and *maqluba*, an upside-down casserole of eggplant, rice, lamb, and cauliflower—and when she felt up to it, I accompanied her on small errands around town. On Friday nights, we sat together on the roof watching the prenuptial festivities down in the street. The *sahra* block party always made her smile and then sigh, a wistful look in her eyes.

As the summer went on, Sitty Halima seemed to grow stronger. Despite being in constant pain, she was determined that Hanady and I should enjoy what would turn out to be our last summer in her company. I learned from my aunt that in fact, Sitty Halima did not know she was dying of stomach cancer. The doctor, who made house calls each week, had described her condition as an inflammation of her gallbladder about which nothing could be done. Sitty Halima accepted his diagnosis with her usual fortitude, and went about her life with as much vigor as the flaring pain in her body would allow.

As for the young man next door, he came around less now that Sitty Halima had live-in companionship, and when he did stop by to check on her, he was as quiet as ever. I don't think he and I exchanged more than a few words in the two months I was in El Bireh. When Sitty Halima died in her sleep a few weeks after my sister and I returned to Brooklyn, it felt like the end of my childhood.

———

Having earned extra credits in a college after-school program, I graduated from high school in eleventh grade. I bid a tearful goodbye to my friends, knowing that despite all we'd shared, I might never see some of them again. My parents did not allow me to attend junior prom. No matter how I tried to argue, they were convinced that everyone had sex on prom night—so my departure from John Jay did not include that particular American rite of passage. One day I was in a morning lineup, chattering with my friends as teachers waved wands around us; three months later I was standing in a different kind of line, waiting to enroll in courses at Kingsborough Community College, overlooking Manhattan Beach.

Almost every weekend, it seemed, we attended weddings. I was seventeen now, an age when many young Palestinian women start to consider marriage. Even though we no longer lived in El Bireh, we had retained the tradition of arranged nuptials. Among my Palestinian girlfriends in Brooklyn, it was very much the norm. My parents had advised that I marry someone who understood our culture, spoke the language, and supported the Palestinian cause. In time, they assured me, mutual respect and shared experience would ripen into love. It had happened that way for my own parents. Their enjoyment of each other and devotion to the family unit had allowed my siblings and me a cheerful, sheltered, and relatively untroubled childhood.

In those days, when I got together with my cousins and girlfriends, the talk often turned to planning our weddings, the style of dress we'd wear, the music we'd play at the reception, and the way we'd decorate the hall. The only missing detail was the groom, but we didn't worry about that. We knew that when the time was right, our parents would offer suggestions. The way it usually worked was that a young woman would attend a wedding or some other social event, and someone would notice her, maybe a mother, a father, or sometimes the young man himself. They might observe her from afar, or have a friendly conversation with the family. Afterward, the parents would contact the young woman's parents, let them know their son was interested in marrying their daughter, and ask if it would be possible for the young people to meet. I felt comfortable with this practice, because I knew Yaba and Yumma would never force me to marry anyone against my will. I knew that some families had already made inquiries about me, but my parents had not considered any of the proposals to be the right match for their headstrong oldest daughter. I was confident that whenever they believed I should seriously consider someone, they would let me know, and a meeting would be arranged. If I liked the young man and felt we could make a life together, then a dowry, the engagement party, and the wedding would follow.

Yaba and Yumma's love story was one of the reasons I always looked forward to Palestinian weddings. There were few occasions more joyful. My friend Fatima's wedding in May of that year was no different. The dance floor was packed. The buffet overflowed. Everyone was in a euphoric mood. Fatima had grown up in the same neighborhood as me. When the time came to be married, she'd traveled back to El Bireh to meet her future husband, a partnership arranged by her parents and his. After the wedding, they would live together in Sunset Park, and she would sponsor him for residency. This was not an unusual scenario. Many of us chose partners from the homeland, where extended families were known and vetted by our parents.

On the night of Fatima's wedding, I was wearing a vibrant red *thobe* embroidered in gold with flowing bell sleeves. I'd drawn dramatic wings at the corners of my eyes with black kohl, and my lipstick was a bold shade of red. I was feeling in my element as I walked to the back of the hall to find my sister Heeba. I meant to pull her onto the dance floor with me. Maybe we'd break out a routine from our dance troupe days, for old times' sake. As I scanned the back of the hall, my eyes landed on a familiar figure—the quiet and serious neighbor who had been helpful to Sitty Halima as her health failed. It was odd to see him here, in a Brooklyn catering hall, so far removed from his home village. He was standing alone, dressed in a crisp white shirt, black slacks, and black tie, his hands shoved deep in his pockets as he watched the dancing.

I went over to him. "Hey, I know you," I said.

He seemed taken aback by my assertive approach. I realized that in his world, young Muslim women didn't usually walk up and start talking to men they barely knew. However, my sisters and I had always conversed freely with anyone we chose, and our father had never criticized us for it. To his credit, the young man rallied, flashing me a smile.

"I know you, too," he said, bowing his head in acknowledgment.

I noticed that above his neatly clipped beard, little gold flecks danced in his eyes.

"I didn't expect to see you here," I said, making light conversation, trying to help him feel welcome in the place I called home.

"The groom and I grew up together," he explained. "I came for the wedding."

We chatted a bit more, exchanging pleasantries, before I continued on my original errand to find my sister. As I walked away, I was thinking how his hazel eyes glittered against the brown of his skin. I realized it was the first time I had ever seen him smile.

———————

A week later, the young man's father called Yaba from Palestine. He explained that his son had seen me at a wedding in Brooklyn the weekend before, and he wanted to ask for my hand in marriage. My father, remembering his mother asking him to consider this man for me, was in a state of wonderment that the question had come around again. He discussed it with Yumma and they decided to bring the proposal to me.

"Why don't you just call him, talk to him for a bit and see how you feel?" Yaba suggested. "He's staying with friends in Boston."

Yumma pointed out that the young man was from a very respected family, that his father had always been good to his wife, and that all his brothers were already married and they were good to their wives, too. And so, because I trusted my parents' judgment and loving intention toward me, I agreed to make the call.

That next night, we talked for two hours on the phone. He told me that Americans found his name, Maher, unpronounceable, and now everyone just called him Mike. I laughed and shared that people in Crown Heights called my dad Nick, even though his given name, Nidal, was really not that complicated. We talked about how different my upbringing in Brooklyn had been from his in El Bireh. As we spoke that evening, I reflected that if my parents had not raised me with such a strong connection to Palestinian culture, our conversation would not have flowed so easily. Because I was familiar with the village where he was raised and many of the people he knew, I had common references with him, and a context for his stories. I was even fluent in the colloquial dialect he spoke, which was fortuitous because he didn't yet speak English very well.

When I put down the phone that night, I thought: *This is a good and wholesome man whom my grandmother loved like a son. And one of the very last things she did before she died was to choose him for me.* That was a powerful testament in his favor. Another was the awareness that if I married him, my children would be fully Palestinian, rather than a generation removed. I was stirred by the idea of my children being as connected to the homeland as I was. My parents had bestowed this gift on their children, and now I had the opportunity to pass it on to mine.

"Well?" Yaba asked as I walked back into the living room after our phone call.

"You seemed to have a lot to talk about," Yumma observed.

"Maybe," I said, and they didn't push any further. I knew they were both being careful not to make me feel pressured. Besides, the young man and I still had to meet again in person. The next step was for my parents to invite him to travel from Boston and visit us for tea or an evening meal. After that, Yumma assured me, I would have a better idea of whether I wanted him to be my husband.

I didn't tell my mother that I already knew my answer.

We were married a few months later, at Widdi Catering Hall, the Middle Eastern venue of choice in Sunset Park. Every formal event in Brooklyn's Palestinian community happened there—engagement parties, weddings, graduation celebrations, fund-raisers, baby showers—and now it was my turn. There were so many people at our wedding I'm convinced it was a fire hazard. I'm also sure it was the most attention my husband ever had to endure.

I would soon learn that the quiet, serious demeanor I had observed in him when he was just the older brother of the kids I played with during summers in El Bireh was his true nature. He was not a man for grand public gestures. He was the sort who made a few friends and kept those friends forever, and who, when his children were born, devoted himself to their protection and care. Perhaps what I most appreciated in those early days of our getting to know one another was that, as my Sitty Halima had promised, he was unfailingly steady and kind.

Chapter 5

Everything Changed

When the security guard on campus told us that a plane had crashed into the World Trade Center, I thought maybe a flock of geese had flown into an engine, causing it to seize. Hadn't something like that happened in the nineties? I imagined a small propeller plane, maybe a news team reporting on the weather. I simply couldn't take in a jetliner full of passengers going up in flames.

I'd been sitting in my 9 A.M. chemistry class at Kingsborough Community College when I heard about the plane. That September morning had dawned clear and crisp, the sky overhead a crystalline blue. By the time the news reached us that one of the Twin Towers was on fire and everyone poured out of class onto the green campus, the air had turned ominous. Scraps of paper wheeled around us, floating down to the ground like confetti. I caught a few pieces and saw that the edges were charred. A chill ran through me as I realized they'd been blown here from the burning tower in Lower Manhattan all the way to the farthest end of Brooklyn. Peering into the smoky sky, I tried to hold on to an innocent feeling. I kept telling myself the inferno on the other side of the river was a terrible accident.

My first instinct was to get to Sunset Park, where my mother was babysitting my two-year-old son, Tamir, and nine-month-old daughter, Sabreen, while I attended class. I waited almost an hour for the bus before someone told me that the entire mass transit system had been shut down. In my lifetime, that had never happened. There was nothing else to do but walk the seven miles from Sheepshead Bay. Grim faced, I headed toward Oriental Boulevard, knowing I'd be on the road for hours. "A terrorist attack—" I overheard someone say as I trudged up the highway. *Oh God, I hope it's not Arabs. Please let it not be Arabs*, I thought.

By the time I reached Bay Ridge, home to the largest Arab American community in New York, it was early afternoon. The place was a ghost town. All the shops were shuttered and the mosque doors bolted and padlocked. A deep hush had fallen over this part of the city. I tried not to think about what was unfolding across the river. I wasn't ready yet to absorb the full horror of whatever could silence the hum of the streets and the underground rumble of trains. I would be home soon enough, I told myself, and then I'd know everything. Head down, I kept on walking, the innocent feeling slipping away.

———

As soon as Yumma saw me coming up the walk, she raced out of the house, car keys in hand. "I have to get DJ," she said. My eleven-year-old brother was in an honors program in Park Slope. With the trains not running, he must have felt out of reach to my mother. She wasn't worried about the others finding their way home. Heeba, Hanady, Hela, and Mo all went to public schools nearby. I assumed Lena, who was newly married, was safely inside the apartment she shared with her husband, and that my father was at his bodega in Crown Heights. At least he had the Chevy and could drive himself home. I watched from the curb as my mother slipped behind the wheel of her red Navigator. But something was strange.

"Yumma, your hijab," I called out to her. "You aren't wearing it."

"Linda, we can't today," she called back. "It's too dangerous."

I felt queasy as she coaxed the car's engine to life and drove away.

In the living room, I checked on my daughter dozing in her baby bouncer, then stooped beside my son, tousling his spiky black hair. "Fire, Mommy," he said, his little hand pointing to the television screen. "Look, Mommy, fire." He kept repeating the word in a kind of daze, and that's when I saw it—not one, but both of the Twin Towers engulfed in flames, and then crumbling one after the other to rock and dust. The two massive structures kneeled almost operatically through dense plumes of ash, again and again in a continuous video loop, papers and documents taking flight like frantic doves. And below the horrific images scrolled the words that would completely alter the life I knew: MUSLIM HIJACKERS ATTACK WORLD TRADE CENTER.

In New York City, almost three thousand people died on September 11, 2001, including 412 first responders. Days later, dead firefighters, medics, and cops stared out from the newspaper in row upon row of photographs. I studied their faces for a long time. That afternoon, my friend Rifah called and asked me to go with her to see her cousin a few blocks away. We strapped our children in their double strollers, hoping that the walk would distract us from the grief we were feeling. On the way we ran into Um Ahmad, an elderly Palestinian woman we knew. Well into her eighties, she was sitting on her stoop, one hand shading her eyes from sunlight as she, too, studied the faces of dead heroes in a newspaper spread across her lap.

"*Assalamu alaikum, cheef halich?*" I greeted her, asking how she was doing in a Palestinian dialect familiar to us both. I walked up the steps and bent to kiss her three times on the cheek. Her thin arms circled my neck, then she patted the concrete step next to her, inviting Rifah and me to sit. She looked at us with her ancient eyes.

"Listen to me," she said, gesturing at our head coverings. "This is not the time to wear your hijab in the streets. Faith is in the heart and God will understand. Right now he wants you to be safe."

Already Um Ahmad saw what might be coming. As a young woman in Palestine during the war of 1948, she had lived through the *nakba*, and now she feared that another sort of catastrophe had been set in motion. By then the nineteen hijackers had been identified. Most had common Muslim names—Muhammad, Said, Ahmed, Khalid—the sounds as familiar to our ears as if reporters were speaking about our own kin. But these men were not our family. They might look like us and share our names, but they had just carried out the worst terrorist attack in the history of my country. And so as Um Ahmad spoke, I understood her concerns, yet something in me resisted her advice.

"Um Ahmad, those terrorists have nothing to do with us," I protested. "A lot of Muslims died in the attacks, too." It was true: sixty Muslims had perished in the Towers alongside their coworkers.[1]

The old lady shook her head sadly. "I know," she said. "But the news is making it about us. Those hijackers shared our faith."

I knew she was right, but I still wasn't convinced that I should stop wearing my hijab. The hijackers may have been Muslim, but theirs was not the faith I practiced. My Islam was an expression of love, devotion to family, service to others, and the pursuit of fairness and truth. I wasn't trying to be stubborn, but my thoughts were reeling: *I'm Muslim. This is who I am. Why should I hide myself in shame?*

I thought about my parents insisting that we speak only Arabic at home. Some days, I'd burst in from school excited about something, my words rushing out in English. "Stop, Linda," my mother would say. "Tell me again in Arabic." Now that I was a mother myself, I was grateful to my parents for raising me to be fully bilingual and proud of my heritage. And then, I had a moment of clarity: if ever there was a time to represent the good in Islam, to act in opposition to the evil those men had unleashed on our world, this was it. I would not take off my hijab.

In the days that followed, I began to feel conspicuous in my beloved Brooklyn for the first time ever. When I walked into our usual supermarket later that week, it seemed as if the very air had shifted. My mother was with me; she, too, had chosen to resume wearing her hijab in public. Some people who on September 10 would have nodded and said hello now held us in their gaze for a beat too long and then looked away. I saw Yumma pull her sweater tight around herself, as if she sensed the chill, too.

Then came the rumors of Muslim men picked up on the street. These men had not been heard from in days. No one knew where they were. To my mind, these stories seemed too *un-American* to be true. Yet on Friday afternoons when we went to mosque, we heard more and more such reports. This woman's husband had been taken from his home. That mother's son had gone missing. This child's father had left for work one morning and never returned.

The men who were missing were not strangers. They were our husbands, fathers, uncles, brothers, and sons, and every week their number grew. Family members begged the imams for help in finding their men, but as troubled as our spiritual leaders were, they had no idea what to do. Worse, they knew they were being surveilled, too. They saw the unmarked cars parked outside the mosques, and the plainclothes agents watching from the corner as the faithful came and went.

Paranoia swept through our communities. In Arab-owned shops and hookah lounges, television sets were tuned only to sports channels, or turned off. The shopkeepers dared not air news programs that could provoke political conversations in case there was an informant in their midst. And if someone, even a friend, asked your opinion of recent events, you wondered if the question was innocent. No one was sure whom to trust. In a matter of weeks, we had all been transformed from ordinary, everyday New Yorkers who happened to worship as Muslims to a suspect class.

In December, I climbed a narrow flight of seventeen stairs to the second floor of a women's clinic, where the Arab American Association of New York (AAANY) was housed. Its executive director, a woman I dearly loved, had called me there. Basemah Atweh was my father's favorite cousin. In fact, he always introduced her to people as his sister. They both had big, loud personalities that lifted and energized any room they entered. Tall and abundantly built, Basemah didn't wear a head covering, and didn't even look very much like an Arab woman. Her bright red or pink or purple lipstick contrasted vividly with her creamy white skin and blond, salon-coiffed hair, but always matched her manicured nails perfectly.

Basemah had divorced her husband as a young woman, raising her son alone at a time when single motherhood was frowned on in our community. Basemah didn't care what people thought. Instead she poured herself into helping women who were in the kind of trouble she herself had faced when she first left her marriage. *What happens to a divorced immigrant wife and mother who doesn't speak the language and has no job?* she asked herself. *Where does a woman suffering from domestic abuse turn to get help, especially in a community where secrets spread like wildfire on dry wind?* Realizing there were no services for Arab women who had fallen on hard times, Basemah resolved to create her own agency. She filed the official paperwork in the spring of 2001, and that summer began meeting with sponsors and clients in neighborhood coffee shops.

Then 9/11 happened. Suddenly, the number of people seeking Basemah's help multiplied. Realizing she needed an office space where the community could find her, she approached Dr. Ahmad Jaber, the obstetrician who had delivered me and all my siblings into this world. Known among Palestinians in Brooklyn for his generosity, Dr. Jaber immediately offered Basemah the empty second floor of his clinic, and in December the AAANY moved in. Dr. Jaber didn't even charge Basemah rent. In fact, for years the center would be funded almost entirely by him—salaries, office supplies, phone usage, electric bills, he paid for it all.

Now, with Muslims under increasing surveillance, Basemah had summoned me. "Linda," she said, "you speak English and you speak Arabic. Come and work for me. We need organizers and translators. We need your skills."

You didn't say no to Basemah Atweh. The very next morning I reported for work at the agency. Tucked between two hookah smoke shops, the office didn't have much in the way of resources. One telephone served the entire place, which was furnished with long white Formica tables and metal folding chairs donated by a local business that was redecorating. The center looked like exactly what it was—an OB-GYN clinic, with sinks in each of the three small offices, and on the walls, posters about women's health. A couple of ancient computers with massive monitors took up entire desks, but the AOL dial-up was unreliable back then, so we researched services for our clients in fat volumes of the Yellow Pages.

The office might have been a bare-bones affair, but with the escalating interrogations and detentions of Muslim men, sometimes for little more than sharing a last name with one of the hijackers, we were busy all the time. I recall as if it were yesterday the very first case I worked on with the family of a man who had disappeared into the abyss of law enforcement. He was Moroccan and had come to the U.S. three years before on a work visa. A manager for an import-export company, he'd been tasked with setting up an office in the New York area. One evening, as he sat down to dinner with his wife and their four-year-old son, there came a knock at his door. When he opened it, he saw standing in the hallway three white men in civilian clothing.

"May we come in?" one of the men asked, and the Moroccan stepped aside. That was his mistake. The men had no search warrant, but once he allowed them into his home, that no longer mattered. Now they could confiscate documents and use them as evidence to arrest him. Many Arab men had already been detained and were later deported in exactly this way. Most were from countries where if the police stood at your door, you let them in and followed their instructions. These men didn't realize that in America, you could refuse to speak with law enforcement without an attorney present. And so when the men said to the Moroccan, "Please come with us," he felt he had no choice but to comply, even though he didn't know where they were taking him, or why.

His wife was distraught. After four days passed with no word from her husband, the imam at her mosque suggested she contact us. She stood in our reception area with her little boy at her side, pleading with us to find his father.

I was still so naive in those days. "What do you mean some men came to your apartment and took him away?" I asked, incredulous. "How is this possible? This is America. You can't just take someone and not even allow him a phone call. Who were these men? Where did they say they were from?"

"I don't know, I don't know," the woman responded, wringing her hands. She spoke Arabic and French, but very little English. However, her son, who was enrolled in a public school kindergarten, was fluent. He stepped forward, tugged my tunic, and looked up at me with round, earnest eyes.

"*Tante*," he said, calling me "auntie" in French, "will you find my *baba*?"

Something about this beautiful child reminded me of my own son— the deep pools of his dark, thick-lashed eyes; the shiny black hair; his absolute innocence and trust. I squatted down so that I was level with him, and I placed my hands gently on his small shoulders. "Yes," I told him. "We're going to find your father."

Though I wasn't at all sure I could manage what I'd promised, I got to work, calling legal clinics at local universities and working with them to try to figure out where this child's father might have been taken. Eight days later, using his Alien Registration Number, we located him in a federal detention facility. It turned out that because he had traveled extensively for his job, his passport had stamps from many Muslim countries, and that had been a red flag for our government. Further investigations had found nothing remotely suspicious in the man's activities, and so when our lawyer petitioned for his release, they let him go.

The next day, the man came into our office with his wife and son, bringing a box of baklava to thank us. As soon as they walked in, the little boy ran over and threw his arms around my waist. Tears welled in my eyes, and I thought how simple this world is, and how complicated at the same time. I met the gaze of the man who had so recently been detained and saw that his eyes were filled, too.

"We are grateful to you," he said. "If you had not come looking for me, I would have been deported."

"Your wife is the reason we found you," I told him. I placed a hand on his little boy's head. "And your son, too."

As I watched this reunited family leave our office that afternoon, the man with one arm around his wife and the other around his son, I thought about my own children. In that moment, I realized that the America in which my son and daughter would grow up was now a much less hospitable place than the neighborhoods of Brooklyn where I had come of age. I was suddenly exhausted beyond expression and sad for my children. And yet, weaving through the melancholy, I felt a strange kind of exhilaration. I knew it was because I had delivered on my promise to a little Moroccan boy, and that had felt profoundly meaningful.

Perhaps it was time to accept that I might never fulfill my childhood dream of becoming a high school English teacher. Basemah had shown me what seemed to be an even greater need, and now all I wanted to do was help the people whose very survival might depend upon my efforts. I understood my place perfectly now. In the shadow of unimaginable tragedy, and the fear and suspicion of Muslims that had followed in its wake, a new flame was ignited inside me, and is burning still.

Chapter 6

Our Sons Are Not Terrorists

It was not yet 6 A.M. as I walked toward 26 Federal Plaza, and yet the line of men stretched down the block and wrapped around the corner onto the next street. The men, virtually all of them Middle Eastern, North African, or South Asian, huddled outside the imposing glass-and-concrete office building, their bodies bundled in coats against the bite of February. Keffiyehs or thick woolen scarves swaddled their faces, and on their heads were kufis or plain knitted caps pulled low over their ears. The ones near the front were wrapped in blankets; they'd been on the sidewalk all night. Some sat with their backs against the building, still dozing. Others paced in tight circles, their faces haunted, their eyes in the half-light as hollow as ghosts'.

The men were queued up outside the Immigration and Naturalization Services (INS) office at that early hour in response to a call for visa holders "of a specified class" to register with authorities. The doors to the building opened at 7:00 A.M., and the men in line intended to be the first cases of the day. Many of them had waited for hours the day before, too, but when the INS office had closed for business at 3:30 P.M., they still had not been called. Advised to return the next morning, they had decided to make the sidewalk their bed. The consequence of being locked out for a second day and possibly missing the registration deadline was more than they wanted to risk.

68

The program, called the National Security Entry-Exit Registry System (NSEERS), applied to all men over the age of sixteen who hailed from any of twenty-five listed nations and who'd been admitted to the United States on visitor, medical, work, religious, student, or other nondiplomatic permits. All registrants were required to present their passports and other immigration documents, be fingerprinted and photographed, and explain their reasons for being in the country. Once in the system, they would have to reregister every year and notify the government of any change of address, employment, or school enrollment within ten days. They were also obliged to check in with authorities before leaving or returning to the country, which they were permitted to do only through specified ports of entry.

The fact that all but one of the twenty-five countries on the list were Muslim-majority nations only formalized what followers of Islam already knew—that after 9/11, we were seen as terrorist threats. North Korea, added to the roster later, would remain the only non-majority-Muslim country on the list. Not surprisingly, the call-in program quickly became known as the "Muslim registry." Announced a year after the extremist organization Al Qaeda claimed credit for the worst attack on American soil since Japan bombed Pearl Harbor in 1941, the call-in program mimicked the registration of Japanese nationals after that earlier attack: flyers emblazoned with the words THIS NOTICE IS FOR YOU! were left in grocery stores and coffee shops, stuck under the doors of mosques, wedged in mailboxes, and taped to bus shelters and lampposts in neighborhoods where Muslims lived.[1]

Civil liberties groups argued that the call-in amounted to flagrant racial and religious profiling. Attorney General John Ashcroft countered that the listed countries had been selected based on knowledge of Al Qaeda cells within their borders. Yet nations like Germany and England, known to have a strong Al Qaeda presence, weren't included. Consequently, the men in line at first light in Lower Manhattan were primarily brown and Black, summoned to appear based on having been born in a place where Islam was the dominant religion. In this equation,

Islam itself was conflated with terrorism, with those who worshiped as Muslims now officially declared as risks to America's national security.

It's almost too obvious to point out that the mass shootings that occur within our borders with such heartbreaking regularity are only labeled as terrorist acts if the perpetrator is a person of color or a Muslim. Never mind that since 1983, white men have committed 64 percent of these mass shootings (defined as a public event in which four or more are shot, not including the shooter).[2] With these events now averaging roughly one per day in America, the victims vastly outnumber those killed in acts of terrorism each year.[3] Yet no calls ever went out for white men to register as threats to national security. In America, when the killer's skin is white, the event is a tragedy. When their skin is brown or Black, an entire race or religion is accused.

As I had many mornings since the Muslim registry was announced, I went to the federal building to offer support to the men in line. Some had previously shown up at our agency, seeking help in deciphering the confusing registry instructions. They didn't know, for example, whether those with pending permanent residency or asylum applications were included in the call (they were). Nor was it clear whether a person born in one of the designated countries who had since become a citizen of another country that was *not* on the list was still required to register.[4] Legal advocates argued they were not, yet many Muslim men who fell into this category were rounded up and detained, and in some cases deported.

Since many of the visa holders were not fluent in English, I'd volunteered to translate for them. As usual, when I arrived at the federal building each morning, I started at the front of the line and moved down the queue, talking to the men and answering questions about the registry. Often, my answers felt inadequate, even to me, given how arbitrarily the rules and regulations were being enforced. But on one point the authorities had been unwaveringly clear: any foreign national not registered by the deadline for their particular country, with the final date falling in April 2003,[5] would be in violation of the law and could be deported. They might also be barred from ever applying for entry permits, amnesty programs, or residency status in the future.

With deadlines looming, the lines outside the INS grew longer every day. As the men inched toward the glass front doors, they brooded. What would happen when they got inside? So many of their friends had already disappeared. Would they be next? Should they even have come here, voluntarily putting themselves in the database of an agency that saw them first and foremost as potential terrorists?

Standing with these men as they waited to be processed, I didn't know how to feel about my role in all this. Why didn't people understand that Muslims had been as traumatized by the events of 9/11 as everyone else, and that we, too, wanted justice and security? Why did our government think the only way to ensure that was to round up innocent family men? I was so distressed and confused by what I was witnessing that I had to become almost robotic just to function.

For most of the men, the registration happened quickly. They'd stand at a public counter on the third floor, present entry documents, get their picture taken, press inked fingertips onto a card, submit proof of address, employment, or school enrollment, done. Some men, however, were questioned more closely: Why had they visited certain Muslim countries? How long had they stayed? Whom did they associate with there? Many of these men were then directed to another floor, and I was not allowed to accompany them there. The first time it happened, a security guard stopped me from entering the elevator. As the doors closed and my client disappeared from view, I turned to the guard.

"Where are they sending him?"

"Tenth floor," the guard said, his accent broadly West Indian.

"What's on the tenth floor?"

Something flickered in the guard's eyes, enough to let me know he was sympathetic to my underlying concern.

"Feds," he said briefly. "It's the office of the FBI."

And so I began to collect phone numbers from the men who got sent to the tenth floor. "Don't be afraid," I'd tell them. "I hope nothing happens, but just in case I will let your family know I saw you here." The men knew as well as I did that they might not be allowed to return home that night, and they wanted me to be able to say, "I was with your loved one at Twenty-Six Federal Plaza on this date, and they sent him to the FBI." At least their families would have a place to start searching.

Perhaps the most galling aspect of the call-in program was the fact that, despite close to 200,000 men registering by the April 2003 deadline, with some 13,000 of them being deported for minor infractions like having expired documentation, not a single registrant was ever found to be connected to terrorist activities. Yet, until the Department of Homeland Security officially removed the twenty-five countries from the NSEERS list in 2011,[6] and the program itself was finally wiped off the books just before Obama left office in 2016,[7] the Muslim registry would continue to incite fear, break families apart, and destabilize once-thriving Arab, North African, and South Asian communities.

Little Pakistan, a one-and-a-half mile stretch along Brooklyn's Coney Island Avenue, was a case in point. By the time the first phase of the special registration ended in April 2003, this community of approximately 120,000 Pakistani immigrants had been decimated. Every day, it seemed, more of its men simply vanished, even those who held green cards or were American citizens. Their grocery stores, coffeehouses, travel agencies, and tobacco shops stayed shuttered with no explanation. Their yellow taxicabs were left parked at the curb, tickets piling up on their windshields. Their seats went unoccupied in college classrooms, and employers wondered why they hadn't shown up for work.

A voluntary exodus followed, with more than 15,000 residents of Little Pakistan quietly packing up their lives and moving to Canada, Europe, or Pakistan.[8] Ironically, these exiles had been fervent believers in the American Dream. They had done everything by the book, toiling in humble jobs when they first arrived, educating their children, opening businesses of their own, climbing the ladder of achievement rung by rung until, through hard work and sheer faith in the promise of their new country, they had achieved steady middle-class lives. It was not lost on me that their path had been identical to the one traveled by my own parents.

Now services at the mosque on Coney Island Avenue, once overflowing with men in white kufis, were almost empty, and local hair salons, pizza parlors, and bodegas tried to weather a precipitous fall-off in business. On bus shelters and lampposts, FOR RENT and HELP WANTED signs jostled for space with flyers announcing the special registry, while abandoned apartments were watched over by friends, just in case their Pakistani occupants should ever return.

Across the country, other Muslim lives were being similarly disrupted. One Afghani national arrived in Iowa City after being invited to interview for medical residencies there. Since he would not know until the following March whether he'd been matched with a program, he'd gone into the local INS office to file for an extension of his visa. The agents initially confiscated the young doctor's passport, then returned it with a warning that he should leave the country immediately. Shaken, the Afghani doctor booked a ticket to travel a few days later. On the night before he was to fly home, FBI agents barged into the house where he was staying and took him into custody. Inexplicably, they moved him from one detention facility to another for months before finally deporting him.[9]

Meanwhile, in San Jose, California, an Iranian-born database manager who had become a Canadian citizen was shackled and flown to a prison in San Diego, where he was incarcerated in a cold, damp cell and forced to sleep on the concrete floor. The reason for his detention: he'd presented himself two days after the deadline for a call-in program that, as a Canadian citizen, he wasn't even sure applied to him. A judge eventually ordered his release.[10]

Another man, a naturalized U.S. citizen of Jordanian extraction who ran an ice cream truck in Chicago, was picked up and held for fourteen days. He never did discover the reason for his arrest. When the authorities finally let him go, they kept his naturalization certificate and social security card. He was forced to retain a lawyer for help in getting the documents returned, because now he was part of a world in which men who looked and worshiped as he did might at any moment be asked to prove their right to exist on these shores.[11]

As had happened in Coney Island's Little Pakistan, many Muslims decided to leave the country of their own accord. One Chicago attorney, after advocating for numerous Pakistani clients detained under NSEERS, became convinced that Muslims could no longer be assured of the American right to due process. "I advise my clients who have no hope to adjust their status to leave with dignity before the registration program ends," he admitted. "They can't imagine that Americans would want to deport them. The dream of America is over for them. The only other option is to live as a psychological fugitive."[12]

Even those of us who did not fall into NSEERS's "specified class" were affected. The worry never left me that my immigrant father and uncles might be picked up by federal agents for no reason, and that my brothers, although American-born, might on any given day be taken into custody, too. Indeed, for years after the official registration period ended, Arab men were still receiving notices to appear before immigration authorities, constant reminders that they were still being tracked.

It was now the spring of 2004, and I was eight months pregnant with my third child, my daughter Sajida. With my huge belly, I was standing at the immigration window inside 26 Federal Plaza one afternoon, translating for a Sudanese man when it occurred to me that some good might yet come of the Muslim registry. Perhaps the fact that I was about to bring another innocent child into this world accounted for my need to find reasons for hope.

And the reason I found was this:

By selectively targeting Arabs, Africans, and South Asians who were followers of Islam, the registry had ensured that Muslims of diverse ethnicities, cultures, and national origins would be forced to recognize our common cause. The experience of being officially vilified brought home to us that we needed representation at the highest levels of government. And so we began to organize, and to develop our communities politically. We realized that if Muslim Americans had been present at the table when the special registry was being discussed, the national security conversation would have been much more nuanced, and the indiscriminate fear and distortion of Islam might never have become so deeply rooted in America's heart.

The speed with which my Muslim brothers were branded as terrorists in the aftermath of 9/11 was dizzying. Of all the stories, perhaps the case of Mohammad Salman Hamdani most epitomized the hysteria. Salman Hamdani was no threat to anyone's security. The twenty-three-year-old wanted only to save lives.

Born in Karachi, Salman had come to New York from Pakistan with his parents when he was thirteen months old. His father opened a candy store and his mother got a job teaching English in middle school. He went to a Catholic academy in Brooklyn, and then attended Bayside High School in Queens, where he was number 79 on the football team and a *Star Wars* superfan. Salman was as all-American as they come, and he had a hero's heart. In college he had been certified as an emergency medical technician and also joined the NYPD Cadet Corps internship program.

Salman graduated from Queens College with a biochemistry degree in June 2001. His sights set on becoming a doctor, he took a job in the DNA lab at Rockefeller University, while continuing to serve part-time as an EMT for an ambulance corps and to put in hours as a police cadet. Salman was hedging his bets. He'd already been accepted into the police academy and was considering becoming a forensic detective—unless he got into medical school. On the eve of 9/11, he was working on his medical school application while also taking care of his father, who suffered from heart disease. On his way to work the following morning, Salman would have stood on an elevated subway platform and seen the smoke pouring from the upper levels of the Twin Towers. Scheduled for an EMT shift later that day, he had his medical bag with him.

Later, everyone who knew him would be convinced that Salman had headed straight to Lower Manhattan, using his EMT and police cadet credentials to gain access to Ground Zero so he could assist the other first responders. That night, Salman never came home. His parents and two younger brothers began calling morgues and hospitals, desperately trying to locate him. Days went by with no news. His mother, Talat Hamdani, prayed fervently that he was not among those who had perished at Ground Zero. Three weeks passed, and the family was no closer to knowing what had happened to Salman. Then the police came to their door.

Two officers sat in the Hamdanis' living room, asking questions about their missing son. Why had he wanted to become a police cadet? Who were his friends? What kind of work did he do at the DNA lab? What were his activities in the weeks before September 11? The officers noticed a photo on the refrigerator of Salman in cap and gown at his graduation from Queens College. Who was the man beside him? they wanted to know. Talat told them he was a fellow graduate and friend from Afghanistan. The officers confiscated the photo. Talat suddenly realized that they saw her son not as a missing person, but as a suspect in the attack on the World Trade Center.

Now she had a new prayer. As the weeks went by and the number of Muslims detained by federal agents climbed past one thousand, she prayed that her son was alive somewhere in a federal prison, a case of mistaken arrest that could be straightened out once they found him. She even wrote to President George W. Bush for help in locating Salman. "He is a Muslim and his first name is Mohammad," she said in her letter. "We all know many different governmental security organizations picked up people at random that day and are still doing it today. We don't have a problem with that. The enemy is among us and it is extremely difficult to identify them."[13] She received no response from the president, but soon learned that her son's cadet photo had been circulated through police departments with a handwritten note: "Hold and detain. Notify: Major case squad." Wanted posters with Salman's photograph showed up in her Bayside neighborhood, sometimes pasted over the family's own flyers asking for information about their missing son. Local newspapers reported that Salman was under investigation, with the *New York Post* publishing a story headlined MISSING—OR HIDING?—MYSTERY OF NYPD CADET FROM PAKISTAN.[14]

Finally, in March 2002 Salman's family learned that his remains, which had been found under the North Tower, had been positively identified using records taken from his dentist. Salman's medical bag had been found near his body, and at last, the true story of the young man's heroism began to be told.[15]

I would later be part of a network of people who supported Talat Hamdani in her campaign to get her son's name inscribed on the World Trade Center memorial with all the other heroic first responders from that day. I was also present with the family when, in recognition of their son and brother's sacrifice, the city renamed the street in Bayside where Salman was raised as Salman Hamdani Way. Listening as politicians and police chiefs praised the young EMT's courage on that terrible morning, I felt a crushing grief at the loss of this altruistic young man who, despite his deepest impulse to guard and protect lives, became a terrorist suspect for a while, simply because he was a Muslim.

———

It is difficult to express the degree to which the systematic targeting of Muslims by law enforcement in the weeks, months, and years following 9/11 emotionally traumatized our community. "It feels like you're under attack all the time," said one Arab American man, a thirty-year-old plumber with no criminal record who somehow ended up on the FBI's no-fly list for a year. The man had been visited at home numerous times by members of the city's counterterrorism task force. He believed that agents placed his name on the no-fly list in retaliation for his refusal to be interrogated without a lawyer present. "They told me they were watching me," he recalled. "They were watching my every move. They knew every contact in my cell phone and every message I sent. They said I would come to regret this and that they were going to take me down."[16]

The young man's mental health suffered. He was anxious all the time, and even broke off an engagement because he didn't want his fiancée to have to endure what he was going through. "The tool of fear: it definitely works," he told a reporter for *The Guardian*. "You can't even turn to the authorities. They are the ones doing it. I know I am supposed to have rights as a citizen, but I think they have a different rulebook for people like me, for Muslim Americans."[17]

With Islamophobia sweeping across the nation, incidents of violence against Muslims were on the rise. One incident in particular struck close to home. On a summer night in 2010, a New York City cabdriver picked up a young white man on Manhattan's East Side. The two men engaged in light conversation until the passenger asked the driver if he was Muslim. The driver replied that he was. The passenger responded with, "*Assalamu alaikum*," then a few blocks later, suddenly yelled, "This is the checkpoint! I have to bring you down!" and lunged across the seat. He drew a knife across the driver's throat before slashing him repeatedly in the face and arm. He fled as the driver, a father of four, stumbled bleeding from the car. Fortunately the driver was taken immediately to the hospital and survived.[18] But he would require months to heal from his injuries, not to mention his mental trauma. Unable even to lift his ten-month-old baby in his arms, he worried about providing for his family.

In my role with the Arab American Association, I heard many such stories. And yet, even I did not fully grasp how the branding of our men as terrorists had seeped into the consciousness of our children, not until a week after the incident with the cabdriver, when a conversation with an eleven-year-old Palestinian American child opened my eyes. This boy would be entering sixth grade at a new school in the fall. He was at our office that day as part of our summer program for neighborhood kids. I asked him how he felt about going to a new school, expecting him to respond with some excitement. Instead, he looked down at his shoes.

"Sister Linda," he said, "what if people ask me if I'm a Muslim?"

"What do you mean?" I said. "You tell them that you're Muslim."

He looked up at me. "What if they hurt me?" he said. "They stabbed that cabdriver. Would it be okay if I just didn't tell anyone I'm Muslim?"

I felt as if a blade were twisting itself inside my heart. I had believed that this precious child was young enough to be sheltered from the pervasive profiling of our men. I was wrong.

"Oh, honey," I said, hugging him to my side, "you don't have to worry. Your parents and your teachers will protect you, and besides, you should always be proud of who you are."

Even as I formed the words, I wondered if I was giving him the proper assurance. Could I really guarantee this boy's security out in the world? The truth was I could not, any more than I could guarantee my own son's. I went home that night in anguish at the realization that even our children believed that as Muslims in America, they were not welcome, and they were not safe.

Chapter 7

Basemah, Beloved

Every other weekend when I was growing up, our family would descend en masse for Saturday-afternoon cookouts at my uncle's house in Canarsie, Brooklyn. Any and all members of our extended clan might show up for these gatherings, but there was one person I looked out for most of all. As soon as I saw her tapping up the walkway in her kitten heels, her bag and shoes setting off her outfit to perfection, her blond hair haloing her face in an eighties-style bouffant, I'd jump up from wherever I was and rush out to greet her. The life of the party had arrived.

Basemah Atweh always walked in like she was the hottest thing in the room. And she was. People would flock to her, marveling at her perfect hair, perfect eyelashes, perfect skin. "Basemah, how come you never wear the same thing twice?" I'd ask her. In a world where women are supposed to make themselves small and not take up too much room, Basemah dominated any space she was in with her confidence. It was clear that she enjoyed and appreciated every inch of her bounteous self, and she inspired people around her to enjoy and appreciate themselves, too. "I don't take shit from anybody, and you shouldn't, either," she'd tell us cheerfully. The lady was one tough cookie, and charismatic. Everything glowed a little brighter and felt more hopeful when Basemah was around.

She was our cousin—second, third, I was never really sure because Palestinians don't much care about those distinctions. A cousin was a cousin, and an elder, whether related by blood or not, was called *auntie* or *uncle*, which made our families sprawling, confusing entities. All I really knew about Basemah's relationship to me was that she had grown up with my father in the West Bank of Palestine; she was my mother's age and one of her closest friends; and she'd always felt like a jolly, conspiratorial big sister to me. I loved nothing more than to see her laugh. She laughed so hard it was almost as if she were having an asthma attack, and everyone would laugh along with her, just to share in her joy.

Other than at my uncle's house on Saturdays, we would see Basemah at weddings and other communal gatherings. We might go to twenty Palestinian weddings a year, which meant we saw her a lot. Every person who met Basemah ended up adoring her, and it wasn't just because of her ebullient personality. It was the fact that you knew within minutes that here was a woman who would give you the hot-pink dress off her back and suit up for any battle of yours that might need fighting.

Basemah had come to America at seventeen years old. She'd married a young man from her village soon after her arrival and settled in Brooklyn. The couple had a son who was around the same age as I was; he and I used to play together as children. When the marriage deteriorated, Basemah decided she could manage better on her own. At a time when most Arab women felt they had no choice but to endure troubled marital arrangements, Basemah divorced her husband and found an apartment for herself and her child. She got herself hired by a health maintenance organization in Sunset Park, where her job was to help families gain access to affordable medical care in Brooklyn.

A local hospital, Lutheran Medical Center (now New York University's Langone Medical Center) noticed her work at the HMO. They noticed, too, how much the community rallied around her. They saw what I'd seen when I was just a kid, that Basemah was the unofficial mayor of Sunset Park. It didn't matter who you were, where you came from, or the color of your skin—if you had met Basemah even once, you were devoted to her. And since Lutheran recognized there was a large community of Arabs and other immigrants in the area that they wanted to reach, they offered Basemah a job as a patient relations representative.

In no time at all, Basemah was the unofficial boss of Lutheran. You could not walk with her in the hospital without fifty people stopping her to chat. Basemah quickly realized she wasn't there just to be a patient relations representative, or at least her conception of that job was much more expansive than the hospital envisioned it. Basemah brought the administrators up to speed in her own inimitable way, pushing Lutheran to add Arabic translations to all the paperwork, brochures, and signage. Basemah also advocated for the provision of modest gowns. Even though she herself did not wear a hijab, she understood that the lack of gowns with long sleeves and more complete coverage of the body could be a barrier to treatment for some Muslim women. Basemah also helped many people get jobs at the hospital, and not just Arabs. She convinced her bosses that if they truly wanted to serve the community, they needed an inclusive, multilingual staff.

Every time my siblings and I went to Lutheran for an appointment, my mom would take us to visit Basemah. Her cubicle was the prettiest one. There were always flowers on the desk, because someone was always thanking her for something. And she always had food. She would open a drawer and pull out some chocolate or a candy bar and hand it to us with a wink. If my mom had received a bill that she didn't understand (our family still didn't have health insurance), Basemah would explain every item to Yumma in a way that struck me, even as a small child, as incredibly patient and kind.

When she first founded her social service agency in the Sunset Park–Bay Ridge area, Basemah's primary goal had been to help Arab women. She knew how to keep people's secrets, and clients trusted her with the most intimate details of their marriages and their lives. Many of the women crossed her path because they had shown up at the hospital battered and bruised. Basemah would go to translate for a patient in the emergency room and the woman would whisper, "My husband threw me down the stairs." Sometimes the woman would be someone from her village, whose husband Basemah also knew. Basemah taught me the value of allowing there to be a space in our community where people could feel safe, where they could tell the whole truth about their traumas, because how else would they begin to get help for themselves and their children?

Above all, Basemah was discreet. Her first rule was to protect the vulnerable from judgment, repercussions, and shame. She sometimes went so far as to allow women and their children to stay in her apartment until she could get them safely settled elsewhere. Indeed, before Dr. Jaber gave up the second floor of his clinic to house the AAANY, Basemah essentially ran the agency out of her home.

One weekend, not long after I'd begun working with her as an organizer and translator, Basemah invited me to lunch. She had heard me say in passing that I couldn't recall the last time I'd eaten *shish barak*, a delicious dumpling stew my grandmother used to make. Next thing I know, Basemah's inviting me over to her house for *shish barak*, which is like an Arabic version of ravioli stuffed with minced meat and pine nuts and simmered in a rich yogurt sauce.

That Saturday, I walked into Basemah's small apartment on Cropsey Avenue in Bensonhurst, pushing my babies in their double stroller. As I greeted Basemah, kissing her on both cheeks, a slender young woman wearing a two-tone blue hijab and a long black sweater emerged from the kitchen. She was carrying a bowl of the stew, which she set on the dining table. She smiled at me and went back into the kitchen.

"Who's that?" I asked as I bent to lift two-year-old Tamir and infant Sabreen from the double stroller. I set Tamir on the floor to explore and held Sabreen against my shoulder, the delicious aromas of garlic and coriander reaching me from the bowl on the dining table. Basemah pulled out a chair in front of the bowl and gestured for me to sit.

"Malika's one of our clients," she said as I adjusted myself in front of the steaming dish of *shish barak*. "She came into the hospital last week, horrible abusive situation at home. She's from Lebanon and doesn't really know anyone in Brooklyn. They were going to send her to a domestic violence shelter, but she hardly speaks any English." Basemah shrugged. "I felt bad. I knew she wouldn't be able to have a conversation with anyone at the shelter. She couldn't ask for what she needed, so I brought her here."

Basemah's houseguest, who I would learn was in her early twenties and four months pregnant, now walked back into the living room carrying two more bowls of stew. She set one down for Basemah on the small rectangular table, and another in front of her own chair, and the three of us ate lunch together, Sabreen on my shoulder, Tamir roaming at our feet, a small improvised family bound by love and need.

———

Basemah and I spent a good portion of our time helping women like Malika build new lives. This might involve enrolling them in language classes, providing temporary financial support, assisting with immigration cases, and helping clients apply for life-saving social services like Medicaid or food stamps.

When I first began working with the agency, I didn't know where to turn or whom to call to help our clients. But I was fluent in Arabic and English, and that allowed me to communicate with people, which made a world of difference to many of them. Meanwhile, Basemah was training me, sending me to classes in crisis counseling, immigration services, and domestic violence intervention. I was a fast learner. Soon I had built my own contact lists and could independently refer people to the services they needed. Yet Basemah never stopped teaching me. She probably had no idea how much I learned just by being at her side.

I remember when we organized our first Eid al-Adha party. Eid al-Adha, also known as the festival of sacrifice, recalled the story of the Prophet Ibrahim's willingness to sacrifice his son to God, only to be stopped at the last moment and told to slaughter an animal instead. Eid al-Adha commemorates obedience to Allah in word and deed. It coincides with the end of the hajj pilgrimage to Mecca, and is one of the two holiest days on the Muslim calendar. Traditionally, our families celebrate the holiday with a community-wide feast and the giving of gifts.

In planning the Eid party, I'd made a list of everything we needed to do—the hall to be rented, food to be catered, party favors for the children, so much more. I didn't see how our little agency could afford it all.

"Basemah, how will we pull this off?" I wailed. "Everything costs too much."

"What do we need?" Basemah said matter-of-factly. We were sitting in her cubicle at Lutheran Medical Center, where Basemah still worked, and from which she still drew a regular paycheck. That allowed her to forgo taking a salary for her position as executive director of the agency, which still operated mostly out of Dr. Jaber's pocket.

I held up my spiral-bound notepad and began to recite the list.

"Book a venue," I said, and before I could mention the next item, Basemah had the phone to her ear and was dialing Widdi Catering Hall. Basemah was no procrastinator.

"We're doing an Eid party for the community in two weeks," she said. "What times do you have available?" A few minutes later she hung up the phone and announced, "Okay, you got Widdi. They're not charging us anything." I would sit there looking at her in awe as our entire to-do list got checked off in exactly the same way.

"What's next?" Basemah would ask.

"Five hundred goodie bags for the kids," I'd say, and Basemah would go to work, calling up a local supermarket, explaining what we needed, then hanging up the phone and saying, "The manager said to just bring a cart and get whatever we need for the kids, his contribution, no charge."

"What about food?" I'd say, and Basemah would jot down the names of women in our community, including my mother. Then she'd start making phone calls, assigning each woman on her list a dish to bring. But instead of asking any one person to make the entire portion of, say, five hundred meat pies, she'd tell five different women, "I need one hundred pies from you." Then she'd call the next woman on her list.

"You're making rice," she'd say, "enough to feed fifty."

"Baked chicken."

"Pasta salad."

"Stuffed grape leaves."

"Shish kebabs."

By the time the last name on the list was checked off, we had a feast, and we hadn't spent a penny.

Next Basemah might call up a local electronics store and get a toaster, a microwave, and other appliances donated for a raffle. Then maybe her old HMO organization would agree to sponsor the entertainment. Next thing you knew, we had booked a band and a clown. That was Basemah. She had the network and the credibility to make things happen. Basemah would call twelve people and fifteen would show up for her. She was just gifted that way.

This was in 2002. Facebook wouldn't be a thing for another three or four years. The secret to organizing, Basemah told me, was relationships. If you want people to come to an event you're holding, you pick up the phone and invite them personally. You remember people's birthdays, and those of their children. You ask about the uncle who had surgery five months ago, the recently engaged young woman, and the progress of teenagers looking ahead to graduation and college. For Basemah, success in any endeavor was based on cultivating relationships, which for her was about letting people know they mattered.

Basemah taught me how to show up for people, and for myself. Most of the meeting rooms we went into were made up entirely of men, except for Basemah and me. She would coach me beforehand, "Don't let those men talk for you, Linda. You speak up for yourself." I took her words to heart, but my best education was simply to watch how she operated and do likewise.

Basemah and I were seated in a wood-paneled conference room with some of our community elders, planning our annual break-the-fast event, Eid al-Fitr—the second of the two holiest days for Muslims. The idea was to invite local priests and rabbis, police officers and shopkeepers, teachers and city representatives, hospital colleagues and other non-Muslim friends to share in the celebration and learn what our practice of fasting from sunup to sundown during the month of Ramadan was all about. There were twenty-three men around the table with Basemah and me, and they were debating who the keynote speaker for the event should be.

Several of the elders proposed that a particular imam should deliver the keynote, and that's when Basemah weighed in.

"That makes no sense," she said from her end of the conference table. Every head in the room swiveled to hear her out, because when Basemah spoke, people got in formation. "English isn't his native language. You know he can barely put two sentences together in English, so how do you expect him to get up there and explain to our non-Muslim guests what is beautiful and special about Ramadan? You need someone who is going to contextualize our spiritual practice, and share why we fast, so people can understand our story. And that's not some guy who just happens to be an Islamic scholar from Egypt but who literally cannot speak to our guests. He's not the person to bring the community together. It's not going to work."

Dr. Jaber, who was also at the table, cleared his throat.

"She's absolutely right," he said to the room.

"And furthermore," Basemah continued, effortlessly holding the floor, "I would highly recommend that we make Linda the emcee of the event. I think it shows that we're bringing more young people into the organizing work we're doing, and involving more women from the local community."

"Well, I agree with that, too," Dr. Jaber said, stroking his short white beard.

Later, Basemah would tease the doctor good-naturedly. "Why did I even have to say anything at all?" she needled him. "If you agreed with me, why didn't you just say it before I did?"

Dr. Jaber held up his hands in surrender. "You're right, Basemah, you're always right," he conceded with a laugh, because he and Basemah often bantered like that. These two giants of our community, both of whom I was lucky enough to be mentored by, had always been the best of friends.

In the end, we hired an African American professor of Islamic studies to be the keynote speaker, and he delivered an inspirational speech about Ramadan as a time of spiritual reflection. As a Black man, he was also able to point out that Islam was not foreign to this country. Muslims have been part of the fabric of American life since the first Africans set foot on these shores, with up to a third of those brought here in the bellies of slave ships being followers of Islam.[1] The tone of the professor's keynote was just right, and afterward, Basemah couldn't have been more pleased. She kept going up to the elders and saying happily, "Didn't I tell you? What did I tell you?" Basemah loved letting people know she'd told them so.

More than any other person on this earth, this brilliant and beautiful woman helped me find and use my voice. My parents described me as the good child, the responsible firstborn daughter who set an example for her younger siblings and made no waves. Basemah taught me to make waves, to stir the pot, to raise holy hell when things didn't sit right or when individuals or communities were in trouble. It would be impossible for me to explain why I do this work without first sharing the life-changing experience of just being at Basemah's side.

I had joined her organization mainly because she asked me to, but when I started watching how she functioned, I knew I wanted to follow her, much like a disciple. Basemah would announce, "We're going to a conference in Washington, DC," and I would respond, "Right behind you," before I even knew what the conference was about. I never questioned her. And as she actively trained me, Basemah became the mother of my activism. "I see a bit of myself in you," she would tell me. It always thrilled me to hear her say that. And she would add, "You, *habibti*, were born for this work."

Now, whenever I am faced with a tough decision or a challenge in my role as a community organizer, I pause and whisper into the silence: *What would Basemah do?*

Part Two

Intersectionality

I have realized that our love . . . is a beautiful form of defiance against a system that seeks to suppress our humanity—a system that wants us to hate ourselves . . . This is why we have to protest. This is why we are so passionate. We protest because we love ourselves, and our people . . . Love is at the root of our resistance.

—Colin Kaepernick,
activist and Amnesty International Ambassador of Conscience

Chapter 8

Breath and Memory

D oug Flutie?" I heard a woman in a leopard-print headscarf exclaim. She was referring to the Boston College quarterback who threw the famous touchdown-scoring Hail Mary pass in the final minutes of a 1984 football game against then national champions Miami. "He's Arab American, too? I had no idea." The Heisman Trophy–winning Flutie, who went on to play in the National Football League and whose forefather had immigrated to the United States from Lebanon, was just one of the many noteworthy Americans included in an exhibit at the new Arab American National Museum in Dearborn, Michigan.

It was May 5, 2005, a cool, clear Midwestern afternoon. Basemah and I, along with Basemah's cousin Angie, and Mona, a Palestinian volunteer with our agency, had driven ten hours from Brooklyn to be present for the museum's opening ceremony. At twenty-five years old, Mona was the same age as me, but she was quiet and shy, while the rest of us were boisterously expressive on that celebratory day. Dr. Jaber and his wife were also in attendance, but they had traveled in another car. Nothing could have kept us away from this joyful occasion. The very existence of an Arab American museum felt like a triumph for our community, with hundreds of people cheering in the street as the ribbon was cut, then flocking inside to explore the glass-and-stone building on Dearborn's Michigan Avenue.

As I strolled through the jam-packed exhibit rooms, I reflected that everything about this place refuted the post-9/11 narratives about Arab Americans. Now, instead of being branded as dangerous extremists, we could proclaim our excellence and pay tribute to our accomplishments as citizens of this nation. At last the contributions of Arabs to American society and culture would be made visible. People would finally know that achievers such as longtime White House press corps dean Helen Thomas, Apple Inc. founder and tech innovator Steve Jobs, basketball player Rony Seikaly, bestselling author of *The Exorcist* William Peter Blatty, labor leader Stephen Yokich, heart pump inventor Dr. Michael DeBakey, presidential candidate and consumer protectionist Ralph Nader, and so many others were people of Arab descent. Indeed, Arabs had been present in America from its inception, yet never before had there been a place where our story was commemorated. And where better to hold such a party than in Dearborn, home to the most con-centrated community of Arab Americans in the country?

The festivities lasted late into the night. At the end of the evening, Dr. Jaber and his wife left to drive back to Brooklyn while the rest of our contingent dined on Dearborn's five-star Middle Eastern cuisine, then went shopping in fine stores for hijabs, traditional embroidered garments, and various Arab delicacies and sweets to bring home to our families. Clothing stores in Dearborn commonly stayed open until ten at night, and many sweets shops didn't close their doors until well after midnight. The next morning, all of us a little bleary from the day be-fore, we rolled out at daybreak for the long trip back to New York.

Angie was at the wheel of the dark green 1994 Toyota Avalon, which belonged to Dr. Jaber. He had loaned us that vehicle for the drive to and from Dearborn, and we knew it was an act of love on his part, because Dr. Jaber adored that car. We used to tease him about the old Avalon. The doctor was a wealthy man, and yet he preferred to drive himself everywhere in that green car, only occasionally borrowing his wife's shiny black Mercedes. But as much as we made fun of the Avalon, we knew that Dr. Jaber's love for the old clunker revealed his humility, and the fact that he would much rather spend his wealth on uplifting his people. Besides, the old Avalon still had a lot of life in her. She was steady on the road, and had brought us to Dearborn without a hitch. Now, as Angie steered us out of the hotel parking lot and toward Interstate 80, Basemah was in the front passenger seat, while Mona and I settled down in the back seat for the ride home.

Soon after we crossed into Pennsylvania, Angie pulled into a rest stop to use the bathroom and get coffee. It was 7:45 A.M., and as we all walked back to the car with cups in hand, Angie held up the car keys and declared she was exhausted. "I'm not going to lie to you, my eyes were closing before we stopped," she said. "I think someone else should take over driving."

The only someone else who could take over was me, because Basemah didn't drive, and Mona was undocumented and didn't have a license. Still, I hesitated. I was an inexperienced driver. I did have a valid license, but with the vast public transportation system in New York, there was seldom a need for me to drive any farther than ten blocks. I couldn't even recall the last time I'd driven on a highway. But Angie was standing there holding out the keys to me, and it crossed my mind that she, like Basemah, was my mother's age, and if my mother were standing there telling me she was too tired to drive, I'd simply take the car keys from her hand and get behind the wheel.

So that's what I did. Basemah slid in next to me in the front passenger seat, and Angie sat behind her and across from Mona in the back seat. I pulled out into traffic on I-80 and was soon cruising along, all of us chatting about the events of the previous day. Presently, everyone else dozed off, and I was alone with my thoughts, covering the miles toward home.

———

Along a rural stretch in Pennsylvania, I started seeing signs announcing roadwork ahead. As the flow of traffic narrowed from four lanes to two, I slowed down, keeping one eye on the tractor-trailer trundling along in the lane to the left of me. To my right was a steep drop-off into a grassy ditch, and no metal barrier to protect us from it. My hands gripped the steering wheel, all my senses heightened. Soon, a long row of orange-striped traffic cones came into view, marking off the construction area. These weren't the small triangular cones that college students steal as trophies for their dorm rooms. The cones were of the larger variety, half as tall as my five-foot-four-inch frame, and shaped like barrels. Up ahead, a cone had fallen over and was lying in the path of the truck beside me. I distinctly remember thinking that the truck was large enough to just roll right over that toppled plastic cone.

But the driver had another idea. He tried to go around the cone, and veered toward me. Panicked, I yanked the wheel to the right, swerving to avoid him. Suddenly, we were flipping over, bouncing down the steep slope and turning three full revolutions before landing upright in a ditch below the highway. It took me several moments to realize we'd come to a stop, and that I seemed to be uninjured. I looked to my right, but the passenger seat was empty. *Where was Basemah?*

I heard a moan from the back seat and turned to see Angie grimacing in pain. Her leg was jammed between the front seats, and was bent at frightening angles. Next to her, Mona, too, had disappeared. *Where could she be?* I realized suddenly that I'd been the only one in the car wearing a seat belt. Had Basemah and Mona been thrown from the car? But that didn't quite make sense, at least where Basemah was concerned, because her door was still closed, the side bashed in. Now I saw that all the doors were crushed and twisted and all the windows had shattered. Maybe Mona had been hurled out of the back window as the car flipped over. She was a petite person, so it seemed possible. Angie's pinned leg had kept her from being thrown from the vehicle, but what had happened to Basemah? She would not have been pitched through a window, or even the windshield. She was a large woman, the seat belt too small for her, which was why she never wore it. Could she have pushed open her door and jumped out as the car spun out of control?

I struggled to open my own door, and eventually succeeded. As soon as I exited the car, I saw Mona, lying maybe forty feet away in the ditch. I started to run to her, but then turned back to try to help Angie out of the car first. She was clearly in a lot of pain, but I couldn't get her door open. Not only was the steel twisted and bashed in, but it was also wedged into the muddy bank of the ravine.

"Angie, I have to find Basemah," I said. "I see Mona but I lost Basemah. I don't know where she went."

"Go, go." Angie waved me on as a new surge of pain contorted her face.

I ran to Mona, who was on her back staring up at the sky.

"You okay?" I asked her stupidly. She was clearly not okay.

"I don't know if I can move my back," she whispered. And then she asked me the strangest thing. "Am I still wearing my hijab?"

"Yes, you are," I told her, reaching down to pull the cloth forward to cover her escaping wisps of hair. Much later, I realized that my own hijab had been knocked off in the accident. I was a sight, my face streaked with dirt, hair flying everywhere, eyes wild with shock and fear. Though I didn't know what was going on with Mona's back, at least she was alive. I still had to find Basemah.

I ran back to the car and circled it, and there was Basemah on the far side, also lying on her back. Her lips were moving, but I couldn't hear what she was saying over the roar of traffic up on the highway. I fell to my knees beside her and bent close.

"I can't breathe," she whispered. "Can't . . . breathe . . ."

"Hold on, Basemah! I'm going to get help."

I looked around us, my eyes roving over the woods on one side then darting to the traffic streaming by on the highway above. I clambered back up to the highway and began waving my arms, trying to flag someone down. A blue pickup truck pulled over and a young white man and his girlfriend got out.

"What's going on?" he asked.

I pointed down into the ditch, where Basemah and Mona lay some distance away from the badly battered car. As soon as the man saw the situation, he took out his cell phone and called for help. His girlfriend ran back to the pickup and emerged with a red-and-black plaid woolen blanket that she wrapped around my shoulders. I hugged the warmth around me gratefully, and then I thought that Basemah must be cold, too. I slid back down the slope to where she lay and spread the blanket over her. She smiled at me weakly, her lips moving soundlessly. She was trying to tell me something. "Shhh, it's okay," I told her. "Preserve your strength. The ambulance is on its way."

Everything seemed to be happening in slow motion, and yet I don't think five minutes had passed from the moment our car flipped until I heard sirens blaring toward us, and the *thump thump thump* of helicopter propeller blades overhead. Police cars with flashing lights blocked off Interstate 80, backing up traffic for miles as ambulances and fire trucks screeched to a halt at the top of the embankment. Paramedics carrying stretchers and first aid equipment raced down the slope to help Basemah, Angie, and Mona. I could tell from their urgency as they worked on Basemah that she was the most seriously injured, even though she didn't have a scratch on her. They cut open her shirt and shocked her heart with electric paddles attached to a defibrillator. Basemah just kept whispering, "I can't breathe," over and over.

At least she's talking, I thought as I retrieved the tartan blanket that the paramedics had tossed aside. Next to me, firefighters were sawing off the top of the Avalon to free Angie, while a few yards away medics had immobilized Mona's broken body and were lifting her onto a stretcher. I saw that two helicopters had landed, and now they loaded Mona into one of them. When I looked back at Basemah, they were shifting her onto a stretcher, too, and starting an IV drip in her arm before rushing her toward the second helicopter. I thought, *Okay, they have her. They'll fix her and make everything right*. It never once occurred to me that this could turn out any other way.

As the helicopters lifted into the sky, I realized that Angie was now out of the Avalon and lying on a stretcher in one of the ambulances up on the road. One of the medics took my arm and ushered me up the embankment and into the ambulance with her. As soon as I was seated inside, he jumped in, too, pulled the doors shut, and signaled his partner in the driver's seat to go. The siren came on, and then we were weaving through traffic toward the hospital.

Angie and I ended up at the same emergency room as Mona, but Basemah was taken to a trauma center. We soon learned that several vertebrae in Mona's back had been shattered. She would have to wear a body brace for years after that day, and have multiple surgeries, but she would eventually heal. Angie had fared slightly better. Her right leg was broken in three places. She might walk with a limp for the rest of her life, but the doctor assured her that she, too, would heal. As for me, I thought I had no wounds at all from the accident until, hours later, I looked down at my left hand and noticed it was covered in dried rivulets of blood radiating from a piece of glass embedded in my wrist. I was a walking PSA for the use of seat belts.

But although I was physically unhurt, an avalanche of guilt pressed down on me. Three women were suffering horrifically because of me. Sitting in the hospital hallway, staring into space, I didn't know what to do but stay close to my friends. A young Palestinian American resident found me there, or maybe he was sent to me by some kind soul. He took me to his home, where his wife encouraged me to clean myself up and eat something.

"Look," the resident said, "I know you're going through a lot of trauma, but you have to get your head straight. Who do you need to call?"

I didn't answer. I thought of Basemah's son, who still lived with her in Brooklyn. And I thought of her eight brothers and sisters. But how could I call any of them to say what had happened without first knowing how Basemah was? Better to wait for news, I decided.

After a while—I have no idea how long—the resident took me back to the hospital. He was with me in the lounge area later when a doctor, an older white gentleman with snow-white hair, walked up to me.

"Is your name Linda?"

I nodded. His expression was so somber, my whole body tensed.

"What is your relationship to Basemah Atweh?" the doctor asked.

"She's my father's cousin and my mentor and she's like my older sister," I said. "She's . . . she's . . . everything to me. She's my . . . Basemah." My words trailed off as I saw the doctor's eyes well up.

"What happened?" I asked him, my voice tiny and scared. "Where is Basemah?"

The doctor sat down next to me, suppressing a sigh. I pulled the plaid blanket tight around my shoulders, but it was a poor armor for what came next.

"Basemah passed away," the doctor said. "We did everything we could to save her, but there was so much internal bleeding."

I looked at him, trying for all I was worth to unhear his words. In my head, a single thought ricocheted like a scream: *Basemah is gone.* I'd never get to hear her laugh with her whole being like she was having an asthma attack ever again.

Chapter 9

Lessons in Activism

The first person I called was my father. I told him there had been an accident. His voice became frantic. "Are you okay?"

"Yaba, I'm fine. Nothing's wrong with me, I didn't break anything. Nothing happened to me." And then I fell silent on the phone, because how do you say the words you know will break your father's heart?

"What about everyone else?" Yaba asked quietly.

I think, by my silence, he knew.

"Basemah is dead," I said.

The strangled sound of my father's cry will never leave me.

He asked for details, and I gave them. My voice was thick and ragged, but I did not cry. I couldn't understand why I felt so detached from myself, as if I were floating outside my body, looking on as unimaginable tragedy took hold. I realized now why I hadn't wanted to call anyone when the young resident urged me to. I hadn't wanted to utter the words that would make the accident real. Now there was no holding back the sorrow and guilt that enclosed me in its fist, or enclosed that other person, the dark-haired woman who had lost her hijab in a ditch next to the highway, who now sat in a hospital lounge draped in a plaid blanket, her eyes as dry as the Palestinian desert as she recounted the story of a beloved's death.

As soon as Yaba hung up the phone, my mother began making calls to let people know we had lost Basemah. Yaba left at once to come and get me, driving the three hours to Pennsylvania and arriving by four o'clock that afternoon. Angie and I both traveled back to Brooklyn with him that evening. Angie's leg had been set in a cast, and she had been given instructions to follow up with doctors back home, but Mona couldn't be moved. She would have to remain at the hospital in Pennsylvania for two more weeks as they worked to stabilize her spine.

As we headed home that Friday, Dr. Jaber was already making arrangements to fly Basemah's body back to Brooklyn for her *janaza* the following day. In Islam, unless there is an official investigation, the dead must be buried within twenty-four hours, and so the imam at Basemah's mosque in Sunset Park began preparations for her service as soon as he heard the news. By the time I lay down in my old bedroom at my parents' house that night, still holding the plaid blanket, the ritual washing of the dead had already taken place, and Basemah's pristine, unblemished body had been wrapped in pure white cotton and was waiting for the funeral service to begin in a matter of hours.

Strangely, I still had not cried for this woman I so loved. It was as if I were moving underwater, everything muted by my crushing remorse at having robbed the world of the bright light that was Basemah. Inside the mosque that afternoon, I could barely process what was happening. The place was packed. The main area held well over two thousand people, and an annexed town hall space had room for another thousand. Both auditoriums were full to overflowing with mourners. Everyone who ever knew Basemah, it seemed, had come to pay last respects alongside her family. In addition to her extended Palestinian community were people of all different races, nationalities, and faiths: her colleagues from the hospital; clients she had once served; local politicians and activists; imams, ministers, and rabbis; people she'd previously worked with at the HMO; in short, practically everyone whose life Basemah had touched over the years. It felt like a huge protest rally in a way, because absolutely no one in that mosque was okay with the fact that Basemah had been stolen from us. It hadn't even been twenty-four hours since her last breath, and yet all these people had put aside whatever plans they might have had for a Saturday afternoon so they could show up for Basemah one last time.

Family members and friends went out of their way to console and assure me that I was not to blame for the accident. It could have happened to anyone, they said. It was just bad luck that I happened to be the one driving when that tractor-trailer swerved into us. I was a mother of three young children, and they were just grateful I hadn't been killed in the accident, too. Even as people hugged me and told me how relieved they were that I'd survived, my thoughts were dark: *Why do I get to live? Basemah was a mother, too. Her son might be grown, but why should he and his future children be cheated of her presence? Why should any of us?*

I didn't go to the cemetery after the *salat*, the prayer service. I knew it would be too much for me to watch Basemah's body being lowered into the ground and hear the dirt thudding onto her casket. Instead, I went back to my parents' house, to my childhood bedroom, and climbed back under the plaid blanket that I had thrown over Basemah as she'd struggled for breath in a grassy ravine. Had it only been one day ago? It seemed I had aged a whole lifetime since then, and now I was another person entirely, broken beyond recognition. I had begged my husband to hold everything together at home without me for a few days. Our children were six, four, and two, and I didn't want them to see their mother so destroyed. I needed my own mother right then. I craved her soft hand stroking the hair back from my temples, and her telling me again and again that Basemah had loved me and would want me to forgive myself and move on.

That night, and for many nights after, I slept clutching the plaid blanket that a kind stranger in a blue pickup had wrapped around my shoulders. The rough wool against my skin felt like the last link to my life's greatest teacher. I had no idea how I would go on without her. And yet I still had not cried.

On Monday morning, I dressed myself and went in to work. At the time, I was on the payroll of the Lutheran Medical Center but stationed at the Arab American Association, because that was how Basemah had arranged it. She'd persuaded her bosses at Lutheran that to make inroads with the Arab American community in Brooklyn, they would need to support their organizations. And so they'd hired me as an off-site ambassador to represent the hospital.

My Lutheran colleagues, who had also been Basemah's colleagues, urged me to take as much time as I needed, but sitting at home, constantly reliving the memory of Basemah lying in the grass, fighting for breath, was hard. The hours felt interminable. I decided it was better to keep busy, keep pressing forward, and so on Monday morning, I climbed the seventeen steps to the second floor of Dr. Jaber's women's clinic and I pushed open the door.

Everyone was stunned to see me standing there. They crowded around, hugging me, insisting it was too soon for me to come back, begging me to go home. And that's when the veil lifted, and the full force of Basemah's death finally hit me. Never again would she move through these rooms, energizing us with purpose and a buoyant spirit, taking care of us all. Without warning I was on my knees, the sobs breaking from me violently, my head and heart consumed by the guilt that had stalked me since I first saw Basemah gasping for breath. Weaving through the remorse was a gathering wave of commitment so powerful it nearly obliterated me. Huddled on the floor of the agency Basemah built, weeping as if I would explode from missing her, I vowed to carry on her huge legacy. This would be my redemption.

When at last I had collected myself, I sat with my fellow staffers and volunteers around the long, white-topped Formica table that served as our conference table, and together we began to make a plan for the months to come. "We have to continue this work for Basemah," I heard myself saying, "because this is all she ever wanted. She didn't dream of riches or fabulous trips around the world. Instead, she dreamed of an organization that would serve women who were like her, and everyone else in our community who might need our help."

That morning, I silently promised myself and Allah and Basemah that the organization she built would live on after her, and that for the rest of my life I would endeavor to make her proud.

———————

In the fall Dr. Jaber and his board of directors voted me executive director of the agency. They shared that for them, the appointment had seemed inevitable. Basemah had prepared me for exactly this, they said. She had invested so much in me, sent me for leadership trainings, taught me how to organize community events, introduced me to influential people, and steeped me in her belief that all our work was, first and foremost, about caring what happens to other people. When I expressed doubts that I was ready for such an enormous responsibility—I was only twenty-five years old—they assured me that there was no one better suited to step into Basemah's shoes. Even as I welcomed their vote of confidence, I knew that no one would ever be able to fill Basemah's red patent leather heels. But I would spend my life trying.

There were some hard days. One of the worst was an afternoon when a young Moroccan woman showed up at the agency, seven months pregnant and bleeding. "I'm looking for Basemah," she told me. "I called her phone but it's disconnected, and I went by her cubicle at the hospital, but she wasn't there."

I remembered the young woman well. Her name was Nadia and Basemah had helped to extricate her from an abusive marriage years before. She had been pregnant then, too. When we had learned that Nadia was newly arrived in America and undocumented, Basemah had filed for emergency Medicaid on her behalf, and—as she had done with so many other young women in trouble—she allowed her to stay in her apartment until the baby came. Nadia gave birth to a daughter, whom she named Basemah after the Palestinian "auntie" who'd saved her.

Soon after, Nadia's mother traveled from Morocco to help with the baby, and Basemah had found the little family a place to live. She even got Nadia a job in a local coffee shop so that she could support herself while her mother watched over her little girl. Basemah had followed up with Nadia for years afterward, making sure she could access all the services she needed to make herself whole—therapy to deal with the abuse she had suffered; English language classes; an application for asylum; infant health care. In time, Nadia got married again, this time to the coffee shop owner, a naturalized Egyptian immigrant. When she'd started bleeding in her home one afternoon in her seventh month, she'd taken a car service directly to Lutheran to find Basemah. Nothing about Basemah's cubicle clued her in that the woman she sought had died. Basemah's coworkers at Lutheran couldn't bear to dismantle her space, and for a whole year had left it exactly as if Basemah had just gone down the hall to pour herself a cup of black coffee.

Nadia looked at me now with huge, frightened eyes. "I think my baby's coming," she said in Arabic. "I need to find Basemah."

I didn't have it in me at that moment to tell her what had happened to Basemah. Besides, I needed to get her to the hospital, to try to save her baby. She was dressed in a navy blue modest tunic and gray jogging pants, through which she had bled. I called 911 and went in the ambulance with her to Lutheran, hoping I could smooth her way as well as Basemah would have. In the ER, the doctor did a quick exam and directed that Nadia be wheeled right to the delivery room. By this time she was writhing in pain, the contractions almost continuous. It was too late to give her an epidural because the baby's head was already crowning.

"Linda, get Basemah," she screamed in Arabic. "Go get Basemah. Please, please. Get Basemah."

I stepped out of the room as if I were going to do as she pleaded, because no way could I tell her at the height of labor that Basemah was never coming. One of the maternity nurses, a tall, robust Black woman whom I knew slightly, followed me into the hallway. "What is she saying?" she asked me. "All I can make out is Basemah's name."

"She doesn't know," I told the nurse, who expelled a long breath.

"Oh, this is bad," she said. And then she saw that I was struggling to control myself, and that my face was bathed in tears. "Oh, honey, don't worry," she said, hugging me to her ample bosom as Basemah herself might have done. "We'll figure out a way to tell her after the baby is born. We'll do it together."

Fortunately, despite arriving two months early, the baby was healthy, and his exhausted mother fell into a deep sleep. I sat next to her in the recovery room until she awoke a few hours later.

Groggily, she asked, "Did she come? Did I miss Basemah?"

By then, the nurse who'd offered to help me break the news had gone off duty. The awful task would be mine alone. As gently as I could, I told the young woman about the accident, and held her as she wept.

———

One of the many lessons Basemah had tried to teach me was that even as you stand in the gap for others, you have to take care of yourself. And you have to take care of your staff, too. It's why she was always creating experiences for us that served no purpose but to bring joy. She'd take our non-hijab-wearing coworkers to her favorite hair salon in Park Slope, for example. Or she'd call us from Lutheran to say someone was on the way over to drop off something, and then a delivery person would appear with platters of delicious Indian food. And on any given day, she might pull a colorful blouse or scarf from a shopping bag. "It had your name on it," she'd say to me or someone else. "I couldn't leave it in the store."

She also created a tradition we called mall days. Maybe once a season, we'd lock up the office and travel en masse to the outlet shops at Woodbury Common in Central Valley, New York. Growing up in Brooklyn with six siblings, I didn't even know what a mall was before Basemah. We couldn't afford such extravagances, or so I thought, until

Basemah showed me the economics of outlet shopping. She would find the best deals—a $600 Coach bag for $75, or a $900 Prada stiletto boot for $100. Basemah wasn't only invested in developing my organizing skills and my social awareness. She was also invested in helping me to realize that I could be a well-cared-for woman who wants to rock a nice bag sometimes or step out in a stylish pair of shoes.

As I grew into the role of executive director of the agency, Basemah's example of incorporating experiences that were simply for joy was the aspect of the job that I struggled with the most. But I would come to understand how critical this particular lesson really was, because social justice work can burn you out fast. Unless you take care to replenish yourself, the burdens you bear for other people will bury you under their weight. Basemah understood this instinctively. We might be organizing a fund-raising gala, working stressful eighteen-hour days, and she'd come in and announce that as soon as the gala was over, she was taking everyone for manicures and pedicures. She knew just how to lighten the emotional load.

I doubt that I will ever be as instinctive and spontaneous at spreading joy as Basemah was, though I try to stay conscious of the need, for myself and for those in the activism trenches with me. In other respects, I would come to see that Basemah had trained me better than I knew. Within a decade, I was able to transform the AAANY from an agency with a $50,000 annual budget to a million-dollar organization. And when Dr. Jaber retired from his clinic, our informal second-floor office suite expanded to fill the entire downstairs area, which allowed us to better serve the elderly and the disabled, as well as mothers wielding strollers with children—all of them had previously been challenged by our steep stairs. Once a shoestring operation with three full-time staff members and a rotating list of ten or so volunteers, the agency now employs more than twenty staff members, most of them women from the local community. The programs we offer have also quadrupled since 2005, along with our client base.

Before, when I was Basemah's right-hand woman, I was supporting someone else's mission, albeit one I believed in passionately. After Base-mah died, I broke through to a great clarity of purpose, and that mission became my own. Unfortunately, I became so single-minded about growing the forest that I sometimes failed to adequately nourish my own foundational trees—my family. I was beyond grateful that I could count on them to watch over my children as I embraced the call to carry on an extraordinary woman's legacy. There were times, though, when I learned of challenging experiences in my children's lives long after the fact. While they never held my absence in those moments against me, it was harder to forgive myself.

Chapter 10

The Pit Stop

My son, Tamir, is a tender soul. I will never forget how at four years old he defended a little girl from an elder's playful teasing. Tamir adored this little girl, who was his age and the daughter of friends from our Palestinian community. My son had declared at a family gathering that when he grew up, he would marry this girl. One of his elder aunts poked fun at his devotion.

"But, Tamir, don't you see how her ears stick out from her head?" she asked him, her eyes twinkling.

Tamir, a stocky little guy with spiky black hair, pulled himself up to his full height and placed his fists squarely against his sides. "God made her ears stick out that way," he declared, "and so they are beautiful."

I was in the kitchen helping my mother make meat, thyme, and spinach pies when I heard him announce this. I whirled around to see his face, stunned by the utter conviction in his voice. It was a fleeting moment, but I felt so proud of my boy—proud of his ability to claim his own truth no matter who might try to undermine it. That was the moment when I understood that as tender as my son's heart was, he was also tough-minded, resilient, and fully his own person. To be honest, I felt a rush of relief, because the world in which he and his sisters were growing up would require all that.

At any moment in America, Muslim children face incursions against their sense of self, condemnations of their faith, and assaults on their community. My children are coming of age in a country that does not love them, does not nourish who they are, and refuses to acknowledge the highest version of who they can be. This was never more painfully apparent to me than when Tamir was in eighth grade and applying to high schools in New York City. He had been scheduled for an interview at Millennium Brooklyn High School, which was located in my old high school building. Soon after I'd graduated from John Jay, the Department of Education had closed the school because of its abysmally poor performance. A couple of years later, they had reopened the campus with four smaller schools located inside the massive building. One of those schools, Millennium Brooklyn, was for high-achieving teens, and it was Tamir's first choice for high school.

Students had to maintain a 90 percent average on their report cards in order to be considered, and they also had to be interviewed. For the interview, they were asked to bring a packet of materials that included their most recent report card, a graded paper on which the teacher's comments appeared, and an essay about why they wanted to attend the school and the strengths they could bring to the community. I knew that other parents had worked closely with their eighth graders on the essay, but my son, aware of how busy his mother was, had pulled the whole packet together by himself.

Now, in a cab on the way to his interview, I asked him to show me the packet of materials, thinking I'd give it a quick once-over before he turned it in to the interviewer. Tamir pulled the manila folder from his book bag and handed it to me. I leafed through the papers until I got to a graded English essay that he had titled "Life Is Like a NASCAR Race." That intrigued me, and I started reading.

"My life is like a NASCAR race," Tamir had written. "My life's engine shuts down, and I have to go in the pit to fix it. A tire goes flat. We go into the pit to fix it. After all that I always go the right way."

The essay went on to recount an experience that Tamir had had in a recent math class. Quiet and reserved, my son was rarely the first to respond when the teacher asked a question, even when he knew the answer. On this day, his math teacher had asked the class to solve a difficult equation that she had written on the board. She offered extra credit on the next test to the first student who came up with the correct answer. She went around the class, calling on different students who'd raised their hands, but everyone got the problem wrong.

"Going once," the teacher said to the class. "Going twice . . ."

At that point, Tamir raised his hand. And he answered the question correctly. Immediately a white boy on the other side of the classroom shouted, "Of course you know the answer. You Muslims are good at math because you need to know how to make bombs."

Reading this, and the rest of my son's essay, tore my heart. Even at thirteen years old in a math classroom in one of the most diverse cities on earth, my son faced hostility simply because of the family into which he was born. So much of my life was spent working to combat Islamophobia and raise awareness about its impact on the Muslim community, yet I hadn't known how directly and personally it was affecting my own child. My son was a typical thirteen-year-old American boy. He loved sports and aspired to become a sports broadcaster. His favorite teams were the New York Yankees, Knicks, and Giants; he enjoyed playing games on his Xbox 360 with his cousins and friends; and he was a big fan of stock car racing, or NASCAR. And yet his classmate had looked at him and seen not my bright, loyal, and kindhearted child but a future bomb maker.

Riding next to Tamir in the cab that morning, I remembered the emotions that had flooded me on the day he was born. I was just nineteen, and how blessed I had felt to become the mother of such an incredible little human. Like mothers everywhere, I had sworn to protect him always, and shield him from harm. Now, thirteen years later, his essay had shown me his maturing heart and mind and forced me to understand that the psyches of even our most sheltered and beloved young people were more wounded than I had imagined. Our Arab and Muslim youth felt alienated, marginalized, and deeply misunderstood.

"Sometimes my culture is portrayed as the evil culture," Tamir had observed in his essay. "But we are probably the most down to earth people anybody would know. One way people have put me down is only thinking of my people as 'The Terrorist.'"

He went on to share that when the boy in his class had shouted that Tamir needed to understand equations so he could build bombs, my son didn't know at first how to react. And so, he wrote, he went into his pit stop to decide how he was going to respond to his classmate's ugly comment. And the way that he chose to respond was by laughing, as if the boy were just telling a joke. My son chuckled and defused the tension, and went on with his day. But when he thought about the comment later, he was troubled. He thought maybe he should have confronted the kid about what he'd said and pointed out his Islamophobia. He wished he'd told his classmates that Muslims are good people; that we believe in God; and that our faith is about love and peace, not bombs and violence.

As I was reading his account of all this, I was bawling my eyes out in the cab. "Tamir," I said, "why didn't you tell me about this? Why didn't you come right home and tell me what happened?" I was thinking that I would have talked to his math teacher about how to bring some sort of restorative justice to the classroom, to make the incident a teachable moment for the students. "I would have defended you," I told my son. "You didn't have to go through this alone."

Tamir looked at me as if I had two heads. "Mom, are you being serious right now?" he asked me.

"What are you saying? I would have supported you."

Tamir shook his head as if I just didn't understand. "Mom," he said, "you have to go into schools with parents of kids who got beat up or bullied. You have to be with moms at detention centers and in courtrooms because their children's fathers are going to be sent to another country. This is not that serious. I'm really okay."

Ever since Basemah's death, my guilt response had been hyperattuned, and now it scorched me with the awareness that my child had so sorely underestimated his primacy in my life because he thought his mom had more dire things on her mind. He didn't understand that nothing was more important to me than what he or his sisters needed, that everything I was doing for our community, I was doing first and foremost for them. It was *their* world I wanted to secure, *their* lives I wanted to protect from the burden and danger of being demonized and feared.

"Tamir, listen to me," I said. "I want you to hear me. You're my child, and you shouldn't have had to go through anything like that alone."

My son wasn't having it. "Mom, sometimes your children are going to have to realize that there are people who need your help more than we need your help. Sometimes instead of you having my back, I need to have your back."

He said those words as we were exiting the car and walking into the Millennium Brooklyn building through the cafeteria door. At that moment, I almost broke down completely. Maybe it was Tamir's essay combined with the fact of being in my old high school building that was making me so emotional, but this wasn't the time—I had to get myself together. I took several deep breaths and dabbed at my eyes with the back of my hand, hoping the kohl I'd applied to them hadn't smeared too badly. Even so, I must have looked a sight, because when we walked into the classroom where the interview was to be held, the teacher surveyed me with concern.

"Are you okay?" she said. "Can I get you anything?"

"I'm fine," I assured her. "I just had a little situation, but I'll be okay."

She didn't press any further. Instead, she gestured for us to have a seat while she reviewed Tamir's admissions packet. My son and I sat at two desks toward the back of the room as she went to the front, opened the folder, and started flipping through the pages inside. Tamir and I glanced at each other when she got to his English essay—and paused. We knew what she was looking at because we could make out the hot-pink marker with which his English teacher had graded the paper. *I am sorry this happened to you*, she had written in the top right-hand corner of the cover page. *Tamir, you have tackled very significant issues here. I can feel your passion and writing from the heart is the best way to go.*

The interviewer turned the cover page and began to read. At one point, she glanced over at us, a strange expression on her face. Perhaps she'd figured out why I looked as if I'd been crying, but she didn't say anything about that after she closed the folder and walked to where we were. "You're an excellent writer," she told Tamir. And then she launched right into asking him about his favorite pastimes, the subjects in school that he most enjoyed, the usual questions. At the end of the interview, she shook my son's hand vigorously, and then mine, and said how much she'd enjoyed meeting us.

When the high school placement notices arrived that spring, my son had been admitted to Millennium Brooklyn. He was ecstatic, and I was proud of him. In his typically unassuming way, he'd done the work and richly deserved this placement in a high school for gifted students. I was also sure that his essay had moved his interviewer, as it had me. I smiled at the irony that in at least one regard, my son's experience as a Muslim American teenager in Brooklyn would be less challenging than mine, because even though he would be going to high school in the same building that I had, he wouldn't ever have to navigate cops storming the cafeteria with weapons drawn.

My son's NASCAR essay became a powerful motivator for me, his math class experience right up there with the question that another Muslim boy had asked me three years before: "Sister Linda, would it be okay if I just didn't tell anyone I'm Muslim?" The message these boys had been forced to absorb was that rather than being prized and valued for who they are and how they conduct themselves in the world, they are vilified in the country of their birth. Almost two decades have passed since 9/11, and yet Arab and Muslim Americans continue to live in one of the most hostile civic environments experienced anywhere. Our youth are confused about how fully to express their identity as they seek to reconcile being Muslim and being American, as if pride in both is mutually exclusive.

Rather than improving over time, the situation has lately deteriorated. With the ramped-up anti-Muslim rhetoric of the 2016 presidential election, anti-Islam hate crimes reached a new high, with mosques being torched, Muslim businesses and homes vandalized, and people who look visibly Muslim being shot, stabbed, or beaten. In New York City and elsewhere, Muslim women wearing hijabs have been particular targets, leading one social media site to offer this self-defense tip to Muslim women: "While you are dressing yourself in the morning, pause and think, 'Are these clothes comfortable enough to allow me to suddenly run if I need to?'"[1]

Yet the hate speech of the 2016 election cycle was hardly new. Since 9/11, the propaganda against our community has been relentless. Indeed, around the same time that my son wrote his NASCAR essay, nasty advertisements were on display in New York City subway stations, depicting the exploding Twin Towers along with a quote from the Qur'an (3:151): "Soon shall we cast terror into the hearts of the unbelievers." With ad space purchased for a reported $77,000 by a notorious anti-Muslim organization founded by blogger Pamela Geller,[2] the billboards aimed to portray Islam's holy book as a terrorist manifesto. The problem was, in combing the Qur'an to find a verse that would seem to prove her false narrative, Geller had completely misrepresented the context of the quote, which referred to a historic battle in which the Prophet Muhammad defended his people against pagan attacks. It's also worth noting that the holy book does not at any point reference Christians or Jews as "unbelievers" but rather considers them as fellow "People of the Book," followers of the same God of Ibrahim.

Consider for a moment if an anti-Christian organization were to take a biblical verse out of context—"I have come to cast fire upon the earth" (Luke 12:49) or "Utterly destroy all that they have, and do not spare them" (1 Samuel 15:3)—in order to associate Christianity with biblically sanctioned violence. This was exactly what Geller's billboards were trying to do with the Qur'an. But even as I grasped the intellectual and spiritual dishonesty of Geller's subway ads, it pained me to think how traumatic those posters of the exploding Twin Towers must have been for those who'd lost loved ones on that awful day. Those ads also endangered my own children, and not just in a physical sense. Ayisha Irfan, one of our Youth Organizing Fellows at the Arab American Association, sought to explain their psychological effect in a Facebook post:

> Even though it's been over 11 years since 9/11, [and] I am now a woman in my mid-20s training youth leaders to never be afraid and I embrace their identity as American Muslim activists, I can't help but have my heart race as I look at a picture of the Twin Towers burning. I can't ignore the very obvious fact that when 9/11 is even mentioned I get a tight feeling in my chest. I can't explain my need to say something yet my want not to entertain a conversation about 9/11. This is the narrative of my generation. We have an inherent sense of guilt for something we had nothing to do with. Every year as the 9/11 anniversary rolls around it hits us again and again that we might never be seen as American enough.[3]

My son, Tamir, and our organizer Ayisha reflect what American Muslim youth across the country are grappling with. As a mother and activist, I contend that it is up to reasonable people of all faiths to stand against hate, whether it is leveled at your child or mine. We need to do right for *all* our children. To use Tamir's inventive analogy about life being like a NASCAR race, let's get ourselves into that pit. Let's do the necessary repairs, educate ourselves about one another, open our hearts, and extend a hand to our neighbors. Let's pause to fix what needs fixing. As Tamir noted in his essay, once we do that, we can get back on the road together, heading the right way.

Chapter 11

A Tale of Two Mosques

The uproar over the so-called Ground Zero Mosque in downtown Manhattan was just another media storm designed to stoke antipathy toward Islam, driving the harmful narrative that bright Muslim boys with an aptitude for math and science were future bomb makers. This particular chapter had begun in 2010, when Sharif El-Gamal, a Muslim real estate developer, purchased a five-story building at 45 Park Place in downtown Manhattan, two blocks from the site of Ground Zero. El-Gamal, a Brooklyn native of Egyptian and Polish descent, was chairman and CEO of Soho Properties. He proposed to construct a fifteen-story Islamic cultural center on the site, one that would welcome people of all faiths and creeds, with a theater, art studios, a fitness center, a culinary school, a bookstore, and a prayer space inside.

To lend some gravitas to the project, El-Gamal partnered with Imam Feisal Abdul Rauf, who had been born to an Egyptian family in Kuwait and had later studied physics at Columbia University. At the time, Imam Abdul Rauf suggested that the location, so close to the site of wrenching tragedy, could be seen as a powerful message of reconciliation. It "sends the opposite statement to what happened on 9/11," he said. "We want to push back against the extremists. What happened that day was not Islam."[1]

Adding to the symbolism was the fact that the Park Place building, which had been leased by its owners to Burlington Coat Factory, had not escaped the World Trade Center attack unscathed: a plane's landing gear had hurtled through the roof and upper two floors, causing catastrophic damage. Fortuitously, no one had been hurt, because the store's eighty employees were, at that hour, assembled in the basement having breakfast. However, the store never reopened its doors. The building had stood empty for almost a decade before El-Gamal purchased it.

An Islamic cultural center overlooking Ground Zero? The right-wing, Fox News–consuming crowd erupted. Even though the local community board had voted to approve the $100 million project, there was frenzied opposition to the center, most of it originating outside New York City, with prominent conservatives weighing in. "Nazis don't have the right to put up a sign next to the Holocaust Museum in Washington," former Republican house speaker Newt Gingrich said. "There's no reason for us to accept a mosque next to the World Trade Center."[2]

In those few words, Gingrich effectively equated Islam with Nazism, and held every Muslim directly responsible for the attack on 9/11. Within days, the project had been dubbed the "Ground Zero Terror Mosque" or the "Victory Mosque," with far-right media pundits speculating that the center would actually be "a recruiting center for jihadists." Coverage of the protests on conservative media outlets like Fox and Breitbart News invented a story of American Muslims as Jew- and Christian-hating fanatics bent on America's destruction, and they spread that falsehood from sea to shining sea.

As the controversy raged into the following year and then the next, it sometimes felt to me as if the very air had been poisoned, and my whole body ached from breathing in the hate. One historian, Jason Tebbe, captured much of what I felt in his description of the spring day in 2010 when he encountered a mob outside the site of the proposed

Islamic cultural center. "The crowd was uniformly white, with eyes full of hard, direct stares with hatred smoldering behind them," he recalled in the online journal *Tropics of Meta*:

> One memory above all stands out to me. I saw a child, maybe nine or ten years old holding a sign. It simply said "Sharia" in red letters dripping with blood. He had such a look of anger on his face that I couldn't avert my gaze. I was chilled wondering how many children were being made to think like this. These were people who had come out in the open for all to see to proclaim their hatred of a group of people because of their religion. It is hard to describe, but there was a feeling in the air that I had never felt before, a palpable feeling of hate that seemed to just emanate from the crowd's bodies.[3]

Tebbe went on to suggest that the paranoia he witnessed that day was driven by something deeper than anti-Muslim sentiment. He saw it as an early indicator of the toxic resurgence of white nationalist fervor in American public life. "At the time I was shaken," Tebbe wrote, "but there were signs that I was witnessing the future, not just an isolated incident. The media, for example, treated the anger at the so-called 'Ground Zero Mosque' as a legitimate expression of patriotism rather than rooted in outright hatred."[4]

Tebbe's analysis would turn out to be spot-on. It eventually came to light that the Ground Zero Mosque protests had been instigated and bankrolled by hedge fund billionaire Robert Mercer, the alleged "dark money" magnate who had thrown his financial weight behind the conservative outlet Breitbart News and the ultimately discredited personal-data-mining firm Cambridge Analytica. Mercer, with his daughter Rebekah, would go on to fund Donald Trump's presidential run to the tune of many millions in 2016.[5] All that is to say the fury whipped up by the proposed Islamic cultural center in downtown Manhattan was chillingly calculated and orchestrated to stir racial animosities in the hearts of white Americans for a deeply cynical purpose: political dominance. If the mainstream media had bothered to combat the ugly Ground Zero Mosque rhetoric back then, Tebbe argued, the "current wave of hate" would not have "crashed down on this nation."[6]

In the end, the Islamic cultural center would never be built. Perhaps strained by the national furor, the relationship between Imam Rauf and businessman El-Gamal soured and the two men parted ways. A year later, Soho Properties' plans for the Park Place location morphed into a forty-three-story luxury condominium complex. I'd had no firsthand involvement with the project at any point, and yet every Muslim in America had been affected by the controversy, which had further poisoned the nation's heart against Islam.

On October 29, 2012, amid the continued tumult over the Ground Zero Mosque, and as incumbent Democratic president Barack Obama campaigned for a second term against Republican nominee Mitt Romney, Hurricane Sandy pummeled the New York metropolitan area and the shoreline of New Jersey. The storm, predicted to be a monster, outperformed, with water pouring over highways, rising over promenades and boardwalks, cascading down subway steps, and pushing into tunnels. As the storm raged through the night, a Con Ed transformer on Fourteenth Street exploded, a huge fireball lighting up the sky and plunging the lower half of Manhattan into darkness. Ambulances lined up in the rain as armies of EMTs ferried patients on stretchers for transport to nearby hospitals. In one neighborhood in Queens, licks of fire whipped from house to house in the high wind, setting one hundred homes burning. And on Staten Island, where the superstorm made landfall at high tide and under a full moon, residents of beachside towns watched their living rooms fill with water, their dining tables, dishes, armchairs, and refrigerators floating.

In Brooklyn, we were lucky. We didn't lose power, although I marveled from the safety of my home at the sight of trees kneeling in the storm. As I watched the news that night with the rest of the country, I knew that the morning would bring a reckoning. Indeed, in the days following the storm, news reports were filled with images of devastated communities. One photograph in particular stopped me cold. It was the image of a plastic bin full of antique dolls, white lace garments soaked and dirtied, limbs broken and tossed together beside the chain-link fence of a house. Next to the bin, sopping-wet jeans, dresses, shirts, towels, and bedsheets had been slung over the fence to dry.

The caption told me the image had been taken in Staten Island's Midland Beach, where seven-foot walls of water had become a raging tidal surge that washed into people's homes and took huge pieces of their lives as the waters returned to the sea. The place looked like a war zone. Trees had been mowed down by the high winds, dragging power lines with them. The storm had made rivers of the streets, and the muddy brown water still hadn't receded. On stoops and sidewalks and in sodden front yards, people stacked up their belongings—couches, mattresses, black garbage bags full of clothing, the contents of so many drawers—hoping the day-after sun would dry everything and hold mold at bay. And they were the fortunate ones. More people had died in Staten Island than in any other area hit by the storm, with twenty-four of the forty-three fatalities in New York City coming from that borough. Most of those deaths were concentrated in Midland Beach.[7] A humanitarian crisis was unfolding in my own backyard, and I wouldn't just stand by.

I called the office of New York State assemblywoman Nicole Malliotakis, who represented both Bay Ridge and eastern Staten Island, including Midland Beach. Nicole is of Greek and Cuban heritage, and like me she is the first-generation daughter of immigrants. She and I had developed a cordial relationship at community events we both attended in Brooklyn. I was a progressive Democrat, she was a Republican, and eastern Staten Island was a conservative Republican enclave, but for both of us, human need trumped partisan politics every time. I asked what our organization could do to help the people who had been most ravaged by the hurricane. Nicole had an idea: Midland Beach was still without electricity or gas, she said, which meant people likely hadn't been able to cook anything since the storm. She suggested we order seventy pies from a local pizzeria and hand-deliver them to local residents.

Within the hour we had rounded up a dozen volunteers and were on our way out to Midland Beach. We ordered several different types of pies and had them delivered to us at a row of folding tables that we set up in the middle of an intersection in town. Alongside the stacks of pizzas we'd laid out toothpaste, toothbrushes, soap, deodorant, detergent, and other everyday necessities. From there, the volunteers fanned out in teams of two, with each pair taking a stack of pies and going door to door. I was partnered with a young Black woman with pink-framed glasses and exuberant natural hair. Together we would walk up to the front doors of houses, knock, and ask the person who answered, "Would you like a hot dinner?" If the person said yes, we would slide a pie off the top of the stack and hand it over, then we'd walk away.

After knocking on half a dozen doors, we had one pie left. The next house was a taupe-colored two-story with white trim and what looked to be most of its contents piled up on the sidewalk outside a narrow front gate. My partner and I pushed open the gate, walked up a short flight of steps to the porch, and knocked. No answer. We could hear the sound of pumps sucking water out of the basement and see the thick black hose emptying the muddy flow into the street. I knocked again. Nothing. We were about to turn and walk back down the steps when the door opened just a crack. A pale, pinched face peered out at us.

"What are you doing?" she asked, frowning. She was clearly confused to find an African American woman with natural hair and a Muslim woman in a hijab standing at her door.

"Good afternoon," I greeted her. "We're in the neighborhood giving out hot pizzas to anyone who wants one. Would you like a pie?"

The woman opened the door wider and stepped onto the porch. She was small and thin, with flat brown hair that lay damp against her head. Her hunched posture inside a man's chambray shirt made her seem fragile somehow.

"I'm so sorry," she whispered.

Now I was the one confused. I thought perhaps she hadn't heard me, or that she might be one of the Russian immigrants who'd settled in this part of Staten Island, who wasn't comfortable speaking English. I thought of my own mother when she'd first arrived in New York and, speaking more slowly, I repeated myself.

"We're volunteers and we're giving out free pizzas—"

The woman interrupted me, waving her hands in front of her face in a gesture that looked poignantly like surrender.

"I'm really sorry," she repeated.

The thought crawled through my mind that she might be mentally unstable, because her words didn't seem to connect to what I'd said.

"Ma'am," I said kindly, "would you like a hot pie?"

"I didn't know," she said. "I just didn't know."

I looked at my partner, who raised her eyebrows and shrugged. She wasn't following the exchange, either.

"I'm not sure what you mean," I finally said.

The woman pulled me by the sleeve to the edge of her porch and pointed to the back of her yard, beyond the waterlogged trees stripped of their bark and leaves. "They were going to build a mosque over there," she said, "right where the old Catholic Church used to be. They were going to use the same building, and everyone said it was going to be bad, and that the people who were coming were dangerous." She paused and wiped her face against the sleeves of her shirt. I saw that she was quietly crying.

"I didn't know," she said again. "I just knew what they told me."

She went on to share that she'd marched against the mosque. "I'd heard all about that 'victory mosque' over there in Manhattan, the one they wanted to put next to Ground Zero. They said it would be the same kind of people."

"What kind of people?" my partner asked, shooting me a glance.

"You know, the Muslims," the woman said. She looked away from us, her eyes roving over her ruined belongings piled up in the street, then up at the now cloudless blue of the sky. "Terrorists," she said at last. "They said they hate us and we didn't want them here. We didn't want them in the neighborhood." She told us that a Catholic priest who'd tried to convince his neighbors to welcome the mosque had been getting death threats, and she herself had been part of the group that had picketed his front lawn.

"And now you're here," she said with a small lift and fall of her thin shoulders. "I should have known better."

I thought of my son, and how he'd wished that he'd told his classmates, "Muslims are good people, too." But this was hardly the moment to lecture this woman on why she didn't need to fear people who were only seeking a place to pray together.

"You know what?" I said instead. "Those same people who wanted to open that mosque, they bought another building a few avenues over, and they're doing great. You don't need to worry about them."

"Oh, good," she said so softly I barely heard her.

"Besides," I added, "now you know better. People can change."

With that, we gave her the last pie and wished her a good recovery from the storm. She stood on her porch holding the pizza and watching us as we walked away.

That night, I reflected that if I had not been wearing a hijab, the woman in Midland Beach would not have known that it was a Muslim who had shown up at her door. She could not know I was Palestinian. More likely, she thought I was Puerto Rican and had converted to Islam. But she did know that while she was pumping floodwater from her basement, two women of color, one who worshiped as a Muslim, had knocked on her door and offered to feed her dinner. I dared to hope that the next time she met a woman in a hijab, maybe at the mall or in the supermarket, she would remember us standing on her porch and her biases might thaw a little.

I had no doubt that she had been as moved as I was by our encounter. She had given me the chance to provide her with some assistance, and to demonstrate that Islam was not a religion of hate. Rather, it was about being there for others in times of need, regardless of race or creed. For a few brief minutes in hurricane-ravaged Midland Beach, we were two women whose politics fell on opposite ends of the spectrum, yet each of us had recognized the other's humanity, and we had both walked away with hearts opened, and hope renewed.

Chapter 12

Love Letter

Nine-year-old Sajida stepped up to the microphone. She would ask the last question of the day. It was an afternoon in May, six months before the November 2013 election that would give New York City its first new mayor in twelve years. Sunlight streamed through the floor-to-ceiling windows of the New York University auditorium where seven candidates now shifted onstage. They sensed at once that their response to this final question, put to them by a child, could make or break their afternoon. The candidates were there to address the city's Muslim community and our allies. People of every description filled the room's six hundred seats, and more attendees stood at the back of the auditorium and against the walls. Black, white, beige, brown, Hispanic, Eastern European, South Asian, young, old, mixed-race, gay, straight, trans—the audience was a uniquely American kaleidoscope of parents, students, community leaders, scholars, and activists. I looked around the room and thought: *I hope these candidates take in how diverse our community really is. We are everybody.*

None of the candidates onstage—six men and one woman—knew that the girl at the microphone was my daughter. I felt a quiet pride as she confidently launched into her question, her beautiful face scrubbed and bright, her black hair pulled into a ponytail, her voice unwavering and sure. "Hello, my name is Sajida and I'm in the third grade at P.S.

169 in Sunset Park, Brooklyn," she began. "In June of 2009 the New York City Council passed a resolution telling the Department of Education to include two major Muslim holidays. Even though fifty city council members voted and thought that this was the right thing to do, Mayor Bloomberg said no way. If you are elected mayor, what would you do to make sure that me and the city's other hundred thousand Muslim students don't have to choose between going to school and celebrating our faith?"

Finally, a cause involving our community that everyone could get behind. And yet the fight to have two Muslim religious holidays added to the public school calendar had already dragged on for seven long years. The campaign had started back in January 2006, when New York's Muslim parents noticed that a critical statewide exam had been scheduled on one of Islam's two holiest days, Eid al-Adha, our festival of sacrifice. It was bad enough that every year Muslim children were asked to choose between observing their spiritual traditions and attending class, but now the stakes had been raised: the results of the statewide exam were a critical component of every public school student's overall record.

When I was growing up, I'd always elected to go to school on Eid. "Whatever holiday plans you've got, we'll do them after three o'clock," I'd announce to my parents. My mother hated that. Most of her other children chose to stay home, but I was her nerdy kid who didn't want to risk falling behind in school. As I recall, I didn't brood much about having to make this decision, in part because being a Muslim in America wasn't nearly as loaded then.

But by January 2006, the environment for Muslim children had become outright hostile. Bullying was rampant, and morale in our community was at an all-time low, which is why I was immediately convinced that Muslim parents needed to petition the New York City Department of Education about adding Islam's two high holy days—Eid al-Adha as well as Eid al-Fitr (marking the end of Ramadan, our annual month of fasting and prayer)—to the academic calendar. After all, Christian and

Jewish high holy days were already observed as a matter of course. Why not the Eid holidays, too? To my mind, the state exam being scheduled on Eid was just one more message to our youth that they simply didn't matter, and I wanted them to know that they did.

At the time, our community sorely needed a win: Every couple of weeks we'd hear about another hate crime against Muslims, or another case of our children being profiled, or, heaven forbid, a terrorist attack on the other side of the world, which somehow always left Americans fearfully convinced that the next 9/11 was hours away. I decided to reach out to the New York chapter of the Council on American-Islamic Relations, or CAIR. Two close friends of mine, Faiza Ali and Aliya Latif, were on staff there, and I knew they were already working with community leaders and imams on a Muslim school holiday campaign.

CAIR's whole mandate was to monitor civil rights abuses against Muslims and intercede on behalf of families and individuals facing discrimination. In this case, the harm to Muslim children was undeniable: yes, the city allowed schools to schedule make-ups for students who missed important exams, but the number of make-ups offered per school was limited, and insufficient to cover the number of Muslim children in the citywide public school system.

The first step was to form a Coalition for Muslim School Holidays to advocate for the cause. Along with then director of CAIR Omar Mohammedi, who had influential contacts in state government, we set up meetings with several state legislators. They understood the point of our campaign at once. In a matter of months, they drafted and unanimously passed a law banning statewide exams on *any* religious holiday, not just for Muslims but also for everyone. Through our campaign, we were able to ensure that not only would this situation never again affect Muslim children, but students who were Christian, Jewish, Hindu, Sikh, Bahá'í, or who worshiped in other faith traditions would also be protected. That would turn out to be the easy part.

The real struggle began when we lobbied the New York City Department of Education to formally recognize Islam's two holiest days by closing school on those days, in the same way that schools were closed on Christian and Jewish holidays. We quickly learned that New York City schools were closed on those days not because of the number of Christian and Jewish students in the public school system, but because of the number of Christian and Jewish *teachers*. Rather than being worried about students missing classes, the Department was concerned about having to find substitute teachers on those days when Christian or Jewish teachers stayed home. Ultimately, officials had decided that it would be more cost-effective to simply close school on those days, rather than go through the headache of hiring and paying substitute teachers.

Since very few of the city's teachers were Muslim, it became clear that our campaign would have to be based on the number of public school students who identified as Muslim. The problem was that city officials held the impression that most Muslim children attended Islamic schools and were not under their jurisdiction. In fact, 95 percent of Muslim children in New York City attended public school, and one of every eight students was Muslim.[1] In other words, roughly 13 percent of the New York City public school population observed the Islamic faith.

Education officials then raised another concern: the dates of our Muslim high holy days were generally based on moon sightings. Indeed, many imams didn't announce when the Eid holiday would fall until a few days beforehand, based on the report of some man in Saudi Arabia who climbed on top of a building and looked at the moon. "Our academic calendar is set a year in advance," one official told us. "We can't wait till the last minute to tell our teachers and students, 'Oh, don't come to school on Tuesday, because it's an Eid holiday.' That's just not going to work."

Our solution was to hire an astronomer to calculate twenty years' worth of dates for Eid al-Adha and Eid al-Fitr, so that the Department of Education wouldn't be tasked with having to figure that out. We did not foresee that our decision to scientifically determine future Eid dates would lead to tension within our own community. It took some persuasion to get imams and Islamic scholars to sign off on the idea of setting the dates based on astronomy calculations and not on real-time observation of the moon's phases. We explained how critical it was that we present a united front, and that without the help of an astronomer, Muslim school holidays would never be adopted.

Simultaneously, we were working to expand our coalition to include non-Muslims who supported religious freedom. Faiza Ali and Aliya Latif, as representatives of CAIR, had settled on three words to define the campaign: recognition, inclusion, and respect. They chose those words because their promise was universal—every community wanted to be recognized, included, and respected. Based on this premise, we collected tens of thousands of signatures on petitions, staged rallies and town halls, and placed op-eds in local newspapers. We were eventually able to bring to the table more than one hundred Jewish, Christian, Sikh, Asian, and Hindu groups, as well as labor unions, civil rights or-ganizations, and even the United Federation of Teachers.

For me, the most gratifying aspect of the school holiday campaign was that immigrant mothers served as its fuel, with Muslim mothers leading the way. As I saw it, the campaign united us in a way that was profoundly needed. We all understood that our children stood to lose or gain based on how effectively we advocated for them, so there was really no room to disagree. American Muslims united across Sunni and Shia theology, and across lines of race, ethnicity, and national origin. If the Muslim registry had demonstrated that we were all targets of government surveillance, no matter our sect, now the Coalition for Muslim School Holidays showed us what might be achieved if we marched in the same direction together.

And here was a perfect cause to rally around, because in post-9/11 America, our children had been made to question whether they be-longed here. The effort to get Muslim holidays recognized by the public school system was our way of saying to our youth, "You matter; your faith matters; you have a right to be who you are and to not apologize for it." In a sense, the campaign was our love letter to Muslim children. We were fighting for them at a time when they often weren't able to stand up for themselves. It was part of why the teachers' union didn't hesitate to join our cause. They knew as well as we did that being able to proudly celebrate their faith would be healing for Muslim students.

Unfortunately, New York City's three-term mayor Michael Bloomberg, who served from 2002 through 2013, didn't see it our way. Even though the city council had passed a unanimous resolution recommending that the Muslim school holidays be recognized, Bloomberg refused to allow it—and his directive to the Department of Education was the one that counted. "I don't care what you do, I don't care how many petitions you gather, this is not going to happen," he told us bluntly when we sat down with him to plead our case. And then he stood, signaling that the meeting was over. "Look," he said before walking out of the room, "you have an election coming up in a few years. Figure it out then."

We were at a stalemate. We had mobilized hundreds of thousands of supporters across diverse constituencies, yet we were now forced to admit that for the time being, there was no way forward. And so in 2009 we stood down, and bided our time.

Four years later, as the new mayoral campaign kicked into gear, Faiza, Aliya, and I decided that we were going to make the Muslim school holiday one of our two main asks of every mayoral candidate. The other issue would be getting candidates to commit to addressing hate crimes and unwarranted surveillance of Muslim neighborhoods. This was the agenda with which we cofounded the first-ever Muslim Democratic Club of New York. We'd begun to realize that organizing in a nonpartisan way just wasn't cutting it. We needed to concentrate our power by engaging in partisan politics, all while embracing the potential of intersectional organizing. The term *intersectionality* had originally been coined in 1989 by African American law professor, feminist, and civil rights advocate Kimberlé Crenshaw, who asserted that marginalized groups could more successfully challenge power networks if they united in common cause. "The better we understand how identities and power work together from one context to another, the less likely our movements for change are to fracture," she explained.[2]

These days, everyone tosses the word around like it's a cool new concept, but Faiza, Aliya, and I had put our faith in the power of intersectionality during that long school holiday campaign. It was the idea behind our mayoral candidate forum at the Islamic Center at New York University. We'd invited every candidate, as well as allies from every group that had previously signed on to our school holiday campaign.

On the day itself, all six Democrats in the race and the one Independent candidate came. Only the Republican was missing. In the run-up to the forum, some wondered whether the candidates would consider our event important enough to show up for, but I had no doubt. I knew that in such a crowded field of candidates, every additional vote mattered. In this equation, Muslims were a sought-after wild card. Our community had never been fully engaged in the electoral process, which meant that a candidate who could expand the electorate and pick up the Muslim vote just might pull off the win. The mayoral forum was an important moment for us, because it demonstrated for perhaps the first time that Muslims in New York could have significant political clout.

In the planning, Faiza, Aliya, and I had identified people in the audience who would ask the pointed questions we intended to put to the candidates. We'd asked Imam Talib Abdur Rashid, a respected African American elder from Harlem, to pose the school holiday question. We felt he had the gravitas that would encourage the candidates to respond to him in a serious way. But at 11 P.M. on the night before the forum, my phone rang. It was Imam Talib.

"Sister Linda, I'm not going to be able to make it tomorrow," he said. "I'm sick and in bed. I'm so sorry."

"Brother, you just take care of yourself; we got this," I assured him, though my thoughts were spinning. Who could we get to replace the imam at this late hour? I called up Faiza and Aliya and we batted around a few names, but ultimately we decided that if the imam couldn't be there, then a child should pose the question. And the child we selected to step up to the mic was my youngest daughter.

Sajida didn't hesitate. And she was pitch-perfect. At the end of her question, all seven candidates onstage broke out in applause. Front-runner Bill de Blasio declared, "You are a role model to us, young lady," and Christine Quinn, former speaker of the New York City Council, joked, "We are all very glad that you are not running for mayor." Then one by one, every candidate present pledged to formally recognize the two holidays. The next day, a reporter cornered the Republican candidate and told him what his competitors had promised. He responded that he, too, would honor the religious observance of Muslim children by closing public schools on Eid holidays.

It was a pivotal moment in a campaign that had lasted seven long years—almost as long as my Sajida had been alive. Two years later, on March 4, 2015, Mayor Bill de Blasio held a press conference at P.S./I.S. 30 in Bay Ridge, a school with nearly 50 percent Muslim student enrollment, to announce the official incorporation of the Eid holidays into the New York City public school calendar. Standing right next to him on the dais was the now ten-year-old girl who had fearlessly addressed a stage full of career politicians and carried us across the finish line.

I heard my youngest daughter whooping and hollering in the next room, then saw her race into my room, rustling a sheet of paper in the air.

"Mama," she screamed, "we did it!"

Bouncing from one foot to the other, she handed me the sheet of paper, which I now saw was the academic calendar for the coming school year, and included on the list of dates when public schools would be closed were Eid al-Adha and Eid al-Fitr.

"You have to send this to Faiza," Sajida said, grabbing my arm. "She doesn't have children, so she won't have seen this." And so I snapped a photo of the calendar with my cell phone and texted it to Faiza as a reminder to us that no matter how pitched the battle or drawn out the fight, if we do not waver, we will prevail.

Chapter 13

Rakers and Spies

O ut of the blue, a video producer from the Associated Press called my office in Brooklyn, insisting he had to see me. His name was Ted Shaffrey, and he had something he needed to show me. It was vitally important, he promised, but he couldn't say any more over the phone. *This can't be good*, I thought. I arranged to meet with him that afternoon.

Now, sitting in my small office, with shafts of light from the window slanting onto the wall behind me, I listened as Ted explained that he worked with the team of AP reporters—Matt Apuzzo, Adam Goldman, Eileen Sullivan, and Chris Hawley—who'd won a Pulitzer Prize the year before for their series on the NYPD's overly aggressive surveillance of Muslims. A cryptic tip from a source—"Ask about Ray Kelly's rakers and mosque crawlers"—had been followed by a steady stream of documents leaked to the Associated Press. The AP's editors assigned a team to go through the papers to see if there was a story. What they found was harrowing.

In a series of reports, the AP revealed that police commissioner Raymond Kelly's task force, trained by a former CIA operative, had dispatched hundreds of informants to infiltrate Muslim student groups and hang around cafes, bookstores, halal shops, and other Muslim-run businesses to "rake up" information. The task force had also sent "mosque crawlers" into houses of worship to report on sermons and listen in on conversations between imams and their flocks, while street cameras mounted on poles covertly photographed the faces and license plates of law-abiding congregants.

Of course, we already knew that our neighborhoods were being watched. The AP investigation only confirmed for everyone else that we weren't being paranoid. Still, the stories, which had appeared in 2011, had been a chilling reminder that Muslims dare not trust even the people they knelt with at *salat* on Friday afternoons, much less the ones who tried to strike up conversation as they sipped coffee in local cafes.

We'd also learned some new details from the AP stories. For one, the NYPD's Demographics Unit ran the surveillance operation. Its agents had extensively mapped the city's Muslim neighborhoods, and had been trained to identify would-be terrorists based on criteria laid out in a ninety-page document titled *Radicalization in the West: The Homegrown Threat*. Authored by two senior intelligence analysts, the report contained this ominous description of likely candidates: "Middle class families and students appear to provide the most fertile ground for the seeds of radicalization. A range of socioeconomic and psychological factors have been associated with those who have chosen to radicalize to include the bored and/or frustrated, successful college students, the unemployed, the second and third generation, new immigrants, petty criminals, and prison parolees."[1]

In other words, as AP reporters Apuzzo and Goldman would later observe in their book *Enemies Within: Inside the NYPD's Secret Spying Unit and bin Laden's Final Plot Against America*, the police "saw terrorists everywhere. The middle class and the unemployed. The aimless and the ambitious. Criminals and college students. Longtime American citizens and new arrivals. Anyone."[2] Indeed, a mere interest in Middle East politics was enough to render a Muslim person suspicious. Simply engaging in discussions about Palestine or bemoaning the plight of Syrian refugees was enough to mark one as radicalized. Never mind that it was entirely natural for Middle Easterners to express such concerns.

The leaked NYPD documents further revealed that the Demo-graphics Unit had declared certain cafes to be potential centers of terrorist recruitment simply because the television was tuned to the Al Jazeera news channel and Arabic newspapers could be read there. At the same time, a Muslim tearoom that prohibited the Al Jazeera news channel was also seen as suspicious, according to the secret files, which accused the owner of trying to avoid "extra scrutiny from law enforcement."[3]

As executive director of the Arab American Association, I'd been ac-tive in organizing protests against these intelligence-gathering tactics for years, and I was as outraged as anyone by the ethnic and religious pro-filing of our community. But I was about to realize that I'd had no clue just how deep inside my own experience the surveillance task force had reached. On that hot August afternoon in 2013 when the AP producer came to see me, he handed me a single sheet of paper. Across the top were the words CONFIDENTIAL INFORMANT PROFILE, along with red ink stamps that said SECRET and NYPD CONFIDENTIAL. Underneath the heading were several bulleted paragraphs identifying our organization as a "terrorist enterprise" and detailing the task force's plan to place an informant on our board of directors. The document even described the characteristics sought in the prospective spy: he or she should be a businessperson, medical practitioner, or other professional of Palestinian, Egyptian, or Syrian descent, preferably middle-aged or older. Clearly, the NYPD had studied the makeup of our board members to come up with this profile of an informant whom they believed would "fit."

I was stunned. The NYPD had been working to insinuate itself into our midst. Now I looked for the date on the document and saw that it was from 2009. Five years—that was how long ago we had been targeted. *Had the task force succeeded?* I considered our board members: most were community elders I'd known my entire life, like Dr. Jaber, so I didn't think our ranks had actually been breached. But how would we ever know? The revelation on that single sheet of paper felt to me like a particularly brutal piece of psychological warfare. There we were, a nonprofit serving primarily women and children; assisting refugees, asylum seekers, and immigrants; offering English classes; connecting families with legal services for men who had been detained; and advocating for parents in the New York City public school system. We were just a regular social service organization, one of hundreds like it in New York City. We even received some of our funding from the city, which meant our books were wide open. We weren't hiding anything. And yet we were suspected of being terrorists just because we were Arabs.

I stared down at that informant recruitment profile for a long time. When I finally looked up, I saw that Ted had raised his video camera to record my reaction. I squared my shoulders and stared into his lens. "I am not a terrorist, I am not a suspect, and neither is my organization," I told him. "So there is no reason why our taxpayer dollars should be going to spy on me or my organization."

I had intended to sound firm, but my voice cracked at the end. Hot tears pricked my eyes, and I just shook my head. I had no words to explain just how betrayed I was feeling. Before that day, I had been fighting to uphold Basemah's legacy, fighting for my community, fighting most of all for my children. But on that afternoon I became a victim myself, and the fight became personal.

The most unsettling part of the NYPD's intelligence-gathering tactics was that the police weren't just sending infiltrators into a town hall to hear what we were saying, or sending rakers into adult language classes to report on conversations we might be having. This was a far more intrusive and dangerous form of surveillance in that they were trying to place an informant on the board of our organization, which would give them access to all our client information and the power to push forward initiatives.

I became justifiably paranoid about people who inquired about joining our board, or even wanting to volunteer. Before, we'd welcomed anyone who wanted to be of service. After all, we always needed the extra hands. Now we buttoned up our application process and started requiring references for all paid and unpaid positions. We also put passwords on all our computers and locks on all our files to guard client information. When it came to our clients, however, I made peace with the fact that we would always be exposed, because we had to keep our hearts open. Chances were, if someone showed up on our doorstep asking for help, they really needed it. At the same time, I was sure we'd had clients who were actually confidential informants, even though I couldn't confirm that. All I really had to go on when it came to the people we served was my Brooklyn-honed gut instinct. And sometimes, it steered me exactly right.

There was the time that a young Palestinian man kept calling our organization, asking to meet with me. He gave his name as Imad, and said he'd recently come to the U.S. from Libya to pursue a master's degree. He wanted my help in finding a graduate program. That was my first hint that something wasn't quite right about his story—he claimed to be an international student yet he wasn't registered in any school, so how would he have secured a student visa? That question circled in my mind as I politely told him that one of our caseworkers would return his call to see if we could help him. He was adamant about wanting to see only me. *Dude*, I thought, *if what you want is referrals to graduate schools, you don't need me, so why are you stressing?*

I made some excuse and got off the phone.

A few weeks later, I left the office at midmorning to get myself some coffee. When I got back, I was walking through the reception area when I heard my name.

"Linda?"

I recognized the voice at once: Imad, the international student from Libya. I turned and saw a man who looked to be in his early thirties, with short-cropped black hair, black-rimmed glasses, and a clipped beard. He was tall and neatly dressed in a short-sleeved button-down shirt and tan dress slacks.

"How can I help you?" I asked him.

"Can we talk?" he asked me in a Palestinian dialect I recognized.

Something about the man still struck a wrong chord with me, but he was here now, standing before me, so I agreed to meet with him. "I have only fifteen minutes," I said, leading the way to my office at the far end of the reception area.

I slipped behind my desk and Imad sat in one of the two chairs facing me. Then, with no preamble, he began peppering me with questions about the agency: Who funded us; who was on our board; what were our main initiatives?

"The answer to everything you're asking is on our website," I said. "All our programs are listed there. All our board members are named. So are our donors, and everyone who sponsors us." I paused, leaned back in my chair and regarded him with narrowed eyes. "So why are you really here?"

He grew flustered, and began to stammer.

"I-I-I'm new in the neighborhood and I—I was just interested in your—"

"You've forgotten your original reason for calling, haven't you?" I said. "Your story about being an international student and wanting help to find a master's program—it was a lie, wasn't it? Because when you first called here, there was a specific thing you wanted to ask me. Or don't you recall?"

He looked trapped and scared. I saw he had no idea how to respond.

I'd had enough of his ruse. "I know exactly what you are," I said. "And I know why you're here. And you're not going to get anything from me that will help you with your handlers. I want you to get up and leave my office right now, and if I ever see you in my community again, I'm going to tell everyone what you are. I will literally post your picture on every pole in the neighborhood and tell people that you're an informant."

His eyes grew round. "What do you mean?"

"You know exactly what I'm talking about," I told him, my voice calm but firm. "I want you to get up right now, walk out of this office, and act like you never met me."

He jumped to his feet without another word and fled.

I wish I could say that was the last I saw of him. But it wasn't. Two months later, I was at an evening event at Barnard College in Manhattan. I had been asked to emcee a reading by the poet Remi Kanazi, a friend of mine who was launching his new book, *Before the Next Bomb Drops: Rising Up from Brooklyn to Palestine*. I walked into the room where the event was being held and immediately I saw him, the man in black-framed glasses who called himself Imad, talking to a group of college kids. I recognized them as members of the Barnard and Columbia chapter of Students for Justice in Palestine (SJP). One of the young men in the group, a wiry South Asian kid with hair shaved on one side and falling over his eyes on the other, looked over at me and waved. I gestured for him to come talk to me.

"Do you know that guy?" I asked him, pointing to Imad.

"No, he just started talking to us," he said. "Never seen him before."

"What's he saying to you?"

The kid shrugged. "Nothing, just regular stuff, asking us about classes, SJP activities, that kind of thing."

"Listen," I told him, "I don't want you talking to him. That guy is an informant. You need to get your friends and tell them that the event is about to start and they should go and sit down right now. Don't trust that guy."

The South Asian kid looked a little rattled. He didn't argue; he was Muslim, too, and he knew that police informants were always trying to insinuate themselves into our circles. I watched as he walked back to his friends and steered them to find seats. Soon, Imad was standing alone, and I went up to him.

"What are you doing here?" I said.

He went pale, startled to see me.

"Well, you said you don't want to see me in your community," he said, gathering himself. "This is not your community."

"All these people are my community," I told him. "Every person in this city who you might inform on is my community. My community is not just a physical place. My community is everybody. So this is how we're going to do this. I am going to walk toward my seat, and you're going to disappear. If I turn around and you're still here, I'm going to go to the mic and announce to everyone that you're an informant. And I can do that, because I'm the emcee."

I didn't wait for him to respond. I just turned and walked to where the chairs were set up, and when I turned back around, he was gone. I never saw him again. I like to think he knew better than to mess with Brooklyn.

The only break we got when it came to the NYPD's rakers and spies was that most of them were not well trained. Imad, for example, couldn't keep his story straight, was painfully obvious in his attempts to solicit information, and folded like a house of cards the minute he was confronted.

While we all understood the need to prevent another terrorist attack, in the decade following 9/11 the NYPD's surveillance of Muslims had far exceeded the bounds of reason and grossly violated our civil liberties. Before 9/11, the department's terrorism task force had numbered some twenty officers. After 9/11, thousands of officers were involved in the intelligence-gathering effort against American Muslims and Muslim immigrants, and they relied heavily on Arab-speaking informants, many of them undocumented.

The police informants were almost never women. Perhaps police believed that in a patriarchal culture, men would be more effective. Often, the young men who became informants had run afoul of the law—they got caught selling stolen merchandise or peddling untaxed cigarettes, or maybe they jumped a subway turnstile or were picked up for drunk driving. Sometimes they were hardworking contributors to society who happened to have paperwork violations. The charges tended to be petty misdemeanors and nonviolent infractions, but they provided enough leverage for police to use.

In one case, for example, a Muslim immigrant who ran a food cart without a street vending license was arrested. Police took him to Central Booking, where a special NYPD unit identified him as a potential informant. He was Egyptian, spoke Arabic, and was undocumented, which allowed them to lure him with the promise of helping him get a green card. The alternative was that he would be put into deportation proceedings immediately. Another Yemeni man was facing ten years in prison after being accused of committing wire fraud. He had five daughters, all under the age of fourteen. The police told him that if he worked with them as an informant they'd drop all charges, and even pay him for his services.

If the prospective informant happened to be a green card holder, the cops would threaten to take away his green card, putting him at risk for deportation. We knew this because some of the families of these young men had reached out to us for help. Some of them had refused to become informants. Others had succumbed for a while and then regretted it, and now sought help figuring out how to get free of their handlers. We'd heard story after story of people forced to inform out of fear that authorities would target them or their loved ones. Others had hoped to win legal status or desperately needed the money.

When people showed up at our agency with this particular problem, we would refer them to an organization at City University of New York School of Law called CLEAR, which stands for Creating Law Enforcement Accountability and Responsibility. The very fact that a service to help Muslims who were being pressured to become informants existed at all spoke volumes. Of course, the most dangerous mosque crawlers, rakers, and spies were those you didn't see coming until it was too late, the ones who seduced and entrapped their way into your life and then delivered you to their handlers.

Osama Eldawoody was such an informant—if that was even his name. An Egyptian immigrant, he wasn't from Bay Ridge, but he was always sitting on the benches outside of coffee shops or hanging out in barbershops, and he'd become a familiar figure in the neighborhood. I never liked the man. I was suspicious of him: he was in his fifties, seemed to be perfectly able-bodied, and was rumored to have a nuclear engineering degree, so why was he at such loose ends during the day? Why didn't he have a job? Who was his family? We would later learn that he'd been paid $100,000 by the NYPD to eavesdrop on Arabs in Bay Ridge, and he'd been under significant pressure from his handlers to deliver a terror suspect.

He eventually befriended a twenty-two-year-old Pakistani American named Shahawar Matin Siraj, who worked in a bookstore next door to the Islamic Society of Bay Ridge. Siraj was known in the community to be intellectually and emotionally challenged, with a tested IQ in the seventies. Eldawoody told the young man that he belonged to a terrorist organization back in his country, and that he had the resources to build a bomb. He proposed that they detonate the explosive in New York City's Thirty-Fourth Street subway station in Herald Square, one of the city's busiest shopping and commercial centers. Over a period of months, Eldawoody enrolled Siraj in this plan, secretly taping hours of incriminating conversations in which he and Siraj railed at the way Muslims were treated in America—tapes that were later alleged to have been tampered with to obscure the extent to which Siraj was being coerced and entrapped. Siraj's parents were convinced that Eldawoody had preyed on their son because of his mental health issues, coaxing him into making radical statements. Indeed, when Eldawoody's police handlers brought the case to the FBI, the feds wanted nothing to do with it, suspecting that the young Pakistani bookstore clerk had been goaded into actions he did not fully understand and that the tapes had been selectively edited.[4]

The NYPD spymasters then offered the case to Brooklyn prosecutors, who decided that even with the questions surrounding the tapes, the case was winnable. Eldawoody had brought another conspirator into his scheme. James Elshafay had volunteered to place a backpack with explosives under a bench or in a garbage can on the subway station platform, since Siraj had insisted he wanted nothing to do with handling any bomb. According to some reports, Siraj had even told Eldawoody that he needed to first check with his mother before going through with the plan.[5] Siraj did agree, however, to scout the Herald Square subway station and draw a crude map.

Elshafay, who according to reports had previously been diagnosed as schizophrenic, made a deal to testify against Siraj in return for a reduced sentence, and in late 2006 Siraj was found guilty of terrorism conspiracy. After the judge pronounced a sentence of thirty years, the defendant's lawyer noted that if the police department believed it had made the citizens of New York safer by convicting Shahawar Matin, it was sorely mistaken.[6]

We never saw Eldawoody around Bay Ridge after that. I imagine that his usefulness as an NYPD informant, at least when it came to Arab communities in Brooklyn, had expired. I still see Siraj's mother from time to time, though. Her son's case turned her into a community activist, and she attends many of our rallies and events. She shows me pictures of Siraj's latest cakes, because her son has become a gifted baker in prison. "At least he's keeping himself busy," she says, her eyes sad and faraway. I always want to hug her when she says that. I know she is imagining what might have been.

Chapter 14

Your Fight Is My Fight

These were the words on the black T-shirts my three children wore to the march that day:

> Walking While Black
> Praying While Muslim
> ARE NOT CRIMES
> #ChangetheNYPD

"What does it mean?" my daughter Sabreen, then eleven years old, asked me.

"You know how cops are allowed to just stop anyone on the street, and interrogate and search them, even though the people were just walking along minding their own business?" I said. "Well, that policy is called 'stop and frisk' and it unfairly targets Black people."

"Like the way they detain Muslims for no reason?"

"Exactly," I said. "But just like they do with Muslims, the police will tell you they only stop and frisk someone when they have a 'reasonable suspicion' "—I made air quotes with my fingers—"that the person might commit a crime."

"How do they know that, though?" Sabreen asked me, her eyebrows furrowing.

"Bright girl," I said.

It was Father's Day 2012, and my three children had chosen to join me in a Silent March Against Stop and Frisk. My friend and fellow activist Marvin Bing, then northeast regional director of the National Association for the Advancement of Colored People (NAACP), was one of the lead organizers. As I walked with my kids toward Central Park, the step-off point of the march, Tamir and Sajida were listening intently to my conversation with their sister. I went on to explain that in a majority-white city like New York, 90 percent of pedestrians stopped by the police were people of color, which is what made the practice discriminatory. I pointed out that not only did the policy violate the Fourteenth Amendment to the Constitution, which guarantees all people equal treatment under the law, but it also breached the Fourth Amendment, which protects individuals against unreasonable searches and seizures.

At the time, a landmark stop-and-frisk case, *Floyd v. City of New York*, was winding its way through the court system, and the fifty thousand people who attended the Silent March that Father's Day were intent on bringing awareness to the lawsuit. Lead plaintiff David Floyd, an African American, claimed that in 2008, New York City police officers had detained and searched him and numerous other Black and Hispanic men without reasonable cause.[1]

Floyd, who lived in the Bronx, had been returning home when a neighbor who lived in the basement of the building his godmother owned asked him for help. The neighbor, who was also Black, had forgotten his keys, so Floyd ran upstairs and retrieved his godmother's master keys. He didn't know which of the many keys on the chain opened the basement apartment, so he and his neighbor tried five or six keys before finding the right one. Before they could enter the apartment, three police officers descended on them and demanded they stop what they were doing. The men explained the situation, but the police did not believe them. They frisked the men and only when they produced identification to prove they lived at the address did the officers concede that they had not been in the process of burglarizing their own homes.

In her ruling, federal judge Shira Scheindlin found that the manner in which the NYPD had been practicing stop and frisk was discriminatory and unconstitutional. The numbers told the story: in 2012, for example, the public advocate's office reported that police had stopped more than half a million pedestrians. Fifty-three percent of them were Black, 31 percent were Hispanic, with only 10 percent white, and 6 percent "other."[2] The NYPD's own records showed that the majority of stops were in Black neighborhoods, especially in Brooklyn and the Bronx, with comparatively few stops in whiter parts of the city like Staten Island, midtown Manhattan, and parts of Queens. Mayor Michael Bloomberg argued that police stopped people in areas with high crime. It was a false equivalency, because even when researchers controlled for crime rates in an area, Black and brown neighborhoods still fielded vastly disproportionate numbers of stops. Indeed, with 143 stops made for every seizure of illicit goods among Blacks, 99 among Hispanics, and 27 among whites,[3] the policy had proved itself spectacularly ineffective in detecting crime.

Yet every time a pedestrian was stopped, whether or not there was evidence of a crime, police were required to make a report, effectively adding that person to the NYPD database. Put another way, despite the fact that illicit goods were twice as likely to be found on white pedestrians, for every 26 whites added to the police database without cause, 240 Black and brown people were also added with no cause.[4] Perhaps to no one's surprise, certainly not to mine, Mayor Bloomberg and Police Commissioner Kelly appealed Judge Scheindlin's ruling, and the practice continued.

Even before the AP video producer showed me the leaked NYPD confidential informant profile, I'd already connected the dots between the department's unwarranted surveillance of Muslims and its stop-

and-frisk policy. The former targeted people based on religion and the latter targeted people based on race. Both were discriminatory police practices, two sides of the same coin, which is why in 2013 our organization joined with more than one hundred civil rights, Black, LGBTQ, Jewish, and Muslim groups (including the Muslim American Civil Liberties Coalition, or MACLC), plus labor unions, educators, and community health associations to call for independent oversight of the NYPD. We were a broad-based coalition called Communities United for Police Reform with a four-point package of legislation titled the Community Safety Act, or CSA.[5] As originally conceived, the CSA proposed to:

1) End discriminatory profiling by expanding the protected categories of race, ethnicity, and national origin to include age, gender, gender identity or expression, sexual orientation, religion, use of a foreign language, immigration status, mental or physical disability, political affiliation, and housing status. As the law stood, the police could harass people who were homeless, undocumented, disabled, queer, or trans. They could behave in a sexist or ageist manner, or stop and question someone simply because they spoke with an accent or wore garments that marked them as being of a particular religion, and those people would have no legal recourse. The CSA aimed to change that.

2) Establish oversight of the NYPD, making police officers accountable to an inspector general who was independent of the department. This particular piece of legislation was authored by a brilliant Muslim lawyer, Faiza Patel, codirector of the Liberty and National Security Program at the Brennan Center for Justice at New York University School of Law, her alma mater. A Pakistani American and counterterrorism expert, she actively advocated against laws that provoked fear of Islam and understood very clearly that the dragnet surveillance of Muslims and the profiling of African Americans by law enforcement were one and the same issue.

3) Protect people against unlawful searches by requiring officers to explain to pedestrians that they had a right to refuse to be searched, and requiring officers to obtain proof of a person's consent to be searched.

4) Require cops to identify and explain why they had stopped a person, and to provide people with a document that included the officer's name and how to file a complaint in each police encounter.

Finding city council champions for the measure was not hard; the legislation simply made sense. In addition, at least one council member, Jumaane Williams, understood firsthand the need for oversight and accountability for the NYPD. Two years before, Williams himself had been unlawfully detained when, during the annual West Indian Day Parade in Brooklyn, he and another city official, Kirsten John Foy, had tried to enter the Brooklyn Museum for a reception. Police officers detained the two men, both African American, outside the building. They claimed the men had been walking along a sidewalk that was closed to the public because of the parade. Williams explained that he and Foy were invited guests at the reception being held inside the museum, and a high-ranking officer had cleared them to enter the building from that sidewalk. Williams even showed the cops his official city council pin on his jacket lapel and produced ID, but the cops refused to believe that a Black man with dreadlocks could be a city council member, and they threw him and Foy to the ground and roughly arrested them.[6]

Both men were ultimately released without being charged, after then public advocate Bill de Blasio, for whom Foy worked as communications director, personally interceded. Williams called the incident "further evidence of the siege mentality the NYPD has unleashed against black men in New York City."[7] Not surprisingly, when our coalition brought the Community Safety Act to the city's legislative body a year later, Williams was a receptive ear. His experience of being racially profiled immediately made this as personal for him as my own experience of being religiously profiled had made it for me. "If I can't feel safe walking down the street as a New York City Council member," he told us, "how is a young Black kid on a street corner in Crown Heights supposed to feel safe?" He and fellow council member Brad Lander agreed to cosponsor our four-part legislation package.

For us, the most important items were the first two—expanding the classes of people who would be protected against biased profiling and creating accountability for the country's largest police force, thirty-six thousand officers. The next largest police department in the country was in Los Angeles, with only nine thousand officers, who were subject to civilian oversight. In contrast, the NYPD was answerable only to the Internal Affairs Bureau—police officers investigating their own. And so we focused most of our energy on getting the city council to approve an independent body that would assess, monitor, and investigate policies and procedures of the NYPD. Its goal would be to ensure that the department was following accepted procedures and settled law and, in particular, abiding by the Patrol Guide, which included such directives as not using dangerous and illegal chokeholds to restrain a person.

My part in the campaign was to help organize Muslims to contact their New York City Council members and ask them to support our bills. I also participated in what we call bird-dogging, which meant we'd stand outside city hall, go up to council members as they walked into and out of meetings, and try to encourage them to vote yes on our legislation. We also did community briefings and rallies—I spoke at so many rallies—and launched an intensive social media campaign.

Toward the end of June 2013, we watched from the balcony area as council members discussed the Community Safety Act. The session had been scheduled for 11 P.M., and the vote itself wasn't taken until after midnight. My mother couldn't understand it when I left home at ten o'clock that night to travel to city hall. "This is crazy," she said. "Who does business in the middle of the night?" In fact, we suspected that the opposition had scheduled the vote for such a late hour in the hope that CSA's advocates would not show up. No such luck. Our coalition turned up in droves. We came in from Brooklyn, Queens, the Bronx,

Harlem; there were so many of us you'd have thought it was high noon. By the time the voting began, the balcony was full of supporters who'd spent the evening bird-dogging council members during breaks in the session. At 2:22 A.M., when the final votes were tallied, we erupted into cheers. On the two most critical pieces of the legislation, we had won.

Mayor Bloomberg, my old nemesis from the Muslim school holiday campaign, immediately vetoed the bills, claiming the legislation would tie up the NYPD in baseless lawsuits and lead to a citywide surge in crime. To override his veto, the city council would be forced to vote on the measure a second time. Given that it was an election year, Bloomberg was counting on softening support of the bill by council members who were up for reelection, who would not want to be branded as anti-police and weak on crime. But he'd underestimated the situation. Even though the vote was once again scheduled for the wee hours, this time on a sweltering August evening, hundreds of observers once again filled the gallery. At just after 1 A.M., both items passed with even more votes than before, a veto-proof majority, and police reform became law.

Three months later, Bill de Blasio would be elected as the new mayor of New York. Among his first official actions was dropping the pending appeal of Judge Scheindlin's ruling on stop and frisk and directing the NYPD to discontinue the practice. He also expanded the Community Safety Act to include even stronger protections against discriminatory profiling of New Yorkers. And, contrary to what Bloomberg had insisted, without the disproportionate targeting of Black and brown communities, the city's crime rate did not go up, and in fact continues to decline.[8]

Under the new administration, Muslims would soon see a similar dialing down of the NYPD's Muslim surveillance operation. In April 2014, de Blasio's new police commissioner, William J. Bratton, announced that the department was shuttering the program and reassigning its personnel. At a roundtable meeting to which Bratton invited some of the former Demographic Unit's harshest critics, including Dr. Jaber and myself, he noted that in the decade since it was formed, the program had generated no actual leads to terrorist enterprises, and had actually served to make New Yorkers less safe by fracturing the trust between Muslims and the police.

After so many years of laboring under a cloud, Muslims began to feel hopeful. A shroud of suspicion had been lifted from our lives and for a brief, bright moment, we walked with a lighter step. We understood of course that the disbanding of the NYPD task force would not mean a complete end to the unwarranted surveillance of our neighborhoods, but we still saw the shutdown as a win, and a testament to our organizing work and coalition building. We didn't yet know that a real estate developer and reality television personality was at that moment sitting in his office in Trump Tower high above Fifth Avenue, contemplating a run for president of the United States. But even if we had known, we could not have foreseen how completely he would revictimize our community by making the condemnation of Muslims, along with all other people of color in America, his rallying cry.

Part Three

The Sisterhood

If you have come here to help me, you are wasting your time.
But if you have come because your liberation is bound up
with mine, then let us work together.

—Lilla Watson,
Aboriginal artist and international women's rights activist

Chapter 15

Social Justice Voltron

I don't remember ever actually meeting Tamika Mallory and Carmen Perez. It seems that, in my life as an activist, they were just always there: a petite, fiery African American woman and a small-framed Chicana with gentle eyes, occupying the same rooms, marching in the same protests, raising their voices for the cause. Yet no one ever thought to introduce us. I think everyone assumed we already knew each other, and in a way, they were right. As we advocated for equality and fairness on different fronts, we had ended up in the same spaces enough times to become familiar with one another's work. These two fierce and loving women were my touchstones even before I knew they were my sisters. I could see their passion and their humanity, and feel how deeply they cared about the people for whom they fought, but I had no idea that the three of us would one day form, as Carmen calls it, an unbreakable "social justice Voltron."

Three years older than Tamika and me, Carmen had been working to end mass incarceration and to develop restorative justice programs for juveniles long before I understood how intricately connected her cause was to my own fight for immigrants' rights and police reform. She had grown up in Oxnard, a farm town outside of Los Angeles, and at seventeen she suffered a devastating loss when her sister Patricia was killed in a car accident. The family suspected that Carmen's sister had died as a result of her association with local gangs. But when police asked her father if he wanted to press charges against the driver of the car that had killed his daughter, he responded, "My grief is hard enough. I would never take another mother's child away."

"I didn't learn restorative justice from studying it," Carmen would say later. "I learned it from a man who would never take another mother's child away."[1] It was within this frame that she began to think about how she could improve the prospects for Chicano youth whose poverty put them at risk for gang involvement, leading directly to violent encounters with the criminal justice system. Carmen studied psychology at the University of California, Santa Cruz, searching for reasons why her brother, "a good guy," was stopped and frisked by police week after week. She began to put the injustices she'd witnessed growing up into their larger racial and socioeconomic context. To combat the systemic bias, she became a youth probation officer after college, and worked on finding community alternatives to juvenile incarceration.

On the other side of the country, Tamika had come of age as a foot soldier in the civil rights movement in Harlem. Her parents had helped the Rev. Al Sharpton found the National Action Network (NAN), and she'd marched in protests as an eleven-year-old Catholic schoolgirl. When she was nineteen, an African Muslim immigrant, Amadou Diallo, was gunned down by police officers as he was returning to his Bronx home. Police claimed they mistook the unarmed Diallo for a suspect in a year-old crime. According to a witness, the officers, all of them in street clothes, had opened fire without identifying themselves. Diallo, who some people later speculated had thought he was being robbed, was reaching for his wallet when police discharged forty-one rounds at him. Nineteen bullets pierced his body.

Amadou Diallo's shooting had galvanized Tamika to push for community policing reform, but an even greater sorrow lay in store. Just weeks after celebrating her son's second birthday, Tamika learned that her child's father had been found fatally shot in a ditch in rural Pennsylvania. The death of her son's father would transform Tamika into a vigorous advocate against gun violence—but from a holistic community-health perspective that sought to heal both the potential perpetrators of violence and the survivors. These two social justice causes—ending overly aggressive policing of communities of color and fighting for gun safety—became Tamika's driving passions. In 2011 she became the youngest executive director of NAN ever.

Carmen, Tamika, and I had all suffered intense and life-altering tragedies at a young age. In each case, the loss of a beloved had served to bring into stark focus our responsibility to care for and protect the lives of people in our communities. It was for each of us a call to action that could not be ignored. In the beginning, we were all organizing in a very localized way, with Carmen working on juvenile justice in Santa Cruz, Tamika involved in community policing in Harlem, and me focusing on immigrant rights in Brooklyn.

In 2008 Carmen moved to New York City to become a national organizer for the Gathering for Justice, a nonprofit founded by the legendary singer, actor, and activist Harry Belafonte. Mr. B, as she called her mentor, sought to connect the wisdom and experience of elders with the vigor and imagination of youth in the fight for equal rights. Carmen was appointed executive director of the organization two years later. In that role, she often partnered with Tamika's organization and mine, as well as numerous other civil rights groups to help pass criminal justice reform that would safeguard our respective communities. Sadly, it would take two more tragedies—the inexcusable deaths at the hands of police of two unarmed Black men, Eric Garner and Michael Brown, in the summer of 2014—to truly explode our hyperlocal focus, widen our perspective, and cement our alliance.

————

Eric Garner, forty-three, was a husband, father of six, and grandfather in Staten Island, New York. At 350 pounds, he cut an imposing figure, but the effect of his height and girth was moderated by his open face and ready smile. Many who knew him used the same phrase to describe him: "a gentle giant." They said he was good-natured, peace-loving, and not remotely dangerous. Nevertheless, on July 17, 2014, police stopped him on suspicion of selling "loosies"—single untaxed cigarettes, fifty cents a stick. A misdemeanor punishable by fines of a few hundred dollars, the black market trade of loosies thrives in low-income neighborhoods where thirteen-dollar packs of cigarettes are often out of reach.

That muggy July afternoon was not the first time police had detained Garner. In the previous decade they'd arrested him numerous times on such charges as driving without a license, marijuana possession, and resisting arrest, often in connection with selling loosies.[2] On one occasion, cops had restrained him, dragged down his pants, and performed a cavity search on the street as people walked by. Garner would detail this humiliation in a handwritten complaint filed in federal court in 2007,[3] but the official complaint hadn't stopped the harassment. In fact, it seemed to Garner's family that it only made him more of a target for local cops.

When police stepped up to him that day, Garner had just broken up a sidewalk fight and was chatting with another man, twenty-two-year-old Ramsey Orta. As two officers surrounded Garner, Orta quietly raised his camera phone, recording as the big man told the cops that he wasn't feeling well, and that he was sick and tired of them always coming after him.[4] He wasn't a criminal. He wasn't armed. He was a man trying to provide for his family.

When Officer Daniel Pantaleo tried to pull back his wrists to handcuff him, Garner shook him off. "Don't touch me, man," he said, and walked away. Pantaleo and his partner, Justin D'Amico, jumped Garner from behind, tackling him to the ground. Pantaleo crooked his arm around Garner's neck in a chokehold maneuver banned by the NYPD. Yet Pantaleo pulled his forearm into the big man's throat and held it there. Other cops swarmed around and pressed Garner's face into the ground. They all ignored him as he gasped again and again, "I can't breathe. I can't breathe."

The video was all over the news by the next day. Everyone could hear Garner hissing, "I can't breathe," not once, not twice, but *eleven* times, yet Pantaleo did not release his hold until Garner's body slumped and went still. At that point the cops began chasing bystanders away from the scene. The city coroner would later rule Garner's death a homicide caused by "compression of neck, compression of chest and prone positioning during physical restraint by police."[5]

I can't breathe.

Garner's final three words echoed viscerally for me. I would never forget Basemah whispering them on the day she died. I simply couldn't fathom how Officer Pantaleo could have heard those rasping words and not have immediately let go of Garner's throat. The video of his suffocation at the hands of men who were sworn to serve and protect was agonizing to witness, and yet I made myself watch again and again. It was as if Basemah were whispering to me, *I can't breathe*, and urging me in the echo of those words to enlarge the scope of my activism, to take it as my personal charge to help turn out Muslims for protests being mounted throughout the city in the wake of Garner's death.

Even as I lent my voice to calls for justice in the Eric Garner case, another senseless execution of a Black man by a white police officer sparked renewed sorrow and outrage. On August 9, Michael Brown, an eighteen-year-old who was due to begin college in a couple of weeks, was walking with a friend down Canfield Drive in Ferguson, Missouri, on his way to his grandmother's house. Officer Darren Wilson approached in a cruiser and told the men to get on the sidewalk. What happened next is contested: Officer Wilson says Brown punched him in the cruiser and then ran when Wilson pulled his firearm and started shooting. Witnesses say Brown did not assault the officer, but ran from the cruiser when the cop started firing, then turned and put his hands in the air and yelled, "Don't shoot!" Yet Officer Wilson kept squeezing the trigger, twelve shots in all. Six bullets entered Michael Brown's body, one through the top of his head.[6]

The noonday execution of this unarmed Black man was shocking enough, but Brown was then left on the street for four hours in the August sun. Only when the sun began to lower itself in the sky was he picked up and thrown into the back of an SUV like a bag of rocks. I remember thinking: *You hear about this kind of thing in Palestine. How is this happening in America?*

The lack of humanity toward these two men—one a family man whom so many had relied on, the other a teenager with his whole life ahead of him—jolted me into the understanding that not only did our movements for justice need to encompass *all* people who were marginalized, but we also needed to mobilize on a national stage. And so, upon hearing about the death of Michael Brown, I picked up the phone and called Mustafa Abdullah, a friend and fellow activist who served as the lead organizer of the ACLU of Missouri. "What are you doing about Michael Brown?" I asked him. "Where are the Muslims on this? We need to stand up."

The next week I got myself on a plane and flew to Ferguson. I wanted to bear witness in person to what had transpired there. It felt right for me, an American Muslim woman in a hijab, to stand in solidarity with protesters from around the country, marching for the sanctity of Black lives. Yet I was still hopelessly naive, because when local authorities confronted us with armored vehicles, tear gas, and riot gear, I was stunned. Muslims faced their own problems with law enforcement, but that week in Ferguson opened my eyes to the state-sanctioned violence that Black people in America had long endured. I had the ridiculous luxury of being incredulous, of thinking: *We're deploying the military against our own citizens.* The scene was one I'd watched broadcast on the news from places like Iraq and Afghanistan. Yet here I was, in the heartland of America, and our government of the people, by the people, and for the people was firing live rounds into crowds of protestors and tear-gassing citizens who were simply exercising their First Amendment rights.

My own son was close in age to Michael Brown. My heart clenched when I imagined how I might feel if what had happened to this young

Black man had befallen Tamir. This was the problem with our country, I realized then. We failed to grieve for other people's children as if they were our own. We failed to see that injustices visited upon "the other" had also been visited on us, which was why as a nation we were so splintered. We had dehumanized certain segments of our society to such a degree that we could not feel each other's pain.

As the case against Michael Brown's killer wound its way through the criminal justice system, Mustafa and I, along with Imam Dawud Walid, an African American religious leader from Detroit, and Muhammad Malik, a South Asian American labor and community organizer from Miami, cofounded Muslims for Ferguson. We wanted to encourage Muslim Americans to embrace the fight against police brutality as a top priority, so we put out a call for Muslims to attend Ferguson October, an event planned by local activists in advance of a critical grand jury hearing on whether Officer Darren Wilson would be indicted. We also arranged for Black Lives Matter organizers to meet with South Asian and Arab business owners in the St. Louis area to foster solidarity between our communities.

Despite our efforts, in late November 2014, a Missouri grand jury declined to indict Michael Brown's killer, saying he had broken no law. A week later, a grand jury in New York reached a similar conclusion in the case of the man who had choked Eric Garner to death. People of conscience were heartbroken and enraged. On college campuses, students lay on the ground to stage "die-ins" in protest of the grand jury decisions. In New York City, Tamika, Carmen, and I helped to organize rallies to close down highways, while protestors poured into Macy's department store and laid themselves down in the aisles. A few blocks away in Bryant Park on that rainy night, people lay shoulder to shoulder on the wet ground, holding up signs that echoed Garner's last words: "I can't breathe." As the traditional media scrambled to cover the protests, citizen journalists tweeted updates in real time. "A whole lot of people are just plain fed up and they're drafting off each other's energy," one wrote. "Something big is happening here. We're waking up."

Marvin Bing is one of the most creative community organizers I know. A conceptual designer and producer of cultural events, he'd been a foster kid growing up, and had done time in juvie in his native Philadelphia. The experience had left him with a lifelong mission to defend youth who are unable to defend themselves. Marvin brought an artist's imagination to all his social justice activations, and an abiding belief in Kingian nonviolence, which urges us to confront the institutions and structures that perpetuate injustice, rather than the individuals who act in their name.

Now Marvin had a new idea, and he wanted me to be a part of it. Before I even knew what he had in mind I was on board, because I trusted him and appreciated that he always made sure Muslims were present around any table at which he sat. That is how I came to be in a meeting on the ground floor of the 1199 Service Employees International Union (SEIU) building in midtown Manhattan, along with nine of the city's boldest and most influential activists and politicos.

Carmen Perez was cohosting the meeting along with Marvin. Also present were people like Angelo Pinto, leader of the Raise the Age campaign to improve juvenile justice outcomes; and Cherrell Brown, a criminal justice organizer working to repeal the death penalty. Among the powerhouse change makers in the room, I tried to act as if I belonged, but the truth was I felt out of my league. But I had shared with Marvin my desire to take my game to a much bigger playing field, and to connect my cause to the overarching fight for justice and equality in our country. It was why he'd invited me to be a founding member of an alliance that would soon be known as Justice League NYC, an intergenerational movement for social transformation. "Look around you," Marvin said to us on that first day. "We are some of the most brilliant people of color in New York City, so why are we not working together? Why are we not organizing together? We are the generation to bring the change we seek. It's time to create something together."

Justice League NYC would go on to engage numerous critical battles on behalf of the oppressed and disenfranchised. Other civil rights groups, labor movements, and police reform advocates would soon join with our initiative, including Tamika Mallory. Tamika, Carmen, and I were now officially working in common cause, and together we pulled off a number of high-profile protests. There was the time when Prince William and Kate Middleton were courtside at a Cavaliers-Nets game at Brooklyn's Barclays Center. We knew a lot of press would cover the royals' attendance at that game, so we staged a mass protest outside the arena to demand that all the cops involved in Garner's death be held accountable. We dubbed the action a "Royal Shutdown." Some of us even wore plastic crowns as a statement on the absurdity of the press being preoccupied with a royal visit when people were being killed in the streets.

It was a cold night in December 2014. Outside the arena, hundreds of us chanted, "I can't breathe," and "All I want for Christmas is to live," and "How do you spell racist? N-Y-P-D!" Thirty minutes later, everyone became quiet and lay down on the pavement. We were a sea of bodies lying side by side in the night, in complete silence. For half an hour the only sounds that could be heard around us were the crackle of police scanners, the hum of street traffic, and camera shutters going off as press photographers and ordinary citizens recorded our protest. Meanwhile, inside the arena at halftime, the Cavaliers' big man LeBron James pulled on a black T-shirt with the words I CAN'T BREATHE across the front, and several other players joined him. Justice League NYC had created those T-shirts, which had been hand-delivered to the players by hip-hop producer and part owner of the Nets, Jay-Z, one of our allies.

Carmen, Tamika, and I quickly became known for these sorts of high-visibility actions, which brought pop culture influencers together with leaders in social justice advocacy. By mixing politics, entertainment, and culture in our messaging, we began to attract young people of color who understood at once that we were out there fighting for them and their communities. Justice League NYC would go on to be honored with the Chairman's Award at the forty-seventh NAACP Image Awards, in recognition of one particularly audacious action that we undertook in the spring of 2015—a nine-day pilgrimage from New York to Washington, DC, to protest the nonindictment of the police officers who'd ended the lives of Eric Garner and Michael Brown.

That convoy of souls across five northeastern states—fueled by grief as much as by the stubborn hope that we could *do something*— would change everything for me. Not only did those nine days bond me to Carmen and Tamika in a profound way, but they also showed me that a magnificent collective stood always ready at my side. When any one of us called, the others would show up without question, knowing that in pressing forward together, we multiplied our effect. Never again would I labor under the illusion that in losing Basemah, I was destined to walk the path of activism with a gnawing sense of being spiritually alone. I now saw that in Carmen and Tamika, and so many others, I was richly supported. God had sent me companions for the journey, and sisters of the heart.

Chapter 16

Nine Days in April

Harry Belafonte sat on a couch in his resplendent, wood-paneled office, telling us not to lose hope. The week before, several of us had been arrested outside Mayor Bill de Blasio's house. We'd gone there to protest the decision not to hold the NYPD accountable for Eric Garner's death, but our action had yielded no discernable result. Now, at a meeting of Justice League NYC, about twenty of us surrounded Mr. Belafonte. We were perched on chairs and literally sitting at his feet. The great man was now well into his eighties but was as vital as ever. Even though his voice bore the slightest waver, his eyes were fiery as he told us about being with Dr. Martin Luther King Jr. and John Lewis on the march from Selma to Montgomery in 1965. Some six hundred people had joined that fifty-four-mile journey along Highway 80. On the fourth day, in a drenching downpour, they had camped out in a soaked field where a single flatbed trailer served as a concert stage from which performers sang and spoke in the rain. Mr. Belafonte had organized it all, using his star power to bring out some of the nation's most celebrated artists—from Mahalia Jackson to Leonard Bernstein, from Nina Simone to Joan Baez, from James Baldwin to Pete Seeger—all to support the cause of racial justice.

Mr. Belafonte described how tired the marchers were, yet how restored in their souls by the performance. Many of the protesters had been beaten and hosed. They'd faced snarling police dogs and some had been arrested, but the rest had marched on for freedom and equality, and so that people like us, sitting in this room, would have the right to vote and raise our voices, too. "There was no other choice but to keep going," Mr. Belafonte told us. "Defeat is never an option." He looked around the room, seeming to hold each person in his gaze at the same time. "All of you here have inherited the mantle from the ones who marched then, and we are all counting on you."

For that entire meeting, I hung on his every word, feeling the great privilege of his belief in us to carry on the struggle. I was in awe of his commitment, which fifty years later was undimmed. *Defeat is not an option*, he had said, and with all my heart I believed him. That night, his grace, authority, and humanity felt like an infinite font of love, pouring sustenance into us all.

A month later the same group was once again gathered inside the same building in New York's Hell's Kitchen, where Mr. Belafonte kept a suite of offices. We were seated this time around an expansive table of highly polished wood that commanded the center of the conference room. Around us, the walls were covered with photographs and awards from Mr. Belafonte's long and illustrious career as an actor, singer, and agitator. The singer Paul Robeson had once told him that "artists are the gatekeepers of truth" and "civilization's radical voice," which is why, in addition to the Gathering for Justice, Mr. Belafonte had founded Sankofa, an organization to connect artists with grassroots organizing and social justice campaigns.

The Gathering for Justice was headquartered inside Mr. Belafonte's suite, as was our own group, Justice League NYC. Our meetings there often lasted well into the night. No one ever wanted to leave. We relished being in rooms that were imbued with Mr. Belafonte's warrior spirit. It reminded us that our efforts were never in vain. However, the great man was not with us on this night, and the mood in the room was glum. "The police are just killing us and getting away with it," Tamika said, throwing out her hands in a gesture of frustration. "This is not justice. We have to make people pay attention."

"We can't just keep doing press conferences," someone else said. "We have to do something really outrageous so people will know we're serious."

Everybody started offering up suggestions, and then Tamika said, "Maybe we should march from here to Washington, DC."

It was as if someone had opened a window in a gloomy place and light flooded in.

"Like Selma to Montgomery," Carmen said, her imagination fired at once. "Mr. B would love that."

"A freedom rally," someone else agreed.

"Our own march to justice," Tamika said, the idea taking hold. "And that's what we'll call it, too, but this isn't 1965, so it's gotta be a hashtag: #March2Justice."

People sat up straighter, looked around at each other with excitement, and then everyone erupted in a chorus of *yes, oh my God, it's brilliant, let's do this, let's go.*

I was caught by the idea, too, but I remember thinking: *New York to Washington—that's a lot of miles.* Two hundred and fifty miles, to be exact. We did the math and figured out that if we marched for ten to twelve hours a day, it would take us nine days to cross the five states between us and the nation's capital. Even to me, who was used to walking everywhere in the city (I didn't have personal security concerns back then), the distance seemed crazy. We agreed we should wait till the winter weather gave way to spring, and in the meantime, we would plan the logistics and build up our physical stamina. Mysonne Linen, a hip-hop artist who was part of our group, offered personal training classes for people up in Harlem. Since I was at the other end of the city in Brooklyn, I went out and bought a $140 treadmill and installed it in my living room the very next day. Every night, no matter how late I got home, I would walk three or four miles on that rickety machine.

We set our step-off date for April 13, 2015. That spring would mark the fiftieth anniversary of "Bloody Sunday" in Selma, and the forty-seventh anniversary of the assassination of Dr. King, and yet all these years later we were still marching for the sanctity and safety of Black lives. As Carmen framed it in our official statement to the press:

> The commemoration of Selma was an important and emotional occasion. We couldn't be doing this work without the sacrifice of Congressman John Lewis and the many others who have marched and paved the way. We honor them and are grateful for their leadership. Yet while we were commemorating what happened fifty years ago, we were also reminded that Selma is now. The people of Madison, Wisconsin, spent the same weekend mourning the death of unarmed nineteen-year-old Tony Robinson, who was killed by police officers. It's important that while we remember the sacrifices made by those who marched in Selma, we ground ourselves in the reality of the times that we live in and recommit to follow in their example.[1]

For months we met in the evenings after work to plan our agenda and itinerary for each day. We plotted our route from the southwest end of Staten Island, Eric Garner's home, following U.S. Route 1 south all the way to the nation's capital. I got busy working the phones to find places for us to dine and rest our heads each evening, and to have a nourishing breakfast before resuming our pilgrimage each morning. Meanwhile, Tamika reached out to affiliated community organizations, houses of worship, and college student groups, all of which pledged to help turn out participants, while Carmen worked on the messaging and press coverage. By the end of March, almost one hundred people had registered, including many 1199 union members. The head of the union, George Gresham, and Mr. Belafonte had agreed to be honorary cochairs of the march. They helped us with fund-raising and sponsorships, and Mr. Gresham even secured two RVs manned by nurses and EMTs and equipped with medical supplies to accompany us along the route. If people got blisters on their feet, they'd provide salve and a place to rest. If people's knees or ankles ached, they'd tape us up so we could keep going. "Two hundred and fifty miles will wear on your bodies," Mr. Belafonte had said when Carmen, Tamika, and I first met with him to tell him of our plan. "The logistics alone are crazy. But I'm on board. I don't know what it is about you three, but I will follow you anywhere."

His words fortified us for the road ahead. Determined that our effort be seen as more than a publicity stunt, Carmen, Tamika, and I, as lead organizers, took pains to establish concrete goals that would yield a quantifiable result. In anticipation of the 2016 presidential campaign, which was already heating up, we partnered with local groups to help us register voters along the way. We also planned morning and evening rallies for each day of the journey to bring awareness to the violence being done to communities of color in the name of policing. At night, we would bed down in churches, mosques, temples, schools, and community centers, and at the end of the journey, we'd gather on the lawn of the Capitol for a performance by artists who supported our cause, along with speeches by leaders in the fight for justice.

During the staged event, we would deliver to members of Congress a three-point justice package that included an End Racial Profiling Act, a Stop Militarization of Law Enforcement Act, and a Juvenile Justice and Delinquency Prevention Act—each one aimed at countering the overpolicing of our neighborhoods and preserving community-based alternatives to juvenile incarceration. We'd even secured the commitment of several lawmakers in Congress to bring the proposals to the floor, where they could be debated and voted on.

Finally, everything was arranged. April 13 dawned unseasonably cool. We assembled at 9 A.M. in Staten Island, where Jumaane Williams and other city council members joined us in the parking lot of a bath and tile store for a kick-off rally. As we marched across the Outerbridge Crossing into New Jersey an hour later, we were all fired up. I surveyed our group, many holding I CAN'T BREATHE signs above their heads and chanting "Hands up! Don't shoot!" in memory of both Eric Garner and Michael Brown. On that bridge with me was every color of humanity, from all walks and experiences. We were Christian, Muslim, Jewish, agnostic, and atheist. We were college students, artists and musicians, PTA moms and soccer dads, ministers, city council members, attorneys, and labor unionists; people who had formerly been incarcerated; community organizers; and even a few longtime civil rights foot soldiers.

Our youngest marcher, Skylar Shafer, a white sixteen-year-old from Litchfield, Connecticut, had signed on to march because she was interested in advocating for children of war. Our oldest marcher, sixty-four-year-old Bruce Richard, was an 1199 union member and former Black Panther. He'd been in the activism trenches since he was twelve, when a police officer lifted him above his head and slammed him down on the hard ground because he and his cousins kept singing doo-wop songs after the officer told them to stop. Another marcher, twenty-two-year-old Shana Salzberg, carried as inspiration a photo of her grandfather, who had survived the Holocaust. Indeed, there were a hundred individual stories and reasons for making this pilgrimage. And every face shone bright because every person who had pulled on their walking shoes to join us that morning understood that we were marching to save lives.

———

Each evening we took the buses from the stopping point of that day's leg of the journey to wherever we would sleep that night. At the end of day three, I pulled off my hijab and stretched out on an air mattress in the women's prayer area of the Al-Hidaya mosque in North Philadelphia, bone-tired but gratified. Around me, my sisters Tamika and Carmen and close to one hundred more people were also settling their weary bodies on rows of air mattresses set up by our advance team, or sliding into sleeping bags spread on the carpeted floor of the men's and women's prayer areas. This beautiful mosque, with its crystal chandeliers, expansive rooms, colorful mosaics, full-service kitchen and dining areas, and blessed availability of hot showers, would be our home for the evening.

When we'd first arrived, Al-Hidaya's imam had been in the parking lot to greet us, along with a dozen members of the mosque, which was the worship home of a large community of Palestinians in North Philly. As we climbed down out of the buses that had transported us from the day's stopping point along Highway 1, we had formed a circle with the imam, who prayed for the success of our journey. He was an immigrant himself, and his English was not very good, but the warmth of his welcome was unmistakable. "We are so honored you are here," he said. "I want you to remember that this house belongs to God, and you are all God's creations, so this is your house tonight. I ask you to treat this house like it is your home."

Most of the people with us were young college students, the majority of them African American. Almost none of them had been inside a mosque before, but they seemed to take the imam's words to heart, because after they had eaten their fill of an abundant meal of steak, chicken, rice, and vegetables and many kinds of dessert, they found brooms and cloths and began sweeping and cleaning up after themselves. Some even went out to the parking lot and swept up little messes they had not made.

While outside with the students, one of our Justice League members, an Iranian filmmaker named Rameen, noticed a black car with tinted windows parked across the street from the gate, with two men seated inside. Now he became aware of a buzzing sound in the sky, and when he looked up, he saw a drone flying back and forth over the gold dome of the mosque. He knew at once what was happening: the mosque and our little band of marchers were being surveilled by law enforcement. Rameen pointed out the black car across the street and the drone overhead to the students; then he got his camera and filmed the drone, which whirred and buzzed above us for the entire night. Many times during the evening, some of the students went out to the parking lot to check if the black car was still there. It always was.

The college kids stayed up late that night, talking with the Muslims in our group and some of the members of the mosque about what it meant to be a follower of Islam in post-9/11 America. It was their first experience of how vulnerable one feels knowing that government agents are watching you, not for your protection, but with the belief that you are a potential enemy of the state. We were marching to take a stand against the criminalizing of communities of color by law enforcement and the state-sanctioned destruction of Black lives, and now the students saw how closely woven with that cause was the struggle of their Muslim brothers and sisters. For me, it was a beautiful thing to watch those connections being made.

Sometime around 11 P.M., Carmen lit some sage and waved it over our group, and spoke prayers for our safety and success. She did this every night before we retired, and every morning before we set off. After that, it was time to shower and get ready for bed. As I was handing out sheets and blankets to people who hadn't brought their own, one of the students approached me.

"Where did our hosts go?" he asked. "There's nobody but us here."

At first, I didn't grasp the weight of his question. "I don't know," I said. "They probably went home to be with their families."

The young man, whose name was Malcolm, stared at me. "What do you mean they went home? You mean they left one hundred strangers in their mosque? There is so much of value here; this place is fancy. They even left the computer lab open. I'm shocked they would just leave all their possessions unprotected."

By now some of the other students had gathered around. "You mean they left us here alone?" they asked, their voices full of wonder. I was surprised by their surprise, and then my heart stung a little because I realized that these students, many of them Black, were used to being looked upon with suspicion in the places where they were not already known.

"What did the imam say to you when you first got here?" I asked them.

"This is God's house," Malcolm said.

174

"Exactly," I continued. "And didn't he tell you this is your house, too? So that means that when the imam went home, he bestowed on you responsibility for the security of this mosque. He didn't hesitate to put you in charge of making sure this place stays safe until he returns tomorrow."

You should have seen those students after that, checking all the windows and doors, going outside to the parking lot to close the gate, making sure everything was as we'd found it, treating that house of worship as if it were their own. I appreciated their care and reverence for the space, just as they appreciated the hospitality and trust that had been extended to them by their Muslim hosts.

I drifted into sleep that night thinking about an experience I'd had the summer before when I had visited relatives in the West Bank. Walking through the town square in El Bireh, I'd noticed a little Palestinian boy selling Wrigley's—they call it taxi gum—five shekels for five pieces. The child was maybe ten years old and not well kept. His red shirt was too small for him, and was torn on one shoulder. Compared to him, I was a relatively prosperous American, and so as I passed by, I flipped him some change and kept walking. The kid ran after me and proceeded to give me a lecture I will never forget.

"Sister, I'm not a beggar, I'm a salesman," he said. "You take your five gums or you take back your five shekels."

Humbled, I took the gum, realizing that when I'd tossed change to a poorly dressed child, I'd assumed I was giving him something. Instead, he had given me a gift far greater—the assertion of his human dignity. And by not allowing me to disrespect what he had to offer, the boy had acted in recognition of my own.

In a way, our hosts at the mosque in Philadelphia had done the same thing for us at the end of an exhausting day. They had given, and we had gratefully received, and in our shared transaction, we had each acknowledged the profound dignity of one human being respecting another, no matter our station, experience, creed, or history. We are all God's creations, the imam had said, and that makes us brothers and sisters. I reflected now that even though he didn't know it, the Palestinian boy in the town square had been, for an unthinking American woman, a reminder of the sacred bonds that connect us all and make us family.

———

At 5:15 A.M. the imam returned to the mosque. I was awakened by his melodic voice giving the call to prayer over the loudspeakers. I sat on my air mattress with my eyes closed, listening to the call. The sound was soft and lyrical, the song of a nightingale, a wailing, haunting refrain that almost brought me to tears. Around me, people started stirring, sitting up, rubbing their eyes, and looking around, confused.

"What's that?" they asked. "What's going on?"

I explained that the imam was doing the *adhan*, or morning call to prayer, and I translated the Arabic words for them:

> *God is the greatest.*
> *I testify that there is no God but Allah.*
> *Muhammad is the messenger of God.*
> *Come to prayer . . .*

Now everyone grew still and just listened, entranced by the sheer beauty of the imam's voice and the way it reverberated in the heart. Some people bowed their heads and said their own prayers, while others stared up at the ceiling or down at their hands in respectful silence.

At around six o'clock we stripped our beds and washed up, then went down to breakfast as the advance team began deflating the air mattresses and rolling up the sleeping bags. In the cafeteria we saw the same smiling faces that had welcomed us the day before, and they had laid out for us a spread of bagels and croissants, scrambled eggs with vegetables, and platters of fresh fruit. Later, as we climbed back onto the buses that would take us to Drexel Hill, our step-off point for day four, our hosts came out to the parking lot holding crates of bananas, oranges, and bottled water.

"You'll need these," the imam said. "We are so grateful for the work you are doing on behalf of all of us."

There were hugs all around as people said goodbye, and when we drove out of the parking lot and past the unidentified black car that was still stationed across the street, I was feeling intensely grateful for our experience at Al-Hidaya. I was thankful that for the students and other non-Muslims who were part of our group, their first experience of being inside a mosque had been one in which they had felt so warmly received. I felt a secret pride, too, because the people at that mosque had been my own people, Palestinian immigrants who were not even trusted to enter a train station with a book bag, and yet they had encouraged busloads of Black and brown people of different faiths to come into their holy space and treat it like home.

As I leaned my head against the bus window and watched the green of rural Pennsylvania sweeping by outside, I reflected that these were the kinds of cross-cultural experiences that dissolved misunderstandings and made it impossible for people to hate one another. I knew without doubt that if any of the students who had been with us at Al-Hidaya was ever in life confronted by an occasion of Islamophobia, they would speak up. They would say, "Oh hell no. I *know* Muslims. They welcomed us into their mosque. They fed and cared for us, and you're just so wrong about them."

For me, that was perhaps the most meaningful aspect of our night in the mosque in Philly—to be able to introduce my fellow marchers to my Palestinian community and my faith. At Al-Hidaya, my people had shown through their hospitality that they, too, were committed to the struggle for freedom, and my Justice League family had felt our communion deeply.

Chapter 17

Road Warriors

D ay four would prove to be the antithesis of our love fest at the mosque. As we headed down Highway 1 toward the Maryland border, we found ourselves passing through towns where every house had a Confederate flag hanging from its windows or fluttering on a flagpole in the front yard. Confederate flags adorned every car and pickup truck, every strip mall and billboard, even every church sign. At one church, a message board with black magnetic letters read TO BE ALMOST SAVED IS TO BE TOTALLY LOST, and tucked right below was a Confederate flag. A few miles on, a purple clown car passed by with a painted sign on the side that said KupKakeKart. Given that three-quarters of our group was African American, the intentionality of the three capitalized *K*s was crystal clear. If anyone had a doubt about the prevailing sentiment toward Black people in this neck of the woods, it was erased as driver after driver leaned out of their cars and yelled the N-word at us, their faces contorted into masks of hate. Others would pull over close enough to blow exhaust smoke at our group while flipping us the bird. "Nigger, go get a fucking job!" they'd scream. Or: "White power! Get off my street!"

I'm not Black, but I wear a hijab, so I knew damn well that all those people didn't like me, either. Some residents would make their hands into the shape of a gun, take aim, and pretend to shoot us as we walked past. I met their cold stares calmly, holding on to the lessons in civil disobedience that Carmen had imparted in her training sessions in the weeks leading up to the march: always meet hate with love, she had reminded us. Never allow other people's poison to find its way inside you. Instead, be a serene mirror for the world, trusting that actions undertaken in good faith will have good outcomes.

Mercifully, as exposed as we felt marching through that part of Pennsylvania, there was no actual violence that day, at least not the physical kind, but try having people yell ugly racist epithets and other vulgarities at you for several hours. Even with Carmen's loving reminders playing in our minds, psychologically it wore us down.

The contrast with our experience the day before was stark. As we'd marched down through New Jersey, through Newark and Trenton toward Philadelphia, people along the route had come out to cheer us on and thank us for what we were doing, and police officers had even escorted us some of the way. Whether for our protection or the townspeople's, we didn't know, but to my mind, those officers reflected my belief that individual police officers were not the issue so much as a system of policing that was corrupt at the core.

To be clear, I have never been against law enforcement. Rather, I am against law enforcement's *brutal conduct*, which I maintain arises from police department policies like arrest quotas that turn too many officers into bad actors. We should not forget that the police force in our country evolved from colonial-era slave patrols in the South and night watches in the North, constituted to control and suppress nonwhite people. In effect, modern-day law enforcement—despite its contract to protect and serve all Americans—still operates based on an original mission to control through violence and mass incarceration a socially subjugated class.[1]

All this played in my mind as we marched through middle-of-nowhere Pennsylvania, headed toward the Maryland border, just beyond which lay the town of Rising Sun and the regional headquarters of the Ku Klux Klan. Here, there was no police protection of any kind, only townspeople who were viscerally hostile. Usually, as we marched each day, we would talk and share stories, getting to know one another. Sometimes we sang anthems as we walked and chanted slogans to evoke our cause. But in the heart of KKK country, everyone grew silent. We pressed forward, braced for anything, knowing better than to surrender vigilance even for a single breath. *What must this moment feel like for the Black people in our group?* I thought. *Do they wonder how many men were lynched in these woods? How many women were raped and children beaten for no reason other than the color of their skin?*

Imagine a long column of people marching, and no one is saying a word, and all you can hear along the side of the road is *shuffle, shuffle, shuffle*, the sound of shoes scraping the earth. The silence of that day is what stays with me, and the weight of people's reflections, which pressed down on us as we put one foot in front of the other and kept on.

That evening, we boarded buses that would take us to Lincoln University, a historically Black college near Oxford, Pennsylvania, where we would convene for prayers and a rally in the chapel, eat dinner on the lawn, and bed down for the night in the school's gymnasium. It was already twilight as our buses entered the campus gates and rolled to a stop in front of the Mary Dod Brown Memorial Chapel, a red-brick building with beautiful stained-glass windows, richly polished wooden beams, and plush burgundy upholstered pews. The students filed into the pews and sat, fatigued and drained. The elders in our group watched them with concern. They understood just how much it had taken for these young people to hold themselves together as raw hatred was spewed at them throughout the day.

Moments later, a young woman named Nicole Webb went up to the altar and began to read a poem she had written when she was a student at Lincoln, in the aftermath of Trayvon Martin's murder in Florida in 2012, and the acquittal of his killer, George Zimmerman, a year later. The poem was in the form of a letter beseeching God to protect and care for young Black men. "Dear God," I remember her saying, "please tell me your first name isn't Zimmerman. Lord, please tell me your last name isn't America."

Suddenly, most of the students were sobbing, wrenching, guttural sounds that rose up from a depth of trauma that was centuries old, an ache these young people had tucked down inside themselves in order to get on with the business of living each day as a Black person in America. Now the wall had been breached, and the students were just bawling their eyes out, some of them on their knees, unable to bear the great weight of that day for a minute longer. The young poet's words had opened the floodgates and we were caught on the rushing tide of emotion that everyone had walled off inside themselves for so many hours along the highway.

The young woman kept reading her poem as the chapel filled with the sound of weeping. I will never forget the torrent of sorrow her letter to God unleashed. By the end, everyone was crying, including me. It was our lowest moment since the march had begun, but even this would turn to gold, thanks to Carmen, the healer in our midst, the empathetic big sister and earth mother. Carmen gathered everyone into a huddle and had us hold one another, arms laced together across each other's backs, heads bowed in tight circles, foreheads touching.

"God loves you all," she kept saying in her soft, soothing, musical voice. "You are so worthy, every single one of you, and you are so loved." She just kept affirming us in that way, especially the students, who had seen so much less than the rest of us, and whose heartache was hardest to bear. "We are all here for you, we are all here together," she told them. "You are wholeheartedly loved. God is right here among us, holding you up. Remember who you are, and why you are here. You are a warrior for justice, and everyone is so grateful for your courage, your spirit, your leadership, your love."

Tamika and I call this "Carmen talk," because that's just who Carmen is. She's the person who can take your broken pieces and make you whole again. That night as the tears flowed, she went around that room and hugged everyone individually, every single person, I swear.

And then she lit some sage and said prayers over us, asking our angels to manifest our highest good, to watch over and protect us, to bring us through the journey with hearts filled to overflowing with nothing but peace and love.

And soon, the sobs began to gentle; we wiped the tears from our faces and tuned in to Carmen's voice ministering to our wounded spirits in her magical, healing way. Her very presence made every one of us feel vitally important to the cause at hand. By the time we filed out of that chapel to have dinner on the lawn outside the gymnasium where we would rest that night, everyone was emotionally spent. And yet, we all felt cleansed somehow, as if our tears had washed away the worst of our sorrow, leaving us spiritually strengthened for the road ahead.

––––––––

Those nine days in April would turn out to be the most powerful experience of my life up to that point, and they would foreshadow another march, a much larger one, in my future. Walking down Highway 1 for hours at a time, alongside so many people who had been directly affected by encounters with police, opened up a new understanding for me about what it means to be Black in this country. Along the way, in towns we passed through, local residents also shared their stories. At a rally in a parking lot in Philadelphia, for example, Tanya Brown-Dickerson recalled the night police shot her twenty-six-year-old son, Brandon Tate-Brown, in the back of the head during a traffic stop. I heard so many other accounts of brothers, uncles, fathers, sons who had been brutalized by police; tales of stop and frisk; the shared horror of watching young Black people like Akai Gurley, Rekia Boyd, Ramarley Graham, Renisha McBride, Jordan Davis, and Tamir Rice cut down in their prime.

I thought I'd understood the need for the Black Lives Matter movement before, but on that pilgrimage I began to grasp in a much deeper way why our tense passage through KKK country had left the African

Americans in our group so shattered. Not many Muslims died in police custody, so for me to witness and hold the firsthand experiences of my African American fellow justice warriors was transformative. As so many Black Lives Matter activists had explained: "Our demand is simple: Stop killing us." I felt as if all my notions about freedom and justice in America were being cracked open, showing how inextricably bound were the struggles of all oppressed people, and how critical it was that we work together. For me, there would be no going back from here.

By the time we approached Baltimore on day six, a Saturday, everyone on the march felt bonded. We slept that night at the Empowerment Temple Church, home to one of the largest African Methodist Episcopal congregations in the country. The following morning our group attended Sunday-morning services led by Pastor Jamal Bryant. Toward the end of his rousing sermon, our cell phones began pinging. With so many notifications going off at once, it was impossible not to check our screens—and that's how we learned that just a few miles away, in West Baltimore, Freddie Gray had died.

Freddie Carlos Gray Jr. was twenty-five years old. He'd lived with his twin sister in a sprawling housing project in one of the poorest neighborhoods in the city. On April 12, 2015, the day before we'd set off on our march, six Baltimore police officers had arrested him for possession of a switchblade. Eyewitnesses report that the cops roughed up Freddie Gray pretty badly before they shoved him into a police van, neglecting to secure him with seat restraints. As the van veered and swerved and cornered on the city's streets, a handcuffed Freddie Gray was tossed against the inside metal surfaces. At the end of the ride, he was found in a coma, his spinal cord severed at the neck and his larynx crushed. Paramedics rushed him to the hospital where, a week later, on that Sunday morning as we worshiped in church, Freddie Gray died.

His death would later be ruled a homicide caused by the arresting officers' failure to follow the department policy of securing prisoners with seat belts for transport. The even greater tragedy was that Freddie Gray should not have been in police custody at all. The small knife found on him was not illegal, nor had he been brandishing it in any threatening way. The knife was merely an excuse that the cops fabricated to justify arresting Freddie Gray after he saw them and ran. And why did he run? One of the cops had beaten him up several times before, and Freddie decided he didn't want to be whaled on again.

Now, as congregants poured out of the church at the end of the service, our group huddled in the parking lot to discuss how to respond to the news that Freddie Gray had succumbed to his injuries. In the end, Tamika made the call.

"Okay, everybody," she announced, "we're going to reroute our march to the western district of Baltimore. No way can we keep going knowing that Freddie Gray died here and we didn't figure out how to stand up for him. It would be unconscionable for us to ignore his death when we're out here marching for his life. We are all Freddie Gray's family right now. So we're going!"

Everyone shouted their agreement and we thanked our church hosts, gathered our belongings, and packed up the buses. Our navigators plotted our new route on GPS, and we all set off on foot to join the demonstration that we'd learned from social media was already happening outside the police precinct in Freddie's neighborhood.

The streets we walked through in the western district were more desolate than anything I'd ever witnessed, with buildings blown out, windows shattered, doorways boarded up, and potholes as deep as my thigh. Being from Brooklyn, I'd seen poverty, but nothing as bleak as this. We passed an elementary school with every window covered by plywood, yet the school was open for business. And on blocks where every building seemed abandoned, there might be an elderly person sitting out on a stoop, or a mother walking with her children, clues that some of the crumbling, roofless structures still housed residents.

At last we arrived at the police precinct, which sat on a narrow residential street that was packed with Freddie Gray's relatives, neighbors, friends, and other supporters. Seventy or eighty people milled around outside the low-slung redbrick precinct house, their emotions raw and fevered.

"Fuck the police!" some people yelled.

"Justice for Freddie Gray!" others cried.

"Freddie was my brother! You fucking murdered him!" a man shouted, his arms around a woman who was crumpled against him, her face pressed into his shoulder.

Amid the cries, the chants, the sobbing, and the yelling, we mixed with the crowd, introducing ourselves, explaining that we had been marching against police brutality when we heard about Freddie. "We're here to stand with you," we said. "We want justice for Freddie, too."

After we'd been there for a little while, one of the police officers involved with Freddie Gray's arrest exited the station and sprinted to his car. The crowd caught sight of him and as if with one mind surged around his vehicle, banging on his windows, rocking his car, howling at him with rage and pain. The mood was dangerous, incendiary, careening out of control. Terrified of what might happen, I looked around wildly, trying to figure out what to do.

Before anyone knew what was happening, Tamika barreled her little body through the crowd of mostly men, all of them bigger than she was. She ducked under their arms, squeezed between them, and pushed past them until she was standing with her back against the window of the policeman's car. I wanted to grab her arm and stop her from wading into that explosive situation, but I made myself stand where I was, trusting that Tamika knew what she was doing when she inserted herself between a crush of angry, hurting Black men and that police vehicle.

She raised both hands above her head, palms open. "I need you all to back up off this car right now!" she yelled over the shouts and cries. "If you love Freddie Gray, and I know you do, then you want justice for Freddie Gray, but this is not the way! If you love Freddie Gray, and I know you do, you do not want to be behind bars today! You are worth more than that. Freddie would not be proud of you if something happens to this police officer. But let me be very clear, I don't give a damn about him. I'm not here trying to protect people who don't care about us, who don't protect us. I'm trying to protect you! You are the ones who matter to me! And I'm standing here right now trying to make sure what happened to Freddie Gray won't happen to you!"

My God, I was in awe of her—all 120 pounds of ferocious courage. I could hardly believe what she was doing, with absolutely no thought for her own safety. As far as Tamika was concerned, these men were her brothers. She could be all glammed up sometimes with her red-bottomed Louboutin heels, but at her core she was a girl from the hood, and these were her people. She'd grown up with them, organized rallies with them, and she knew their rage in this moment was born of sorrow, and so she talked to them as if she were talking to her own family, with fierce empathy and sisterly love.

"I am not protecting this police officer!" she repeated, shouting to be heard above the crowd, "'cause we all know this police officer don't give a damn about you! I am here to protect you! I know you're angry and I want you to be angry, but right now we need to let this police officer go wherever he is going. We don't need more dead Black men out here in these streets, because we've got work to do!"

It was extraordinary to see those men's faces soften, to see their recognition of how much Tamika cared about them, how much she understood them, to behold her instinctive leadership. She took up so little space physically and yet she commanded that crowd with such power and eloquence. She made them feel her love. "You matter to me," she kept saying. "I'm standing here for you."

That afternoon in the western district of Baltimore was yet another pivotal moment on our march. I had witnessed Carmen's motherly leadership in the chapel at Lincoln University, and now I was seeing Tamika's fiery integrity and bedrock commitment to the people she fought for every single day. These two women put everything on the line in the fight for justice, and I felt so privileged to stand with them.

That day outside the precinct, the demonstrators slowly backed away from the policeman's car and let him through.

The sad postscript is that while all six police officers were subsequently indicted, they were cleared of all charges.[2] In the cases of Eric Garner and Michael Brown, no indictments would ever be issued, although the police officer who put Garner in a chokehold would be fired from the force five years after the fact. For many of us who marched that April, it would be a hollow victory. The truth is we're still fighting for justice for Freddie Gray, Eric Garner, Michael Brown, and so many more as the roll call of dead Black men and women grinds on without end.

On Monday evening, April 20, as the Union Temple Baptist Church in Washington, DC, came into view, a chorus of sobs broke from the marchers. We had made it. Carmen, Tamika, and I put our arms around each other, all of us overcome with a complicated mix of joy, sorrow, triumph, pride, humility, and, most of all, *hope.*

Above us, the sky was a brooding shade of violet, ripped every few moments by spectacular forks of lightning. We had marched that day through gusts of wind and rain, and now we marveled at the pyrotechnical display above the place where we would rest our heads on the final night of our journey. I think some of us wept because of all we had been through, and all the stories we had shared. Our bodies ached, our feet bore blisters, and our throats were parched. Still, we had pressed on, crossing rolling farmland and woodland, traveling under bridges and overpasses, along rushing highways and lonely two-lane roads.

The night after the protest in Baltimore for Freddie Gray, we had slept inside the historic Masjid Muhammad ("the Nation's Mosque"), where Malcolm X had once prayed and preached. On the final afternoon, as we approached the West Lawn of the Capitol, our number swelled from a hundred hardy souls to some two thousand strong as people came out to join the last leg of our journey. My own organization, the Arab American Association of New York, had sent a busload of supporters from Brooklyn, and the 1199 union had sent a couple of busloads as well. Our honorary cochairs and a lineup of actors and musicians were also with us on that last day, as were gun violence survivors; immigrant rights advocates; women's groups; Black Lives Matter activists; LGBTQ, Latinx, and Asian American organizations; and hundreds upon hundreds of everyday American citizens.

At the Capitol, we gathered for speeches and musical performances and the presentation of our three-point justice package to members of the Congressional Black, Hispanic, and Asian caucuses. There wasn't a dry eye as a twelve-year-old girl named Heaven spoke to us about her father, Bobby Gross, gunned down by Metro Transit police just weeks before. And later, Georgia Representative John Lewis riveted us all. I had the honor of introducing him, with Carmen and Tamika at my side. As the congressman stepped up to the podium to speak, I shivered at the significance of being on this stage, for this purpose, with this man. I remembered what Mr. Belafonte had said, that we are the descendants of the giants of the civil rights movement, who had marched for our freedom and who were still out here fighting alongside us.

That evening on Capitol Hill, as twilight crept over the west lawn, John Lewis recalled that when he'd marched from Selma to Montgomery on Bloody Sunday, the batons of Alabama state troopers had fractured his skull. "We were beaten, teargassed, trampled by horses. But we never gave up. We never gave in," he told us. "You must never, ever give up or give in. You must keep your faith, keep moving your feet, and keep putting your bodies on the line."[3] And then he thanked us for marching, heartened that a new generation had taken up the torch of freedom and would carry the flame. "We cannot be silent while our brothers and sisters lose their lives," he boomed from the stage. And the crowd roared.

By the end of that year, all three items in our justice package had been introduced in Congress, with the Juvenile Justice Delinquency Prevention Act winning the votes needed to be authorized.[4] The third bill, proposing independent oversight of how police departments gain access to tear gas and other militarized devices of the sort deployed against citizens in Ferguson, did not pass the floor, but President Obama subsequently moved to reform federal guidelines on the provision of military hardware to civilian police departments.[5]

We had posted a significant victory in the fight for law enforcement accountability and oversight, but the larger struggle was still far from won. And so like all the brave and stubbornly hopeful road warriors who had come before us, we would, as Congressman John Lewis had charged us, "continue to walk and work together, until we redeem the soul of America."[6]

Chapter 18

Silence Will Not Protect You

A s the events of the next year would make abundantly clear, the soul of America was going to require the concerted effort of a lot of redeemers. By the start of 2016, the U.S. presidential election campaign was in full fever, with Hillary Clinton and Bernie Sanders duking it out for the Democratic nomination, and Donald Trump nastily baiting a crowded field of Republican candidates. We all know how that turned out, so I won't belabor how the election unfolded. Instead, I want to give a shout-out to Bernie Sanders, the Jewish senator from Vermont, and the transformative effect of his campaign on my Muslim community—and on me.

I was a surrogate for the Sanders campaign, and my inside view of that operation left me with a profound respect and affection for the candidate I came to call Uncle Bernie. While he might sometimes come off as gruff and crotchety, the man has courage, and his heart is pure gold. To this day, Bernie Sanders is powered by an unshakable belief in our nation's capacity to express its highest good, rather than wallow in the muck and tribalism of gutter politics.

My first clue to the tenacious idealism that animated Bernie Sanders's political ideology came when I was introduced to Winnie Wong, cofounder of People for Bernie and mother of the #FeeltheBern hashtag. Through her, I met senior-level staffers who asked me to be an official national surrogate for Bernie Sanders. *You're Muslim and Palestinian American*, they said, *and we want you to bring all that to our campaign. We want to give you a platform, not to recite hollow talking points but to go out there and express what is true for you and for your community. Say whatever you want. We want to know what matters to you. We're reaching out to effective organizers from many different communities around the country, because we want to build a movement that includes the whole glorious spectrum of American voices, represents the diversity of their interests, and understands their needs.*

I'm paraphrasing their words, but that was the gist of what they said.

I was astounded. My entire life, people had told me that to make it in the mainstream of America, I would need to appear "less Palestinian." *Middle East politics is a divisive issue*, they'd say. *It's too controversial. Doors will close if you continue to advocate for Palestinian human rights and make your Muslim faith a central part of your identity. People will say you're anti-Semitic, that you're against the state of Israel.* Yet here were senior staffers asking me, on behalf of the first major Jewish candidate for president, to be a surrogate for his campaign—and to be my whole, authentic, unapologetically Muslim self while doing it. For me, this was momentous, because Bernie was effectively saying to Palestinians, and to all Arabs, *We see you, we believe in your fight, we hear your concerns, and we want you to come into the tent with us.* Since Bernie Sanders's progressive policy positions on issues like immigration, student-debt cancellation, universal health care, and his diplomacy-centered approach to foreign policy already resonated with me, I signed on to his campaign and pledged to do all I could to bring my community with me.

It's worth noting that no other U.S. presidential candidate had ever put a woman in a hijab front and center in a national campaign. I could hardly have been more visible. At political events, I was often the one warming up the crowd and introducing the candidate. It was a far cry from the time when Obama staffers in Michigan had moved two hijab-wearing women out of the camera frame at a campaign rally. Obama had been outraged when he found out, and he'd called the women afterward to apologize. Nonetheless, the message had been sent: The support of Muslims was a political liability. We were not seen as patriotic Americans, but rather as the suspicious "other."

This was true even before 9/11. Muslims have not forgotten that, during her bid to become the senator from New York in 2000, Hillary Clinton returned $51,000 in campaign contributions from Islamic groups so as not to be publicly associated with them.[1] And then there are the Republicans, who routinely deploy the terms *Muslim* or *Middle Easterner* as shorthand for *terrorist*, ginning up fear and antagonism to drive their white xenophobic base to the polls.

Bernie Sanders was different. He openly proclaimed his belief that Palestinians should have a homeland, and that the nation's next president had a humanitarian responsibility to work toward that goal. His push to engage Muslims in the electoral process would lead to a historic political upset in the Michigan Democratic primary in March 2016. Even though Sanders had been down twenty points in the polls, he eked out a victory over Clinton in the state that was home to the largest population of Arab Americans in the country.[2] Without a doubt, Muslims gave him the edge. I had predicted before the primary that Sanders would win. I'd guessed that the polls had missed a whole swath of the state's demographic: Arab voters. Pollsters seldom call people for whom English is a second language, while Muslims, understandably cautious in post-9/11 America, seldom indulge strangers asking their opinions on politics over the phone.

Even in states without a large Muslim presence, the Sanders campaign put me in front of the camera in a way that was unprecedented. A month after the Michigan primary, I was in Wisconsin warming up an almost completely white audience. "I am unapologetically Muslim," I'd declared from that stage. "And yet we are the same because we all want the best for our country. And I know all of you here can #FeeltheBern, too!" The crowd went wild. To have that audience embrace a Palestinian woman in a hijab was something I needed my people to see because, with the exception of Jesse Jackson's presidential campaigns in the eighties, my community had never felt invited into the American political process.

And while other candidates chose media professionals to carry their message in postdebate spin rooms, Bernie chose the community organizers, including visibly Muslim me. He went to mosques, spoke openly about his views on fostering Middle East peace, sought a path to citizenship for the undocumented, and happened to have been born and raised in Brooklyn just like me. Sanders understood that when you reach out in an authentic way to communities that haven't been engaged by other candidates, you just might come up with a surprise. He proved that when you sit with a community and respectfully say, "What are your needs? I want to hear you," you just might get answers.

Bernie Sanders took the time to say to Muslim voters, "I want your support," and he showed that he supported us in return. He would go on to win in Wisconsin and carry several other primary contests as well, but he ultimately came up short in the race for delegates. That summer, Hillary Clinton became the Democratic nominee for president, facing off against the Republican candidate, Donald Trump.

I'd believed in Sanders's potential to lead our country and was disappointed that he would not have the chance. But I abhorred the idea of Trump in the White House, which meant I needed to join the volunteer effort to get out the vote for Clinton. I wanted to do everything possible to ensure that the man who had branded Mexicans as criminals and rapists at the kickoff of his campaign, who consistently instigated violence against Black and brown people at his rallies, and who had called for a ban on all Muslims entering the country would never become president.

That is how I came to be walking through a suburban neighborhood of Cincinnati, Ohio, on a chilly October afternoon, canvassing for votes for the Democratic nominee with a fellow volunteer. In this part of the state, the houses were spaced far apart, many of them with Trump signs decorating their lawns. As we passed one house, I noticed a woman in a hijab come onto the porch and hand a glass of water to a man in a rocking chair. Just as quickly as she appeared, the woman slipped back inside the house. Now I was puzzled, because there was a Trump sign staked in the front yard.

This particular house was not listed on our canvassing route. Nevertheless, I motioned to my fellow volunteer that I'd be right back, and started walking up a long path toward the man in the rocking chair. Standing at the foot of his porch steps, I introduced myself, explained why I was in the neighborhood, and struck up a conversation. I learned that the man's family hailed originally from Egypt and they had lived in Ohio for twenty years. It didn't take me long to ask my burning question.

"So why do you have a Trump sign staked in your yard?"

"It makes me feel safe," the man said with no hesitation.

I nodded, because this made perfect sense to me. In a country where middle school children like my own son were equated with terrorists, living under the cover of Trump in a swing state like Ohio was an act of security, if not survival.

"I get that," I said, nodding. And then I pushed a little more. After all, I had helped Bernie take Dearborn, Michigan, with decisive numbers, and I was eager to make similar progress with the Muslim community here.

"But you're not actually going to vote for him, right?" I prodded.

The man looked around, as if to make sure no one was listening. When he spoke again he had switched to Arabic.

"What if Trump doesn't win?" he asked me. "Who do you think his supporters will take revenge on first? They'll blame us. They'll come for us."

His response stunned me.

When Donald Trump won the election just one month later, this man's words haunted me. How many people had voted for the Republican nominee out of fear of reprisals in their local communities? How many people had pulled the lever for Trump because they understood the potential for violent retribution by his base, which for months had been whipped into a white nationalist frenzy at his rallies? And yet, I knew the Egyptian's surrender to fear was misguided. Rather than averting the dire consequences of a Trump presidency, his silence had helped assure the nation's descent into a nationalist ethos fueled by Trump's virulent rhetoric against all nonwhite people. The result would be nothing less than a new age of tyranny.

———————

I spent most of November 8, 2016—Election Day—in Brooklyn, helping to turn out my community to the polls. Then, starting around five that evening, I was booked for back-to-back interviews with almost every media outlet in the city. "We cannot afford to have this Islamophobic, xenophobic man as president," I asserted in one interview after another. As I traveled between studios, I kept telling myself there was no way that Trump could win the election. And yet there was something in my gut that cautioned, *Don't be too sure.*

Perhaps it was my awareness that Trump's race-baiting agenda, his flagrant promotion of the supremacy of whiteness, had slipped into a welcome groove for his base. And there were many others whose disenchantment with establishment politics had made them willing to draw the wild card. Many of these voters did not consider themselves racist; nevertheless, they calculated that they and theirs had little to fear from the Republican candidate's white nationalist agenda. And why should they not cash in on their white privilege? It wasn't as if they had personally planted their heels on the throats of their nonwhite brothers and sisters, so why shouldn't they vote to elevate their own?

At about ten thirty that night, I was in an outdoor media booth in Rockefeller Center, getting ready for yet another interview. A BBC producer was clipping a microphone to my coat lapel as I watched the election returns on a huge jumbotron set up above the skating rink next to us. I kept waiting for states like Michigan, Pennsylvania, and Wisconsin to start flipping from red to blue, but it wasn't happening. This night definitely wasn't going the way all the pollsters had predicted.

Right before I went on air with the BBC reporter, I saw that my son had called. I tucked the phone inside my coat pocket, thinking I'd call him back right after the interview. Then he called again. And again. The phone kept vibrating in my pocket. This was so unlike Tamir. He was the kind of kid who would call me one time, and if I didn't answer, he'd just move on. Yet on this night, he kept blowing up my phone. I finally lifted a hand to halt my interview. "I've got to go," I told the BBC reporter. "My son keeps calling. Something is obviously wrong. I'm so sorry, but I need to go home to my family."

I removed my mic and handed it to her, then stepped out of the booth to call my son. Tamir answered his phone, sobbing and screaming. "You said this couldn't happen!" he cried. "How could this man be winning? He *hates* us! He hates Muslims! They're going to round us all up if he wins. What are we going to do?"

I was devastated. To hear my big, stalwart seventeen-year-old boy, this steadfast soul who hadn't cried a day in his life since he was a toddler, so emotional because of who might win the presidency just broke me. As I traveled back to Brooklyn in an Uber car that evening, I stayed on the phone with Tamir, trying to reassure him that we would all get through this terrifying moment in our nation's history.

In my mind, I was already organizing a grassroots resistance to Trump's blatantly racist and Islamophobic proposals. But my son's horror that such a man could ascend to the highest position in the land of his birth unnerved and frightened me. As my driver sped through the New York night toward home, my heart hammered in my chest and the blood was a roar inside my head. I felt more afraid for my community than I had at any time since the planes had flown into the Twin Towers fifteen years before. Yet I could not have imagined what was still to come.

Chapter 19

The Women Who Marched

In the days leading up to the election, when I'd knocked on doors in Ohio, I'd met a beautiful little boy named Yahya. The son of a local imam, he had a bright round face and eyes that held far too much worry for a five-year-old. "Sister Linda," he had asked me, "is Donald Trump going to win the election?" I had knelt beside him and assured him that no, that man would not win the presidency; we would not let it happen. His face beamed like the sun broke through when I said that. Moved by his innocent belief in my words, I took a picture of us together and posted it on social media. "Yahya is why we will continue to fight," I wrote under it, "so he can grow up in a country that will embrace his brilliance and all his adorable complexities, and see him like any other child." My promise to Yahya is a part of the reason it took me so long to accept what was unfolding before our eyes on election night.

How many people could not get out of bed on the morning after? How many others pushed forward into the day, disbelief giving way to dread as they mourned the loss of the world they thought they knew? I had stayed up all night with my own children, watching every last vote get counted. My two daughters, fifteen and twelve, folded themselves against me, the three of us wrapped in a throw blanket, our eyes like saucers in the television's unforgiving glare. My son was on the other couch, his elbows on his thighs, his face often buried in his large hands. *His hands are so like his father's*, I thought, my breath catching a little.

Abu Tamir had gone to bed hours before. Knowing his gentle heart, I understood that the tears of his children had been hard to bear. No doubt he'd discerned that the reprieve we were all holding out for would elude us, and he didn't want to see the moment when our hopes would be crushed underfoot. Long after I knew he was right, my children and I kept watching the returns, praying that the votes still coming in would be our salvation. Surely our belief in the promise of America would be rewarded, and this nightmare would dissipate in the brightness of day.

Salvation never came. As the first glimmers of light outlined the rooftops of Brooklyn, we all sat in silence, finally understanding that the worst had happened. The man who had called Muslims "a sick people," and branded Mexican immigrants as "rapists and murderers," and described African Americans as being "lazy" and "low IQ" had won. The man who refused to disavow the support of the Ku Klux Klan, and who had been accused by nineteen women of being a sexual predator, would be our next president, even though, just one month before the election, an *Access Hollywood* tape of him saying he could just grab women "by the pussy" because "when you're a star . . . you can do anything" had played on airwaves from coast to coast.

Despite this man's bigotry and sexism, exit polls suggested that 52 percent of white women had voted for him.[1] Weaving through my grief (because that is what the morning after felt like to me—as if a beloved had died; as if an ideal of my country had been murdered) was sincere bewilderment: How could *any* woman have voted for Trump? How could more than half of white women have endorsed his bid? It made absolutely no sense to me.

At the other end of the spectrum were Black women, 98 percent of whom were reported to have voted against the man.[2] Black women understood what much of white America did not seem to grasp—that while Trump might not target them as directly as he had targeted Black and brown communities, they, too, would suffer from the fallout of his policies, which were nakedly racist, Islamophobic, xenophobic, anti-immigrant, antigay, antidisability, antiwoman, anti–poor people, anti-everyone but straight white men. And not all of them, either—just the rich ones who could pour money into his own coffers. Yet a swath of "Make America Great Again" voters in the economically ravaged heartland had underwritten Trump's candidacy, based on little more than his promise of making whiteness supreme. His red-cap-wearing MAGA base had failed utterly to comprehend that they, too, would be sacrificed to the president-elect's lies and fearmongering, his power lust, shallow intellect, and unending greed.

As shocked as I was by Trump's win, and by the number of white women who had voted for him, the frontline position that Black women had taken at the polls did not surprise me one bit. As an intersectional organizer, I'd developed one tried-and-true principle: follow Black women. Trust Black women. "Ask a Black woman how she's voting and why she's voting that way and then do what she does," I often told people. "Black women will never lead you astray." I reasoned that, as the most marginalized in our society, African American women had felt the pain of oppression most keenly, and those who had historically been closest to the pain had become, for their very survival, the most informed about remedies.

In weeks to come, this particular belief of mine would be tested, debated, and challenged as women of color joined forces with white women who were as dismayed as we were on the morning after to plan a Women's March. Our feminine energy would become a beacon of power and political purpose, a magnificent guiding star pointing the way forward. In nine short weeks after the election, women of all colors and creeds would come together to birth a global movement for change. In the end we were seven million strong, with more than a million souls gathering in Washington, DC, on January 21, 2017, the day after Trump's inauguration. It would be the largest single-day demonstration in U.S. history, a moment when our brilliance and resolve inspired the entire world, and in the light and likeness of so many women, a new resistance was born.

Not that this alliance of women happened easily. Indeed, swamped by our immense sorrow and disappointment at the outcome of the 2016 election, the organizers of the Women's March on Washington would have to dig deep. We would also have to wade into uncomfortable and sometimes passionate discussions about the nature of our sisterhood before arriving at a consensus, and forging a spirit of trust and unity from which we could stake out common ground.

———————

I know that other people might tell this story differently, but as I experienced it, this is how everything went down.

Two days after the election, I was scrolling through Facebook when I saw an event page for a Million Women's March, set for the morning after Inauguration Day. The event creator was calling on all women to stand in unity and solidarity with feminist leaders, Black women, Latina women, immigrant women, queer and trans women—there was a whole list, but it didn't include Muslim women. That really bothered me, given that banning Muslim immigration and inciting fear of Muslims had been such a driver of the Trump campaign. Even when Hillary Clinton talked about Muslims, it had been in the context of national security. I clicked on the event and commented: "This is a great endeavor. I hope you will also include Muslim women and Muslim communities."

My comment immediately went viral. Just a few hours later it had garnered thousands of likes, with people widely agreeing with the sentiment. Then Tamika Mallory called me. "I see you're commenting on the Women's March page on Facebook," she said. "Why don't you come and help us organize?"

I'm getting ahead of the story. Let me rewind.

Almost as soon as the election results were confirmed, women across the country began communicating on social media about a protest, but it was a retired attorney in Hawaii named Teresa Shook who made the first event page. Like so many, she'd logged into a Facebook chat group, wanting to commiserate about what had happened. As comments scrolled up her screen, Teresa had an idea. "I think we should march," she wrote. A million women marching on Washington—how could the world ignore so many women? But most of the people in her chat group didn't see the vision.

"Too cold," they said.

"Too hard to organize."

"Too soon."

Then one woman responded, "I'm in," and for Teresa, that was all it took. She logged out of the chat group and set up a private Facebook event she called the Million Women's March.

By the next morning Teresa's event had ten thousand responses from people who said they planned to attend, with another ten thousand who were interested. Meanwhile, in New York City, a fashion designer named Bob Bland also had the idea for a march, and she, too, had made a Facebook event. A friend pointed her to Teresa's page, which now had fifteen thousand confirmed attendees, and the two women agreed to merge their events, with Bob taking the lead on planning. Suddenly, women from all over the country who didn't know one another were talking online about meeting up in Washington for a protest demonstration the following January, on the morning after the inauguration.

A few days in, some of the women in the chat, including Vanessa Wruble, noticed that the group was all white. Vanessa knew they would need to reach out to women of color for the event to be truly inclusive. As the founder of OkayAfrica, a media platform that showcased the culture and politics of the African continent, she realized what some of the other women did not—that as horrified as they were by the election outcome, the prospects were exponentially more chilling for Black and brown women.

Vanessa asked Michael Skolnik, a writer and activist she knew on the board of the Gathering for Justice, to connect her with women of color who could join in organizing the march. "I know just who you need," Michael told her. "They're a trio, a Latina woman, an African American woman, and a Palestinian American woman, and they can organize in their sleep." He was talking about Carmen, Tamika, and me.

Vanessa called Tamika first, and put her in touch with Bob Bland. Tamika had already heard rumblings about the march: the word in her community was that white women were planning a post–Inauguration Day protest and women of color weren't included. Bob explained that this characterization of the event was exactly what they were trying to get past. Bob happened to be in the hospital in labor with her second child when she met with Tamika. By the time Bob delivered her daughter Chloe, Tamika was fully on board, which meant Carmen and I would soon also be on board, because when one of us asked, the others simply didn't say no.

The first order of business was to change the name of the march. The Million Women's March echoed the name of an action in Philadelphia twenty years before, when Black women had marched to shine a light on issues that affected them. To be fair, the white women organizers hadn't been aware of the earlier event, but in their ignorance they'd created some offense among African American women, who only knew that an all-white group had co-opted the name of a march that had been about the uplift and empowerment of Black women. This kind of miscommunication was why the organizers needed women of color in the mix, not just Carmen, Tamika, and me, but a whole roster of brilliant Black and brown women who now joined us at the table. With so many impassioned women from different backgrounds, we had some fences to mend, and we set about creating an open dialogue that would allow us to do just that.

The group eventually settled on calling the event the Women's March on Washington, in homage to Dr. Martin Luther King Jr.'s historic March on Washington fifty-three years before. Tamika took the extra step of reaching out to Dr. King's daughter, Dr. Bernice King, CEO of the King Center, to get her blessing on the name.

Another issue was the fact that the planning team was loose and decentralized, with members spread across the country and communicating mostly online. We all knew that the effort had to be headquartered somewhere, and New York seemed a logical choice. After speaking with Mr. Belafonte, Carmen offered the offices of the Gathering for Justice. With the Gathering's direct action experience and strong ties to social justice and artistic communities, she knew it was the right move.

Next, the group decided that Carmen, Tamika, Bob, and I would be the cochairs for the march, with Janaye Ingram, a political organizer from New Jersey, spearheading the tasks of securing permits and handling on-site logistics, and Paola Mendoza, a filmmaker, overseeing the onstage program. On any given day, there might be more than forty women in the Women's March headquarters, working on different aspects of the campaign. Over the next few weeks, Mr. Belafonte, Gloria Steinem, Angela Davis, LaDonna Harris, and Dolores Huerta also signed on as honorary cochairs, giving us instant street cred with their various constituencies and making it easier to bring high-profile cultural influencers like Toshi Reagon, Alicia Keys, America Ferrera, and so many others on board. Indeed, almost everyone we approached to take part in the event agreed at once, and helped spread the word to their social media followings. We were starting to understand that this thing was going to be huge—as many as a quarter of a million people might show up. We thought we were dreaming big.

———————

Given that Inauguration Day was only nine weeks away, everyone had a role to play, with Tamika holding us accountable. As Carmen and I knew well, Tamika did not mess around. If someone had committed to a task, she expected it to be done. To pull off such a gargantuan effort in so little time, there was really no other way to approach it. However, some of the white women in our group were not used to answering to a fierce, bristling ball of fire in the body of a petite Black woman. Nor were they used to centering the opinions and issues of women of color, but since we were the ones with the most experience in organizing protest movements, we didn't hesitate to advocate for our communities. That made some of our meetings contentious, but I was convinced that the difficult conversations they provoked were essential to our success.

We had many discussions, for example, about exactly why we were marching. What did we stand for? What was our platform? It seemed to me that many of the white women at our table simply wanted to vent their outrage that a misogynist, sexist, patriarchal racist had been elected president. And to be honest, we were on the same page; we were disappointed and outraged as well. We also knew that so much of what the white women in our group were newly angry about were conditions that women of color had been dealing with for decades. "Look, we're with you," we told them. "But you have to remember that there are communities in this country who have been grappling with racism and misogyny for a long time. So we need to be clear that we're not just marching from a place of rage. We need to be proactive about demanding change."

We agreed that Carmen and I would convene a diverse group that included Jewish, African American, Latina, Muslim, indigenous, and queer women to come up with a platform that would speak to as many communities as possible. The result was the Women's March Unity Principles, which we unveiled in advance of the march. The full text, as found on the Women's March website, begins:

We believe that Women's Rights are Human Rights and Human Rights are Women's Rights. We must create a society in which women—including Black women, Indigenous women, poor women, immigrant women, disabled women, Jewish women, Muslim women,

Latinx women, Asian and Pacific Islander women, lesbian, bi, queer and trans women—are free and able to care for and nurture their families, however they are formed, in safe and healthy environments free from structural impediments.[3]

The Unity Principles projected a vision that would allow people to feel as if they were marching *for* something—namely the right for everyone to live freely and practice their religion and have economic, racial, and social justice. And while we definitely appreciated all the celebrities who'd agreed to perform or speak at the march, we also wanted to hear from the young Pakistani undocumented immigrant, and the woman from Flint whose children were being poisoned by contaminated water, and the Mothers of the Movement—African American mothers who had lost their children to police and vigilante violence.

For the four cochairs, highlighting the experiences of marginalized women was a no-brainer, but we had to help some of the white women in our group understand why that was so important. Women of color had long felt excluded by white liberal feminism. As far back as the first women's rights convention in Seneca Falls, New York, in 1848, the feminist movement had sidelined Black women. The white suffragists who campaigned so vigorously to end their own disenfranchisement at the polls openly embraced racial segregation at their rallies, and forced Black women, who risked their very lives to participate in the protests, to march at the back of the line. Even Susan B. Anthony and Elizabeth Cady Stanton, the heroes of women's suffrage, had opposed the Fifteenth Amendment, which in 1870 gave Black men the right to vote.[4]

They did not consider that justice for any marginalized group was a giant step forward for every marginalized group, or that their own aims could be connected to the needs of others who had also felt the sting of oppression. Certainly there was no instinct for the value of intersectional organizing back then. Instead, white feminists had viewed their liberation only through a white lens, and as far as Black and brown women were concerned, that myopia had persisted to the present day.

It explained why women of color had initially refused to have anything to do with the march. "White women don't respect our voices," they told us. "They don't center our issues." Some African American women had even publicly criticized Carmen, Tamika, and me for signing on to help organize the event. They said we should have known better than to cast our lot with white women when more than half of them had helped elect Trump. Still, we were convinced that this moment could be transformative. We really did believe that white women's liberation was bound up with ours, and the march was an opportunity for them to become true justice warriors for *all* women.

That meant making significant blind spots visible and relatable. For instance, many of the white women in our group didn't see that if you want to be paid the same as a man, you have to reconcile the fact that Black women still don't get paid the same as white women. And indigenous women don't get paid the same as Black or white women. You can't talk about economic justice without talking about racial justice. You can't talk about reproductive rights or gender justice or immigration issues without talking about racial justice. And if you claim to be a feminist who stands up for the rights of all women, then you have to also stand up for—to cite an example that hits close to home for me— Palestinian women in the West Bank and Gaza.

While looking at issues through a racial justice framework was natural for the women of color in our group, it was brand new to many of the white women. They accused us of being divisive by constantly bringing it up. Others completely understood where we were coming from, but they worried about upsetting and alienating white women outside our organizing body who might want to join our march. They didn't see how that concern in itself was problematic, because centering the experiences of marginalized women was not about upsetting white women; it was about helping them to recognize how they were consciously or unconsciously aiding and abetting the very patriarchy that they claimed to be fighting against.

During those insanely grueling weeks of planning, we slogged through many such conversations as we navigated uncharted corners of our sisterhood. I remember one meeting when a deadline for an order of branded merchandise was missed. The person responsible was somewhat nonchalant about dropping the ball and didn't appreciate everyone else's annoyance that now, to get the order completed in time for the march, we'd have to pay an extra $5,000. "I'm feeling marginalized in this room," the woman declared in response to what she internalized as personal criticism. "I feel as if I am being treated like a second-class citizen." And then she started crying.

I was dumbfounded. Yet I could see that what she was feeling was real for her, and so, knowing that my own leadership style can come off as a bit aggressive, I took a deep breath and chose my words carefully.

"I'm really sorry that you're feeling hurt," I said to her. "But I think this is also our moment, as a group that's building a family together, to educate one another about the implications of the words we use. So for example, being able to say 'I feel hurt, I feel unheard, I feel disrespected,' those are absolutely valid feelings and I am so sorry that anybody in this room is making you feel that way. And if I'm making you feel that way, I deeply apologize. But," I continued, "it's not right for you, a white woman, to sit in a room with Black women, with Latina women, with undocumented women, with indigenous and queer women, and say that you feel marginalized and like a second-class citizen. You are organizing with women who have had family members killed by police, and you really have no idea what it means to live in a country where you are a second or even a third-class citizen."

I don't mean to imply that these sorts of clashes of culture and lexicon permeated the whole movement. Our group included extraordinarily conscious white women who would say: "Teach us how to be genuine allies." Many of those women are still organizing with us to this day. But neither do I want to sugarcoat the fact that there were definitely some who complained loudly that three of the four cochairs were women of color, who felt as if we had co-opted *their* movement. Carmen, Tamika, and I knew we had to push through that, because each of our communities was counting on us to pitch a large and inclusive tent, one that would allow the whole beautiful rainbow of women in America to find their place in this march, too.

––––––––

For the organizers, the Women's March would turn out to be the most monumental undertaking of our lives. People have no idea. They think of it as something they just showed up to one day, because they felt that they had to *do something*. Meanwhile, we had devoted every atom of our beings to the planning. We lived and breathed for the cause. I'd worked with Paola Mendoza on developing the onstage program, but my primary involvement was in fund-raising: we had to raise enough to cover security, staging, and production, and to ensure full compliance with the Americans with Disabilities Act, including the construction of ramps and lifts, and the hiring of sign language interpreters. We had to budget for the installation of huge jumbotrons and sound systems, so the people at the back could see what was happening onstage. And we had to be able to livestream the event, which meant setting up hot spots for Internet access. There was also a medical fee for ambulances and other emergency services to be on standby, whether or not we used them. Additionally, there were all the permits, the tents and food for organizers, volunteers, speakers, and performers, and airfare and accommodations for everyone, including every member of a musical artist's accompanying band.

Then there was the cost of branding and merchandise. We had partnered with Amplifier, a design lab that produces art for social change as a way to magnify the voices of a movement and bring awareness to wider audiences. That Shepard Fairey poster of a Muslim woman in an American-flag hijab that you saw people carrying at the march—that was a part of the "We the People" campaign created for us. As a hijab-wearing Muslim woman, I particularly loved that poster and its message, "We the people are greater than fear." For me, those words encapsulated why I do the work I do. We cannot ever allow ourselves to be immobilized by fear.

When all was arranged, decided, and done, we would pay out more than $2 million so that women and our allies could stand shoulder to shoulder in opposition to tyranny and in solidarity with women's rights everywhere. In the process, the self-care mandate that is rule number one in any activism handbook was sorely neglected by practically everyone involved in the planning. The pace of our days left us physically exhausted and emotionally depleted, all the more so because during those nine weeks of nonstop emails, fund-raising and sponsorship meetings, permit coordination, and daily conference calls, we hardly ever saw our families.

One evening, about a month before the march, I was in a hotel room in Washington, DC, with Tamika and Carmen and a couple of other organizers. After a long day of meetings with local agencies, I had collapsed in a chair to catch my breath. I was on my phone, scrolling on Facebook, when I saw a post my son had made. "Couldn't be more hyped right now!" he had written, and posted above was a photo of his first college acceptance letter. The effusive notice not only welcomed him to the next freshman class, but also detailed a substantial four-year scholarship.

I lost it. Suddenly I was bawling, because my son had gotten into his first college and hadn't even called to tell me. *What the hell am I doing?* I thought. *Why am I not home with my family?* My firstborn was stepping into manhood and I hadn't even been there to tell him how proud he makes me. For weeks I had been clocking eighteen-hour days, coming home to Brooklyn long after my children were asleep and waking up when they'd already left for school. I'd been away so much that my own son hadn't thought to share this important milestone of his life.

Carmen and Tamika rushed over to me and held me as I cried. Their eyes were wet, too, because they understood exactly what I was feeling. Tamika hadn't seen her college-age son in months, while Carmen had missed Thanksgiving with her family in California, and even though her beloved father was in his nineties and in frail health, she would miss the Christmas holidays, too.

After several moments, I composed myself enough to call Tamir. I meant to congratulate him, yet instead I launched into a hurt tirade—how could he let me find out this momentous news on Facebook? Why hadn't he called me at once? How could he have excluded me? Tamir listened as I spoke my piece, and then he said calmly, "Mom, you're working hard. You're organizing a big march. This is really not that big a deal." His reasonable tone reminded me of four years before, when he was applying to high school and had written that "Life Is Like a NASCAR Race" essay without ever telling me about the boy who accused him of being good at math so he could grow up to build bombs. I felt much the same way as I had then—distressed that my child did not understand that no matter what I was doing, he and his sisters came first for me.

"Tamir, it *is* a big deal," I told him. "I really need you to understand that. It's a very big deal." Eventually, I worked my way around to an apology for how I had lit into him, and expressed how deeply proud I was not just of his acceptance, but also of the way he always took responsibility for his life. So few people really understood what it took to mobilize communities, but my son had witnessed it firsthand, and he'd tried to give me the space I needed to be who I was, to do what I do. When I was able to see his assurance in that light, my heart swelled with gratitude for him, and for my entire family, who always had me covered.

A few days before January 21, 2017, we all began to realize that the Women's March turnout was going to be huge. Not only was there a main march planned for Washington, DC, but numerous other cities across the country were staging companion marches, and we'd received word that people were also planning to march in countries as far away as South Africa, New Zealand, and even in Antarctica. On social media, photos proliferated of planeloads and busloads of women wearing pink knitted hats with "pussy" ears (in repudiation of Trump's *Access Hollywood* vulgarity), headed for the nation's capital. We also heard that Amtrak had added more trains for that inaugural weekend, because all their regularly scheduled cars were completely booked up, and not by the "Make America Great Again" crowd.

Inauguration Day was as disturbing as expected. The new president's speech was dystopian and divisive, and a dark mood hung in the air. People in red MAGA hats were everywhere in Washington, but mixed in with those red caps were women of every race and age and description, wearing pink knitted hats with peaked ears, arriving on trains and planes, in cars and on buses, flooding into the city not for the new president's swearing-in, but for what came after.

On the morning of the march, the organizers rose before daylight and headed to the intersection of Independence and Third, where the main stage was set up. The onstage program was scheduled to begin at 10 A.M., but we wanted to get there early, to make sure everything would go off smoothly. At five o'clock on that unseasonably balmy January morning, it was still dark outside, and yet, when I walked out onto the stage, thousands of people were already there, holding signs and posters and stretching as far as my eyes could see. Adrenaline shot through me, and I climbed down into the crowd to thank these steadfast souls for showing up. The excitement and love they exuded as we talked and embraced one another was a tangible force, and that's when I knew for sure that this day would be epic. But the sight that moved me most of all was the number of women who were carrying our Amplifier posters, including the one with the Muslim woman in her Old Glory hijab. My skin tingled at the sight of her, because in my country, on this day, a Muslim woman in a hijab had become a potent symbol of American freedom.

Seven million people around the world marched for freedom that day, with 1.2 million of us in Washington. People had traveled from every corner of our nation to be there, and they'd transformed the murk and gloom of the previous day's inaugural proceedings into a movement for change that was hopeful, brilliant, and sustaining.

When it was my turn to go up on that stage, my mother and my three children were beside me. We could barely contain our wonder. As I took the mic, I looked out over the sea of pink hats and homemade signs and those beautifully rendered "We the People" posters of brown and Black women, and I couldn't see to the end of the crowd. People were spread out in peaceful protest to the farthest horizon and beyond. Standing up there in my hijab, I felt a great joy and pride in being able to visibly represent the millions of Muslim women who marched with us, and the millions upon millions of my people around the globe who were watching the live broadcast. Among them, I knew, were members of my own family, gathered around a television set in Palestine, cheering us on.

I would tell the crowd that morning that I was my Palestinian grandmother's wildest dream. "*Assalamu alaikum*, may peace be upon you, brothers and sisters," I began as I introduced myself as one of the cochairs of the march. "I stand here before you unapologetically Muslim American, unapologetically Palestinian American, unapologetically from Brooklyn, New York . . . Sisters and brothers, you are my hope for my community."

I went on to declare my resistance to a president who "won an election on the backs of Muslims and Black people and undocumented people and Mexicans and people with disabilities and on the backs of women," even as I pointed out that "the very things that you are outraged by during this election season—the Muslim registry program, the banning of the Muslims, the dehumanization of the community that I come from—has been our reality for the past fifteen years." The tone that I used, my defiance and confidence on that stage, made me an emblem of resistance as much as every other woman who stood up that day and refused to step quietly aside. We had put the forces of hate and division on notice that we were marching to center stage, and they'd better get ready because the reckoning was here, and we would bring our sisters, mothers, and daughters along with us, and the men who were our allies, and together we would change the world.

Chapter 20

Stand with the Dreamers

The backlash came almost at once. By the time I woke up on the Monday morning after the March, there was already a furious defamation campaign against me—far-right Islamophobes claimed that I was a radical Islamic supremacist, that I was anti-Semitic because I advocated for the human rights of Palestinians; that I wanted to institute sharia law in America because I wear a hijab; that I was connected to terrorist groups. The accusations were ridiculous and untrue, yet they were being circulated through conservative media outlets in a dangerously toxic way. Meanwhile, on social media, people wrote the most despicable things.

"A good Arab is a dead Arab."

"You're getting two bullets to the head."

"Your time is coming."

The hardest part of this torrent of hostility was its effect on my family. "Can't you sue these people?" my son asked in frustration.

My sister Hanady sat next to us at the dining table, frowning at my laptop screen as she concentrated on disabling my Facebook messages.

"But we're trying to catch threats and report them," I protested.

"I don't care," Hanady told me, her face fierce. "Let them find some other way to threaten you. This is just too much. You don't need to read this garbage. Don't even let these people in your head."

Later that night, my daughter Sabreen, who had been lying in bed scrolling through the comments on my Instagram account, burst into my room, distraught. "Why are they saying these awful things about you?" she cried, waving her cell phone in the air. "Who are these people? They don't even know you!"

I went to her, my tall, beautiful girl, and folded her in my arms, one hand smoothing her glossy mane of hair.

"Mom, these people are threatening to kill you," she whimpered. She held her phone up to my face. "Look," she said, "they even doxed you. And they doxed Grandma and Grandpa, too."

A chill shot through me as I saw that not just my address but also my parents' address had been posted online for the crazies of the world to see. Sabreen and I held on to each other for a long time, no longer speaking, our minds roaming to frightening places. I could feel my child's body trembling against mine, and I wondered for the millionth time whether my activism was worth the toll it was taking on my family. How I wished I could shield my children from the avalanche of hate that was now pouring down on their loudmouthed mother, and affecting them. The obvious intent was to neutralize any influence I might have gained through my visibility as a cochair of the Women's March. I had gone from being a local organizer to having a national profile, one that some people found all the more objectionable because I was a proud, hijab-wearing Muslim woman.

Ironically, the ugly clamor grew even louder when a wide range of people stepped up to defend me. As part of this countercampaign— that I did not ask for but for which I was grateful—Bernie Sanders tweeted "Thank you [Linda Sarsour] for helping to organize the march and build a progressive movement. When we stand together, we win. #IMarchwithLinda." Numerous others joined him in supporting me—elected officials, celebrities, authors, Jewish leaders, movement allies, faith leaders, organizations like the ACLU, and hundreds of thousands of regular Americans all had my back. Their full-throated response to the smear campaign against me was heartening: "If you come for @lsarsour, you come for all of us," one reverend wrote. "When, like @lsarsour, what you do counts & you stand courageously for the oppressed, cowards attack you. #IMarchWithLinda," another supporter wrote. "Thank you @lsarsour for inspired leadership and inclusive vision. #IMarchWithLinda because when hate targets LGBT, she marches with us!" tweeted another.

I especially appreciated the defense of my Jewish allies, because the worst parts of the defamation campaign were the stories accusing me of being anti-Semitic because I had called out Israel's human rights violations against the Palestinian people. This particular criticism boggled my mind: As a Palestinian Muslim woman, why would I not want freedom for my own people, as indeed I advocated for the right of all oppressed people to live free? The fact that so many Jews completely understood my position gave me hope.

"#IMarchWithLinda b/c she shows up for me + my Jewish community just as fiercely as she does for her own. @lsarsour is my sister," one woman tweeted. "Hell no you will not attack @lsarsour with your Islamophobic rhetoric. This Jewish female is proud and inspired to #MarchWithLinda," another declared. Soon, my name was trending on Twitter as more and more people tweeted their support of me. They pointed out that for the Women's March, I had worked closely with groups like the National Council of Jewish Women to develop the Unity Principles, and that for years I had organized with Jewish groups that had challenged Israel's treatment of Palestinians.

Unfortunately, this wave of support only incensed my adversaries and made them more determined to destroy me—to delegitimize my role in the Women's March, to silence my calls for the humane treatment of Palestinians, to undermine my work in police reform, and ultimately to make me so radioactive that no one would have anything to do with me. The end goal was to ensure that the universities that invited me to speak on their campuses, the news programs that booked me to comment on issues, and the political campaigns that asked me to be a surrogate for the Muslim community wouldn't want to go near me. But it wasn't working. In fact, the smear campaigns were actually bolstering my national profile, because as the hate rained down on me, all the constituencies I worked with moved to encircle and protect me.

Still, I had to accept that I had become a target of the extreme right, and my life would not be the same. It got to the point where I no longer felt safe in my own city. People who vocally expressed disagreement with my positions were understandable. I'd always expected vigorous debate. It was something else entirely for my opponents to post messages on social media threatening my life. "We have formed a new militia specifically to take you and your followers off the map," one commenter said. "Don't believe me? Remember this post when they come for you."

If the threats against me were unsettling, even worse was the way my adversaries went after my family. My brother Mo worked at a kosher barbecue restaurant in Crown Heights, which was located right next door to where Yaba's grocery had stood for thirty-five years. The owners of the establishment knew and adored my father, and they had watched his children grow up in his store. They'd admired my brother's cheerful outlook and his work ethic, and had hired him part-time in the restaurant while he was still a teenager. From there, Mo had worked his way up to become the manager, and the restaurant's Orthodox Jewish clientele loved him.

But a local attorney, an avowed Zionist and one of my chief antagonists, discovered where my brother worked. He printed up flyers announcing that Mo was the brother of "Hamas organizer Linda Sarsour," and calling for Jews to boycott the restaurant. For weeks this man stood outside the restaurant, handing out flyers. He also had people calling and harassing the owners until, reluctantly, Mo decided to go. Never mind the ludicrous claim that I was a Hamas organizer; how did this man know where to find my brother? Mo is the most apolitical human being I know. He isn't involved in activism of any sort; he's just trying to live his life. Our paths were so different I barely even saw him. So how did my opponents know to go after him?

I would soon discover that I had been under surveillance by more than U.S. law enforcement for almost a decade. According to a May 26, 2018, article in *The Guardian*, which was headlined ISRAELI INTEL FIRM SPIED ON PALESTINIAN-AMERICAN LINDA SARSOUR, REPORT SAYS, a dossier had been compiled not just on me, but also on my family. Noting that I was a loud-and-proud supporter of the Boycott, Divestment and Sanctions (BDS) movement, a global effort to encourage governments, corporations, and universities to boycott Israel over its occupation of Palestine and treatment of Palestinians, the report disclosed that "an Israeli private intelligence firm spied on the Palestinian-American activist and Women's March co-chair Linda Sarsour and her family in an apparent attempt to collect damaging information." The dossier had been supplied to the heads of American universities and, among others, to "American billionaire and Donald Trump backer Sheldon Adelson."[1]

I'd always suspected that the effort to defame me was no random undertaking, but rather a concerted campaign. Now I saw that my opponents were powerfully connected and willing to spend millions to take me down. They were messing with the wrong woman. Carmen liked to say that my hijab is my cape, my superpower. And as I'd told the crowd gathered in the nation's capital on the day of the Women's March, "Fear is a choice." Not only did I refuse to cave in to fear, I actually saw all the right-wing threats, slander, and alternative facts leveled against me as proof that I was making inroads.

Of course, my unrepentant stance only further inflamed my critics. It didn't help matters that I had dared to link the liberation of Palestine to the women's movement in an interview with *The Nation* magazine. "You can't be a feminist in the United States and stand up for the rights of the American woman and then say that you don't want to stand up for the rights of Palestinian women in Palestine," I said. "It's all connected. Whether you're talking about Palestinian women, Mexican women, women in Brazil, China, or women in Saudi Arabia—this feminist movement is an international global movement."[2]

The editors had titled the piece "Can You Be a Zionist Feminist? Linda Sarsour Says No." That alone caused a minor uproar. The week the interview appeared, one of my friends, a rabbi with whom I had often worked on direct action campaigns, called me out of concern.

"Linda, I tried to defend you," she told me. "But you said you can't be a Zionist and a feminist."

"I actually didn't say that," I clarified. "Did you read the piece?"

"Not yet," she said.

"Read it and call me back. I'll wait."

A little while later, she called. "I see what you mean," she said. "I actually agree with everything you said here. It's just the headline—"

"Which I did not say," I reminded her. "Magazine editors have the right to title their stories however they choose."

What I had said, and now reiterated to my friend, is that if you do not believe that Palestinian women deserve equal treatment and the right to self-determination, and that they deserve access to basic health care and to deliver their babies safely in hospitals, then you're not a feminist. Because feminism is about believing in *all* women's rights, all over the world, regardless of their ethnicity or socioeconomic status or religion or the chain links of a fence in Gaza caging them in.

"Who can argue with that?" the rabbi said with a sigh.

The new administration wasted no time fulfilling our worst expectations. Just one week into his term, the president issued an executive order barring citizens of seven majority-Muslim countries—Iraq, Syria, Iran, Libya, Somalia, Sudan, and Yemen—from entering the United States for ninety days, with refugees from Syria prohibited indefinitely. It was the Muslim ban he had promised during his divisive campaign.

I was sitting with a group of colleagues at a training workshop in Los Angeles when I heard. Tamika and Carmen were with me in the room when the word of the ban popped up as news alerts on our phones. I felt so deflated. It hadn't even been a week since the March, and already the president had launched his campaign of hate—and he'd started with my people. "I have to get back to New York," I told the women gathered around me. "I need to be with my family."

Even though we were supposed to be in Los Angeles for two more days, Tamika decided to fly back to the East Coast with me. She and I traveled together to the airport, and as we pulled up to the terminal, an amazing sight greeted us. Thousands of people had swarmed the arrivals building in a spontaneous rapid-response protest of the sort that speaker after speaker had called for just the weekend before. Their signs, too, were reminiscent of the homemade signs carried at the Women's March, as if the current action was a dynamic extension of that global movement.

WE WILL LOVE AND PROTECT EACH OTHER, one sign read.

WILL SWAP 1 TRUMP FOR 10,000 REFUGEES, read another.

And this one, which made me laugh through my tears of wonder and gratitude: FIRST THEY CAME FOR THE MUSLIMS AND WE SAID NOT TODAY MOTHERF***ER!

I truly believed people were still feeling the hope and solidarity of the Women's March, and were acting on that heightened consciousness now. When we had asked people to show up for Black women, for Muslims, for refugees, for the undocumented, Americans had heard the call, and now from all walks of life they had descended on the nation's airports, along with lawyers and human rights activists, ready to advocate for arriving Muslims who might otherwise be turned away.

The following Monday, I became the lead plaintiff in a lawsuit filed by the Council on American-Islamic Relations to prevent authorities from acting on the president's directive. The case, *Sarsour v. Trump*, contended that the executive order condemned and harmed Muslim communities by portraying them as disposed to terrorism. Meanwhile, the American Civil Liberties Union and the National Immigration Law Center also petitioned the courts to halt Trump's Muslim ban pending a review of its constitutionality. In months to come, to circumvent legal action, the president would put forward two more iterations of the ban, with the Supreme Court of the United States ultimately upholding his right to issue a revised version of the order. Even so, my fellow citizens had continued to register their vigorous opposition to the Muslim ban. In a striking turnaround from the usual vilification and rejection of Muslims in post-9/11 America, they had kept their voices loud and their feet marching in the streets, this time to defend my people.

That day in Los Angeles, as Tamika and I waded through the crowd and into the terminal, people recognized us at once. Everyone started applauding, and someone passed me a microphone, and right then and there, I addressed the protesters. "Once this administration comes for the Muslims and the refugees, they're going to come for others, too, but if we stand together their efforts will fail," I told them. It was my usual spiel. I don't think I could have begun to express right then the depth of my appreciation at seeing so many people showing up in support of Muslims.

Later, as I sat next to Tamika on the flight home, I allowed myself to believe that our massive, women-led movement of a week before had propelled the resistance to new heights, and that in my hijab, I had played a part in that. What if I hadn't been front and center at the Women's March? What if there had been no mass mobilization on the day after the inauguration? Would we still have seen the sparked-up civic engagement among people who had never considered themselves to be activists and organizers?

Now imagine if, the day after the inauguration, nothing had happened. Remember that distress and despair people were feeling? What if they'd had nowhere to put those emotions, no way to transform the darkness into hope and promise? Instead they woke up to the Women's March—to seven million people around the world saying: *We stand with immigrants, we stand with Muslims, we stand with all women, including Black women and indigenous women and queer and trans women, and together we are building a movement with people who have everything at stake, and we will move our feet for justice, and win.*

I still believe passionately in this promise, even though there has been a disheartening coda to the story of the Women's March. The backlash that stalked me in its aftermath also ensnared my fellow co-chairs who had helped to create such an epic campaign. Tamika Mallory, Carmen Perez, Bob Bland, and I all found ourselves embroiled in a controversy driven by white women who claimed that we had hijacked their movement—never mind that our mission had been to create entry points for *all* women to be part of the Women's March. A year later we were being accused of anti-Semitism, religious fundamentalism (because I wore a hijab), and financial improprieties that were investigated and found to have no basis in fact.

It turned out that some of the very same white women who had reached out to women of color for help in organizing the march now resented our being the faces associated with its resounding success. The criticism expressed on social media and eventually in mainstream news outlets became so pitched as to feel abusive, especially when leveled by women who had walked through the fire with us in the nine weeks leading up to the march. As some of our white sisters sought to disavow our contributions and malign our reputations, they demanded that we relinquish leadership of the Women's March organization. I could not help but be reminded of how early white suffragists had similarly discounted the efforts of Black women, relegating their participation to a mere footnote in the history of feminism's first popular campaign. Fortunately, as an aggrieved chorus of voices rose against Tamika, Carmen, and me, a robust refrain of other voices, including many white women and Jewish allies and a contingent of nine rabbis, came to our defense, refusing to allow us to be maligned in the wake of a movement for freedom and justice that had galvanized the entire world.

Chapter 21

We Are Not Here to Be Bystanders

Sitting onstage inside Harlem's famed Apollo Theater, surrounded by academic dignitaries at the graduation ceremony of City University of New York's School of Public Health, I felt nauseated. I had been chosen as the commencement speaker, and I was nervous, which was so unlike me. I never got butterflies before public speaking events, but today felt different. It was the afternoon of June 1, 2017, the sixth day of Ramadan, our holy month of fasting and prayer. *Maybe I'm just hungry*, I thought. It was true that my last meal had been hours ago, before sunrise, yet I knew that wasn't the cause of my queasiness. I tried to push away the thought that once I walked out to the podium at center stage, not even my security detail standing in the wings could protect me from a madman who might have sneaked in with a firearm, intent on doing me harm.

When CUNY's dean had asked me to speak, I'd been honored to accept, excited by the opportunity to inspire a new generation of leaders. However, the weeks leading up to this day had been brutal, with the usual suspects mounting an unusually bruising campaign to get me disinvited. Leading the charge was a well-known Zionist assemblyman from Brooklyn's Borough Park, who had long had me in his crosshairs. He'd insisted that I was anti-Jewish and should not be allowed to speak at a publicly funded university. He had gone so far as to send the governor of New York a letter signed (he said) by one hundred Holocaust survivors. As part of the evidence of my anti-Semitism, he pointed to an October 2015 tweet in which I had posted on a photo of a little Palestinian boy facing a line of Israeli police in riot gear and armed with assault rifles. The boy, who could not have been more than five years old, stood squarely in his blue polo shirt and sandals with rocks in his small hands. "The definition of courage," I had written.

"You can't support a terrorist and then be the commencement speaker at a university that my taxes help pay for," the assemblyman had declared in response. He did not think to mention that my tweet was made in a week when more than two hundred Palestinians had been killed in clashes with Israeli security forces, which is why that little boy's defiant stance had moved me deeply. Still, I did not plan to mention Israel or Mideast politics in my speech, and said as much publicly. That did nothing to stop the hate-peddlers from spewing twisted narratives about me.

An impressive roster of Jewish and civil rights organizations and individuals spoke out on my behalf, including Jews for Racial and Economic Justice, and the Center for Constitutional Rights. Brooklyn city councilman Brad Lander sent a letter to CUNY noting that while he and I did not always agree on matters concerning Israel, I had raised more than $100,000 from Muslims nationwide for the repair of desecrated Jewish cemeteries in Missouri, where his own grandparents had been laid to rest. CUNY administrators, too, stood firm in supporting me, and the hashtag #IStandWithLinda was trending on social media.

At a rally in front of city hall, Tamika Mallory answered the nonsensical claim that I wanted to impose sharia law in America. "We support Christianity, even though the Bible says that gays should be blown up," she pointed out. "But we don't agree with that. We don't always agree with everything that is in our religious faith." Then, speaking directly to the assemblyman who was my nemesis, Tamika added: "Do not call her the terrorist when you are the one spewing hate . . . We don't just stand with Linda, we stand in front of Linda. We will walk with her, we will be with her, we will pray with her, we will keep her because she is us and we are her."[1]

I was out of the country when this rally was held, but when I read reports of it in the news and online, my heart was full. I couldn't believe how many people had come out for me, their voices drowning out for the moment the litany of hate. But the opposition was impressively well funded, and it clapped back. A few days before commencement, my opponents staged a rally outside CUNY's midtown center, with a giant platform set up under a #CancelSarsour banner, and wires snaking all over the street to power huge sound systems. The cast of characters wasn't surprising: white supremacist Richard Spencer was in the mix. So was Pamela Geller, who years before had inflamed the Ground Zero mosque controversy with Islamophobic posters in subway stations. Breitbart News enfant terrible Milo Yiannopoulos, who had declared me "a Sharia-loving, terrorist-embracing, Jew-hating, ticking time bomb of progressive horror," was also among the speakers at the rally.[2] Even Aaron Schlossberg, a Manhattan attorney recently in the news for his tirade of hate speech unleashed at Spanish-speaking restaurant workers, was out on the street that day, yelling that my Jewish supporters were "fake Jews."

The whole campaign had been so assaultive that I'd elected to resign my position as executive director of the Arab American Association of New York, to spare my coworkers the continued ominous phone calls. Now, sitting onstage, I scanned the audience, not knowing whether they would cheer or jeer. I was not yet aware that outside the theater, members of Jews for Racial and Economic Justice and Jewish Voice for Peace had turned out to stand in solidarity with me, as indeed they had stood in solidarity with my community for the past fifteen years. In a peaceful demonstration, these allies had assembled at the front entrance of the Apollo to distribute roses to the graduates and their guests as they walked into the theater through a gauntlet of police officers. Each rose was tied with a ribbon bearing a small tag with the words WE STAND WITH LINDA. I would not learn of this deeply moving show of support until after the ceremony, because for security reasons I had been whisked into the theater through the back entrance, where more police officers stood guard.

As the dean introduced me, I glanced toward the wings of the stage, locking eyes with my security detail, drawing confidence from their presence there. On cue, I rose from my seat and walked to the podium. Polite applause rose from the audience as I adjusted the mic, my hands not quite steady. I took a deep breath, smiled bravely into the spotlight, and began.

I had decided to use my platform that evening to honor three white American heroes in Portland, Oregon, who had stepped up a week before to defend two young women of color, one of them wearing a hijab. A white man on a commuter train had been hurling ugly racial slurs at the women, cursing Islam and threatening their lives. Three men, also white, had tried to reason with the raging passenger, placing their bodies between him and the women. As the train pulled into the next station, the angry passenger lunged and stabbed each man in the neck before running away. The other commuters called the paramedics and stayed beside the men, two of them mortally wounded.

I said their names: Rick Best was a fifty-three-year-old military man and father of four. Twenty-three-year-old Taliesin Myrddin Namkai-Meche had recently graduated from Reed College. His smile in photographs was joyful. As he lay dying, a Black woman, a single mother of five on her way to community college classes, knelt at his side. She removed her tank top and pressed it to Taliesin's neck, whispering, "Stay with us. What you did was pure kindness. You are such a beautiful soul." Soon the medics arrived. As they placed him on a stretcher, he said to the woman, "Tell everyone on this train I love them." They were his last words. The third man, a twenty-one-year-old poet by the name of Micah David-Cole Fletcher, mercifully lived.

"What does it mean when we say we are social justice activists and organizers committed to justice and equality for all people?" I asked the graduates that afternoon. "It means we have made the decision that we will never be bystanders." And I added: "In an age of alternative facts, fake news, and emboldened racism and xenophobia, we cannot be silent. We cannot allow the voices of hate and divisiveness to be louder than the voices of solidarity and love."

As I walked back to my seat, the graduates and their guests leaped to their feet in a thundering standing ovation. Relief washed over me. I felt weak and light-headed, and this time I knew it really was from hunger.

———

That night for *iftar*, the evening meal at which Muslims break our daily fast during Ramadan, I joined hundreds of activists and allies from MPower Change, a Muslim-led grassroots social and racial justice organization I'd helped to found, and members of the New York State Immigrant Action Fund. Our two groups had decided to hold that evening's *iftar* outside of Trump Tower on Fifth Avenue in Manhattan, as a form of peaceful protest against the administration's continued anti-Islam rhetoric. We had invited people of all faiths to break the fast with us. By the time I got there from the CUNY graduation ceremony, huge blue tarps had already been laid on the ground between police barricades and the sidewalk, and people of all descriptions had been welcomed into the space.

First, we knelt and prayed and gave thanks for the power and blessings of community, and as soon as the sun dipped below the horizon, people started bringing out trays of food, setting them on tables in our midst. With the fifty-eight floors of Trump Tower looming above us, and a line of police officers looking on, we began sharing plates, sitting knee to knee on the tarps, hijab- and kufi-covered heads bent in communion with blond ponytails, stop-sign Afros, Asian man buns, Jewish yarmulkes, and close-shaved crew cuts. We wore every kind of dress, from tank tops and jeans to business suits and abayas, and everyone was chatting and enjoying a delicious spread of chicken and rice, hot crusty bread, spinach pies, pizza, and vegetables.

At a certain point, I noticed a cluster of people in red MAKE AMER-
ICA GREAT AGAIN baseball caps watching us from behind the barricade.
Maybe it was all the spiritual reflecting I'd been doing for Ramadan,
or the warm standing ovation of the CUNY audience, but I was feeling magnanimous, and keenly aware that despite the racial antagonism
that our current president tried to exacerbate, we were all still God's
creations, which made us brothers and sisters under the skin.

I got up and walked over to the MAGA hats. "Would you like something to eat?" I asked them pleasantly.

They shuffled their feet and cocked their heads at me but didn't
answer. But neither did they walk away. "We have more than enough,"
I went on. "Whenever we order food during a fast, we always end up
ordering a bit too much."

They seemed curious and possibly interested. One young couple
had the aura of newlywed tourists; they seemed poised to push aside
the barricade and enter our blue-tarped dining area. The woman's eyes
met mine, a smile flickering.

"You can help yourself to food," I said, my tone warm. "But the only
thing I ask is that if you come inside the barricade, you must take off
your hat. It is triggering and hurtful to many of us here, so if you come
into this space, I ask that you respect it."

The couple hesitated then, and then smiled and shrugged and shook
their heads *no*. Nor did the rest of the group accept my invitation to
share in our *iftar*. But I did note that their demeanor was friendlier and
less guarded than when I'd first walked over.

Baby steps, I thought.

I nodded politely and returned to my friends and my meal, hoping that at least the people in the MAGA hats would remember that
they'd been welcomed in. And I prayed, too, that they would come to
understand that Muslims are not their enemy, and they need not be
distrustful of my hijab or my culture. Perhaps they would accept, finally,
that people who look like me also call America home, and we love our
country as much as they do, and we want her to thrive.

This is my life now—keeping my voice loud and showing up for social justice causes that might need a hopeful spirit and tireless feet. And so I was once again in Washington, DC, participating in an act of civil disobedience outside Speaker of the House Paul Ryan's office, demanding that he meet with us to hear the concerns of undocumented people. We were there to protest the Trump administration's call for an end to the Deferred Action for Childhood Arrivals (DACA) program that former president Barack Obama had put in place to confer temporary legal status on some seven hundred thousand undocumented immigrants brought to America as children.[3] Demonstrations were happening across the country in the run-up to the March 5, 2018, expiration of DACA protections, as announced by Trump. Ultimately, the Supreme Court would delay the shutdown of the program by up to a year to allow Congress to take action on the DREAM Act, a bill that would grant a pathway to permanent legal status for DACA recipients. I'm convinced that our direct action campaigns, like the one outside Speaker Ryan's office, helped to bring about that outcome.

With me in the halls of the Capitol that day were Muslim and Jewish leaders, joining with the immigrant rights groups and undocumented people, many of them from Central America. I remember there was a little Mexican girl there, maybe six years old, and she was wearing butterfly wings. For undocumented people, butterflies symbolize freedom because they can fly over borders and roam the world. This little girl's butterfly wings were almost larger than she was. She walked up to an imam whom she had heard speaking Spanish—he was a Texas-born convert to Islam—and, gazing into his bearded face and kind eyes, she said, "*Quiero volar como una mariposa*"—I want to fly like a butterfly.

Another imam overheard the request and smiled down at the child from his six-foot-five height. He called over a third imam, also a man of towering height, and the two spiritual leaders lifted the child above their heads and the little girl laughed gleefully as she flew. Everyone clapped and cheered, and the child's mother, looking on, put one hand over her heart and swiped at her wet eyes with the other.

I took a picture. I keep it on my phone because moments like these sustain me. The memory of them, these human exchanges infused with love and optimism, are my armor. They help me confront atrocities like children ripped from their asylum-seeking parents at the southern border and locked in cages for months while their parents are deported without them. The little Mexican girl with butterfly wings, flying joyfully with the help of two imams, also bolsters me when my own life feels at risk, and I am plagued with questions about whether to keep going with the work I do.

Perhaps the worst moment came on November 4, 2017, in Phoenix, where I had been asked to give the keynote at the annual conference of the Arizona chapter of the Council on American-Islamic Relations. As soon as I was announced as the speaker, CAIR-Arizona began receiving threats. "There will be a lot of Muslims and Muslim lovers in one space," noted one commenter on the organization's Facebook page. "Don't waste the opportunity." And a week before the event, a local paper ran a story under the headline LINDA SARSOUR IS COMING TO PHOENIX—AND HATERS ARE LOSING THEIR DAMN MINDS.

On the day itself, as I exited my car in front of the hotel where the banquet was being held, a line of about twenty white men in camouflage clothes and red MAGA hats stood along the curb with AR-15s at their shoulders and growling dogs at their feet. Nearby, a cluster of women in bedazzled Trump T-shirts screamed slurs at me through bullhorns. One yelled again and again that I should have my head cut off, while her companion menacingly slashed the air with a huge American flag.

I kept my head high and my stride bold as I walked past the protestors in my peach-colored formal gown and deep burgundy hijab, my security detail beside me. As the doors opened onto the hotel lobby, I heard a woman screaming into a bullhorn, "Linda Sarsour is a damn terrorist. She's not welcome in Arizona! We don't want terrorist Linda Sarsour here!"

Right then my cell phone beeped. My mother was texting me from Brooklyn. "You got a package," she wrote, and then sent through a picture of a bulky manila envelope with tape everywhere. The sender was "Sarsour for NYC Council," and the return address was on Manhattan's Upper West Side. I knew right away that something wasn't right about that package.

"Don't open it," I texted my mother. "I'm going to call DJ."

My brother was out in the neighborhood riding bikes with his friends. I told him about the package and asked him to go home at once and see what it was. In Yumma's kitchen, he pulled on some rubber gloves and carefully tore the package open. "What the hell?" he texted me, and then he began sending photos of the package's contents. It was a scrapbook of sorts. On the cover was a crudely painted portrait of me under the title *A Jihad Grows in Brooklyn*. Below that the author of the book was listed as—*me*.

I was so confused. *Is this a joke?* But no, it was the opposite of a joke, because now DJ was texting me pictures of the inside pages of this book, and it included chapter after chapter of inflammatory, outright lies about my life. Even more disturbing were the mislabeled pictures of me and various members of my family, personal photos that had never been in the public domain. One image of a cousin was said to be me without my hijab. Swiping through the cell phone photos DJ kept sending, I thought about the men with assault rifles and dogs outside the hotel, and the women with their bullhorns, and in that moment I felt as unsafe in the world as it was possible to feel.

I've often reflected that God made me so tenacious and stubborn because he knew I'd need such qualities in my line of work. I called on those resources now as I marched into that banquet hall and gave my keynote as planned. And I was as unapologetic as ever. "Who cares what they say about CAIR now?" I asked the audience. "Fifty years from now, they're going to say that CAIR was one of the most effective civil rights organizations of all time. It's like how, fifty years from now, people are going to be walking down Colin Kaepernick Boulevard. Sisters and brothers, this is how history in this country works."

The truth was I'd been badly shaken by the appearance of that mysterious scrapbook at my parents' house. After hiring a lawyer to investigate, I would learn that it had been put together by the same man who had previously cost my brother Mo his job at the kosher barbecue restaurant. But that came later. On my flight back to New York that evening, I huddled against the window, wrestling with a crisis of confidence. My organizing work had been born out of love for my community, but again and again it had put my family in jeopardy. That night, I wondered more seriously than I ever had whether I should go on. Maybe it was time to stop doubling down, to step out of the spotlight for a while, until things quieted down.

Then I looked down at my hands, which were absently playing with the wooden beads that I always wore on my right wrist. The beads, given to me years before by my beloved Basemah, had been made from the shavings of olive trees, which grow and thrive on the rockiest terrain in Palestine and live for thousands of years. Remembering Basemah now, I could feel the force of her love flowing through me, and my breath became less ragged, my heartbeat steadier, my mind calm. Touching each olivewood bead on my wrist, I reflected that, like Basemah, I was connected to a strong and resilient people, whose roots grew deep in the same rocky places as those enduring trees. And I thought: *If Palestinians refuse to surrender in the face of the longest military occupation in modern history, how can I bow to the intimidation of extremists who don't begin to comprehend my abiding love for my people and my commitment to justice for all?*

By the time my flight touched down in New York, I was newly resolved. My purpose had always been to protect my children, to make them proud, to do my part to create a world where they and all children could feel safe and cherished, and in which there would be no ceiling on their dreams. This was my single most important task as a mother, and also as an organizer. And so I would not quit. I would do what Basemah had trained me to do. I would keep the flame burning, and carry on.

Love Is Not Done

I was at a faith retreat in Minnesota when I heard about the bombs.

As a senior fellow at Auburn Seminary, I met a few times a year with a circle of fellow activists to share insights and strategies for building multifaith movements. I always welcomed the opportunity to learn from some of the most progressive and morally courageous voices in the Christian, Muslim, Jewish, and Sikh faiths. At Auburn Seminary, we coached one another in the organizational skills and spiritual resilience needed to lead communities in making change. My seminary group had been a lifeline. Time and again these thoughtful faith leaders had helped me to rise above the vitriol that came at me by the hour.

I was glad to be at the retreat on the day the news broke about the bombs. I'd felt grounded by the company of dedicated movement builders like the Rev. Dr. William Barber II, founder of the Poor People's Campaign; Stosh Cotler of Bend the Arc, a movement for justice and equity in the Jewish community; the Rev. Dr. Jacqui Lewis, an advocate of racial reconciliation, LGBTQ rights, and economic justice; Imam Dawud Walid, director of the Michigan chapter of the Council on American-Islamic Relations; Rev. Peter Heltzel, a progressive Evangelical pastor in New York City; and the Rev. Dr. Katharine Henderson, president of Auburn Seminary, author, and interfaith bridge-builder. These warriors for justice helped me to stay centered when we learned that a series of pipe bombs had been mailed to fourteen prominent critics of the current commander in chief, including to former presidents Obama and Clinton and their first ladies, and the offices of CNN, which Trump had decried as "fake news" and the "enemy of the people."

Of course, I knew there was a possibility that I could be targeted, too, so I'd excused myself to call my family, cautioning them to be careful about the mail. I texted them news photos of what the envelopes containing the pipe bombs had looked like, and asked that if any such package showed up, they should leave it outside the house and call the police at once.

At the end of my restorative week in Minnesota, I traveled home on the same day that the pipe bomber was apprehended in Florida. Fortunately, none of his devices had detonated before law enforcement got to them. I'd been back in Brooklyn for only two days and was alone at home when my phone rang. The caller was from a foundation that helped sponsor women's education programs at the Arab American Association of New York. "Two FBI agents were just here looking for you," the young woman on the line told me. "They wouldn't say why."

My anxiety spiked. Adrenaline flooded my senses as the caller described the men: both white, dressed in jeans and sneakers, with puffy down vests over flannel shirts. I was dubious. Didn't government agents usually show up in suits and ties, with an identification lanyard dangling around their necks? And why did they visit one of AAANY's sponsors, and not my former agency itself? I thanked the young woman, hung up, and immediately began making calls, trying to ascertain if the men were in fact from the FBI. If they were, then fine. I'd get my lawyer and we'd talk. However, given recent events, these men sounded like something more sinister. Their descriptions were a closer match to the Trump supporter who had walked into a Kroger grocery store in Kentucky days before and murdered two Black grandparents; or the white terrorist who'd opened fire in a Jewish synagogue in Pittsburgh, killing eleven worshipers just one day after the pipe bomber was arrested. With Trump having recently declared himself a nationalist in the run-up to the 2018 midterms—a declaration everyone understood to be his way of tele-graphing to his base that he was with them on the white-supremacy agenda—I couldn't discount the possibility that some of his more unhinged followers might have concluded a race war was at hand.

I was on the phone with my friend Winnie when I heard a sharp rapping on my door. I opened it to find two men who matched the description I'd been given. I put Winnie's call on speaker, and with my phone still in my hand, I stepped outside, pulling my front door shut behind me. Calculating that I might be safer on the street, I waved at the construction workers renovating the house next door.

"Can I help you?" I asked the men.

They flashed their badges, just the way you see on television. "We're from the FBI and we need to talk to you," one said.

As the former executive director of the AAANY, I'd counseled numerous Muslim families that when law enforcement knocks on your door, you don't answer their questions or go with them until you call your lawyer. And so I took my own advice, telling the men that I would not speak to them without my attorney present.

"That's your right, ma'am," the taller of the two men said. "But we're not here to investigate you or anyone you know. We have information pertaining to your personal security that we believe you should be informed about."

Against my better judgment, knowing I'd be too agitated waiting for my lawyer to get there while wondering what they knew, I caved.

"Okay, I'm listening," I said.

They told me then that an "enemies list" had been found among the belongings of the Florida man who had been arrested as the pipe bomber. The suspect, who'd lived out of a white van emblazoned with images of Trump, along with pictures of the president's critics with gun sights over their faces, had apparently intended to mail his homemade terror devices to everyone on the list—and the next name was mine. Even though the bomb maker was now in custody and the evidence suggested he'd been working alone, the FBI felt it important to notify everyone targeted.

After the agents left, I sat alone in my living room, feeling utterly numb. I was due in Washington, DC, the next day for a press event. My ride would be arriving soon. I got up, packed a small bag, and sent off texts about what I'd just learned to a few colleagues. I decided that since the FBI believed the immediate danger had passed, I'd spare my family this new worry. They knew to be careful with the mail, and I didn't want to give them more cause for concern. They'd already been through so much.

That evening, as I rode down I-95 with three colleagues in a dark car, the numb feeling persisted. Nothing felt quite real. I think now that I was traumatized by the news the FBI agents had given me, and I disassociated so as not to feel fear. I refused to feel resigned or despairing. I refused to feel outraged. While often useful, anger would have been too destabilizing an emotion right then. I needed to think, to plan, to be strategic, because only then could I help to do what John Lewis had charged us to do during our March 2 Justice three years before.

Redeem the soul of America, he had said.

And so, I am calling on everyone who reads this book to join me in the struggle for a redeemed nation, one that will heal its divisions and affirm the sanctity and sovereignty of every life as it paves the way for a better world. And what might that world look like? I often play a game with myself that I call "Fifty Years." In it, I envision the society I fight for with breath and body every single day, the world I want for my children and yours, the world that I tell myself will be our reality within fifty years. Visualizing this world helps make very clear to me exactly why I am out in these streets, organizing communities for justice. Because the world I would have my children and grandchildren inherit bears no resemblance to a Monday afternoon with FBI agents on my doorstep.

Instead, it looks more like what happened on November 6, 2018, the night of the midterm elections. After all the votes were tallied, an unprecedented number of women and people of color had been elected to political office, with more than one hundred women now serving in the House of Representatives, up from the previous high-water mark of eighty-five. The overwhelming majority of them ran on the Democratic ticket, many of them flipping seats from red to blue in states that had gone for Trump in 2016. Among them were Rashida Tlaib of Michigan and Ilhan Omar of Minnesota, the first Muslim women ever elected to the House. Rashida's and Ilhan's victories were more than symbolic for me, as I counted both women as dear friends. Not only had I witnessed their trials and watched them triumph, but the fact that Ilhan wore a hijab while Rashida did not was, for me, a beautiful expression of the independence and diversity of Muslim women.

African American women, Latina women, and Native American women also won big on election night, most of them running on progressive platforms calling for health care for all, tuition-free college education, environmental protections, gun law reforms, and a path to citizenship for undocumented immigrants and refugees. With twice as many women running for political office as in previous midterms, it was clear that the Women's March and our subsequent Power to the Polls voter registration and mobilization campaigns, as well as MPower Change's #MyMuslimVote national initiative, had helped secure the win for candidates who so recently had been outside the realm of what a typical politician "looked like." Without a doubt our grassroots movements had helped to harness the collective power of women to elect public servants who were guided by the values that seven million people across the globe had marched for two years before.

But there is still so much more to be done: for one thing, a disappointingly high number of white women, 49 percent, voted against their own interests by supporting Republican candidates who echoed the policies of Trump.[1] Clearly, some part of our message of intersectional solidarity did not resonate with these women. And so we must find new ways to build that bridge, because until we do, all marginalized communities will remain at risk.

A recent case in point: Just one block from the corner in Crown Heights where my father's bodega once stood, a young Black man, Saheed Vassell, was fatally shot by police. He had been holding a metal pipe when police approached him. Saheed's neighbors all knew that he had bipolar disorder, and was harmless. No one was afraid of him. He used to do odd jobs for the barbershop on the block, sweeping and taking out the trash. He was close to my age, thirty-four, when he died, which meant we would have passed each other often in the neighborhood.

When Yaba heard the news about Saheed, his usually jocular demeanor grew somber. "He must have come into my store," he reflected, wiping a large hand down his suddenly weary face. Yaba thought he remembered the man's parents, too, both of them hardworking Jamaican immigrants.

"There's a protest for Saheed tonight," my father messaged me the next evening.

"I'll be there," I responded.

I was at the office of Justice League NYC with Carmen and Tamika when I got his text. I told them where I was going, and they both said they were coming, too. That evening, on the corner of Montgomery and Utica, hundreds of my Brooklyn neighbors thronged the street. "Mental illness should never be a death sentence!" some of the protestors chanted, while others yelled "Murder!" again and again. Several speakers pointed out that the police could easily have subdued Saheed without killing him. "My son was a good young man," his mother told the crowd. "I want to make sure people know he was good."

And then it began, full-grown African American men coming up to me, asking me, "Aren't you Nick's daughter? I used to see you in his store." Again and again it happened, men twice my size enfolding me in bear hugs, thanking me for being there for Saheed, for them, asking me, "How's Nick?" and "Tell him I said hello." I saw in their faces the ghosts of children who bought quarter juices in my father's bodega after school, boys whose names Yaba knew, whose parents he asked after as he folded down the tops of brown paper bags in his precise, punctuated way. *One of these men could be Jerome,* I reflected, remembering the hungry boy who had shoplifted and was met not with punishment but with kindness and my father's belief that he would do better next time. *No wonder I am an activist*, I thought with a sudden sense of surprise. Even when I hadn't known it, I was being trained.

Now, standing a block from the place where Linda Sarsour's Spanish & American Food Center had served the neighborhood for thirty-five years, I was flooded with memories. I hardly noticed when someone handed me a megaphone, but as I lifted it to my lips, I felt the pain of Saheed's loss, and the conviction that he'd deserved better, that we all deserved better. "Saheed was one of us!" I shouted into the crowd. "We will fight so that what happened to our brother Saheed will not happen to anyone else!"

After I finished speaking, I handed the megaphone to the next person, my eyes searching for Carmen and Tamika on the crowded street. Both women, with fists in the air, were chanting "Justice for Saheed!" Their eyes burned in the twilight. Soon the streetlights came on, illuminating the faces of people I had grown up with in my beloved Brooklyn, and the two women who now marched by my side. As I made my way through the roar of voices toward my sisters, my own fist pumping in the air, no one but God heard me whisper: *This is where I belong.*

Acknowledgments

This book belongs to those who believed in me, the people who shaped and encouraged me, motivated me, and supported me throughout my years. To my family: You have held me up through my darkest moments. You have given me the space to commit myself to this movement because you know I love and fight for you every day with every particle of my being.

To Dr. Ahmad Jaber, who delivered me as a baby and was the first voice I heard saying the call to prayer: you ushered me into the world as a brave, compassionate activist under your thoughtful mentorship and leadership. The Arab American Association of New York will always have a special place in my heart. It's where I stepped into my power and became the movement organizer I am today.

Every time I thought I couldn't go on any further, Faiza Ali and Murad Awawdeh sent me funny memes to reignite my dimmed fire, even as they reminded me where I came from and why this work is my purpose. Tamika Mallory and Carmen Perez are my rocks. Our sisterhood is unbreakable, and without it, and the many profound moments we shared, my story would be incomplete.

As I've traveled the country to raise awareness of social injustices and to organize, my gratitude goes to my MPower Change family for holding down the fort and helping me build the largest grassroots, Muslim-led movement in the country. The Rev. Dr. Jacqueline Lewis and the Rev. Dr. William Barber II, you have been my spiritual center, always a phone call or a text away. We may not share the same faith, but I love you as creations of my God who have shown me the love and compassion that I know your Christianity calls you to.

As attack after attack was levied against me, I remained steadfast knowing that Jews for Racial and Economic Justice and Jewish Voice for Peace would stand boldly in my defense. Your organizations are the embodiment of allyship, and I will never be able to repay you. You taught me that solidarity is not just words but also action.

Rashida Tlaib, you were the activist organizer I strived to emulate as a young person. You showed me how powerful it was to be unapologetically Palestinian American and encouraged me to never tone down my Brooklyn attitude. Thank you, Zahra Billoo and Imraan Siddiqi, for checking in on me and strategizing with me when I felt as if I knew the destination but didn't know how to get there.

To the senior fellows at Auburn Seminary, thank you for your constant prayers and for committing yourselves to a faith-rooted movement for justice. Our time together reaffirmed my own faith and gave me the determination to help build an interfaith movement that centers the most heartbroken people in America.

Winnie Wong, Ana María Archila, and Ady Barkan, you are my movement warriors. You always go where you are needed and you take me with you. When I thought I was too exhausted to get out of bed, your battle cries for justice were all I needed. Eric Ward, you are brilliance personified. You invested in me, you believed in me, and you are available to me in a way I don't always feel I deserve. Maria Mottola, my neighbor and dear friend, you saw my nonprofit leadership before I realized it was my path.

To my Justice League NYC sisters and brothers, you are my superheroes. You fly in at the right time and are ready for whatever fight is to come. You are my protectors and I am brave because of you. I am also grateful to the Women's March team for your work and sacrifices.

Women's March has been one of the most difficult spaces for me to organize in, but it is also one of the most rewarding in terms of how much I have learned and evolved as a leader.

Sister Aisha al-Adawiya, you are the calm breeze on a summer day. Thank you for your pep talks, your wisdom, and your history lessons that have rooted me in my lineage as a Muslim and as a woman. Imam Omar Suleiman, Imam Zaid Shakir, Imam Talib Abdur-Rashid: Thank you for showing up to the front lines when called and for demonstrating the beauty of our faith. You have come to the aid of the most pained and hurt in our society in the path laid by our beloved Prophet Muhammad (may peace and blessings be upon him).

Thank you to the Ross Yoon Agency for pursuing me although I didn't answer emails for weeks because I didn't think I would have time to write a book. Thank you to Dawn Davis, my extraordinary editor, whom I fell in love with as soon as I met her. I knew in my heart that you would be the one to get my story out to the world. Thank you to Simon & Schuster for giving me this platform. The words flowed on these pages because Rosemarie Robotham championed me and used her brilliance to birth this work. Thank you, Rosemarie, for taking me back on my life's journey and for helping me to create a space to inspire others.

I stand on the shoulders of those who have come before me. Sitting at the feet of Harry Belafonte, aka Mr. B, and Ruby Sales, I soaked up your words, your resilience, and your wisdom. You have centered me and placed me on the timeline of a journey toward the promised land.

There are so many other friends who stepped up for me over the years: Patrisse Cullors, Sarab Al-Jijakli, Imam Khalid Latif, Tahanie Aboushi, Manar Waheed, Alicia Garza, Nadia Firozvi, Shaun King, Sunny Alawlaqi, Mohammad Khan, Rama Issa-Ibrahim, Kayla Santosuosso, Ashleigh Zimmerman, Said Durrah, Chris Rominger, Jennie Goldstein, Shahana Masum, Rasha Mubarak, Ahmad Abuznaid, Philip Agnew, Fatima Salman, Steve Choi, Jumaane Williams, Brad Lander, Carlos Menchaca, Aliya Latif, Ali Najmi, Father Khader El-Yateem,

ACKNOWLEDGMENTS

Zeinab Bader, Aber Kawas, Dalia Mogahed, Mark Thompson, Julianne Hoffenberg, Brea Baker, Jennifer Epps-Addison, Cassady Fendlay, Mysonne Linen, Kirsten John Foy, Habib Joudeh, Nadia Tonova, Maha Freij, Sarah Sophie Flicker, Abed Ayoub, Sophie Ellman-Golan, Paola Mendoza, Rafael Shimunov, Jose Antonio Vargas, Alida Gardia, Nihad Awad, Cathy Albisa, Zein Rimawi, Rinku Sen, Dr. Abdul El-Sayed, Dove Kent, Somia Elrowmeim, Amardeep Singh, and many, many more.

To the institutions that have held me up: Arab American Association of New York, MPower Change, Council on American-Islamic Relations (CAIR), Islamic Circle of North America (ICNA), Muslim American Society (MAS), and the Muslim Legal Fund of America—I'm so grateful for all that you do for our communities.

To every activist, organizer, and movement leader, I see you and I love you. The stories I share in this book would not be possible without you. You are the true patriots. You love our country so much that you are willing to sacrifice everything to make it a truly great nation for all people. I am humbled to be making this walk of love and faith with all of you.

Notes

Introduction: What Is Your Jihad?

1. bell hooks, "Sometimes people try to destroy you, precisely because they recognize your power—not because they don't see it, but because they see it and they don't want it to exist," Facebook, June 12, 2018, https://www.facebook.com/bellhooksfans/posts/sometimes-people -try-to-destroy-you-precisely-because-they-recognize-your-powern /10155777244467635/.
2. Chris Geidner (@chrisgeidner), "Hey you people scare-sharing Linda Sarsour's speech, read this transcription, which I just made because you all are trash misquoting her," Twitter, July 6, 2017, 3:28 p.m., https://twitter.com /chrisgeidner/status/883090260619612160?lang=en.
3. Linda Sarsour, "Islamophobes Are Attacking Me Because I'm Their Worst Nightmare," *Washington Post*, July 9, 2017, Opinions, https:// www.washingtonpost.com/opinions/linda-sarsour-no-i-did-not-call -for-violence-against-trump-heres-what-jihad-means-to-me/2017/07 /09/c2acb086-64b6-11e7-9928-22d00a47778f_story.html?noredirect= on&utm_term=.a17fe70db202.
4. Sarsour, "Islamophobes Are Attacking Me Because I'm Their Worst Nightmare."

Chapter 1: The Choice I Made

1. Nassim Hatam and Derrick Evans, "The Iranian Trailblazer Who Removed Her Headscarf," BBC News, produced by Elaine Jung, December

7, 2018, https://www.bbc.com/news/av/world-middle-east-46426844/the-iranian-trailblazer-who-removed-her-headscarf.

Chapter 2: El Bireh to Brooklyn

1. Zack Beauchamp, "What is the Nakba?," *Vox*, May 14, 2018, https://www.vox.com/cards/israel-palestine/nakba.

Chapter 3: Broken Windows

1. Libby Nelson and Dara Lind, "The School-to-Prison Pipeline, Explained," *Vox*, October 27, 2015, https://www.vox.com/2015/2/24/8101289/school-discipline-race.
2. Nelson and Lind, "The School-to-Prison Pipeline, Explained."
3. "2015–16 Civil Rights Data Collection: School Climate & Safety," U.S. Department of Education's Office for Civil Rights, accessed December 29, 2018, https://www2.ed.gov/about/offices/list/ocr/docs/school-climate-and-safety.pdf.
4. Nelson and Lind, "The School-to-Prison Pipeline, Explained."
5. Mimi Kirk, "Staunching the School-to-Prison Pipeline," CityLab, October 31, 2017, https://www.citylab.com/equity/2017/10/staunching-the-school-to-prison-pipeline/544247/.
6. Kirk, "Staunching the School-to-Prison Pipeline."

Chapter 5: Everything Changed

1. Samuel G. Freedman, "Muslims and Islam Were Part of Twin Towers' Life," *New York Times*, September 10, 2010, On Religion, https://www.nytimes.com/2010/09/11/nyregion/11religion.html.

Chapter 6: Our Sons Are Not Terrorists

1. Louise Cainkar, "Special Registration: A Fervor for Muslims," *Journal of Islamic Law and Culture* 7, no. 2 (Fall/Winter 2002: October 1, 2002): 73–101, https://epublications.marquette.edu/cgi/viewcontent.cgi?referer=https://www.google.com/&httpsredir=1&article=1007&context=socs_fac&sei-redir=1.
2. Mark Follman, Gavin Aronsen, and Deanna Pan, "A Guide to Mass Shootings in America," *Mother Jones*, accessed January 2, 2019, https://www.motherjones.com/politics/2012/07/mass-shootings-map/.

3. "U.S. Mass Shootings, 2019," Mass Shooting Tracker, acessed May 28, 2019, https://www.massshootingtracker.org/data/2019.

4. Cainkar, "Special Registration."

5. Cainkar, "Special Registration."

6. "Removing Designated Countries from the National Security Entry-Exit Registration System (NSEERS)," *Federal Register*, April 28, 2011, https://www.federalregister.gov/documents/2011/04/28/2011-10305/removing-designated-countries-from-the-national-security-entry-exit-registration-system-nseers.

7. J. David Goodman and Ron Nixon, "Obama to Dismantle Visitor Registry Before Trump Can Revive It," *New York Times*, December 22, 2016, https://www.nytimes.com/2016/12/22/nyregion/obama-to-dismantle-visitor-registry-before-trump-can-revive-it.html.

8. Michael Powell, "An Exodus Grows in Brooklyn," *Washington Post*, May 29, 2013.

9. Cainkar, "Special Registration."

10. "Canadian Passport 'Meant Nothing' to U.S. Immigration Officials," CBC News, January 13, 2003, https://www.cbc.ca/news/world/canadian-passport-meant-nothing-to-u-s-immigration-officials-1.374872.

11. Cainkar, "Special Registration."

12. Cainkar, "Special Registration."

13. Joyce Purnick, "Metro Matters: Praying for a Son to Be in Jail," *New York Times*, October 29, 2001.

14. William J. Gorta, "Missing—or Hiding?—Mystery of NYPD Cadet from Pakistan," *New York Post*, October 12, 2001, https://nypost.com/2001/10/12/missing-or-hiding-mystery-of-nypd-cadet-from-pakistan.

15. Sharon Otterman, "Obscuring a Muslim Name, and an American's Sacrifice," *New York Times*, January 1, 2012, https://www.nytimes.com/2012/01/02/nyregion/sept-11-memorial-obscures-a-police-cadets-bravery.html.

16. Rose Hackman, "American, Muslim, and Under Constant Watch: The Emotional Toll of Surveillance," *Guardian*, March 27, 2016, https://www.theguardian.com/us-news/2016/mar/27/american-muslim-surveillance-the-emotional-toll.

17. Hackman, "American, Muslim, and Under Constant Watch."

18. N. R. Kleinfield, "Rider Asks If Cabby Is Muslim, Then Stabs Him," *New York Times*, August 25, 2010, https://www.nytimes.com/2010/08/26/nyregion/26cabby.html.

Chapter 7: Basemah, Beloved

1. "Islam Has Been a Piece of the American Religious Fabric Since the First Settlers Arrived in North America," National Museum of African American History & Culture, accessed September 10, 2018, https://nmaahc .si.edu/explore/stories/collection/african-muslims-early-america.

Chapter 10: The Pit Stop

1. Kirk Semple, "'I'm Frightened': After Attacks in Paris, New York Muslims Cope with a Backlash," *New York Times*, November 25, 2015.
2. Pete Donohue, "Group's Ads Link Islam to Terrorism," *New York Daily News*, January 8, 2013, https://www.nydailynews.com/new-york/group -links-islam-terror-article-1.1235963.
3. Linda Sarsour, "Life Is Like a Nascar Race," January 12, 2013, http://linda sarsour.blogspot.com/2013/01/life-is-like-nascar-race.html.

Chapter 11: A Tale of Two Mosques

1. Brendan O'Connor, "The Sad, True Story of the Ground Zero Mosque," *The Awl*, October 1, 2015, https://medium.com/the-awl/the-sad-true-story -of-the-ground-zero-mosque-dc222bd2c02f.
2. O'Connor, "The Sad, True Story of the Ground Zero Mosque."
3. Jason Tebbe, "The 'Ground Zero Mosque' Controversy Was a Harbinger of Our Times," *Tropics of Meta*, March 21, 2018, https://tropicsofmeta.com /2018/03/21/the-ground-zero-mosque-controversy-was-a-harbinger-of -our-times/.
4. Tebbe, "The 'Ground Zero Mosque' Controversy Was a Harbinger of Our Times."
5. Keith Boag, "Money Man," CBC News, accessed January 2, 2019, https:// www.cbc.ca/news2/interactives/sh/wex94ODaUs/trump-robert-mercer -billionaire/.
6. Tebbe, "The 'Ground Zero Mosque' Controversy Was a Harbinger of Our Times."
7. Michael Wilson, "On Staten Island, Haunting Memories of Those Killed by Hurricane Sandy," New York Times, October 27, 2017, https:// www.nytimes.com/2017/10/27/nyregion/hurricane-sandy-staten-island -deaths.html.

Chapter 12: Love Letter

1. Louis Cristillo, "Religiosity, Education and Civic Belonging: Muslim Youth in New York City Public Schools," Teachers College Columbia University, April 30, 2008, p. 4, https://www.edweek.org/media/musnyc report.pdf.
2. Kimberlé Crenshaw, "Why Intersectionality Can't Wait," *Washington Post*, September 24, 2015, Opinion, https://www.washingtonpost.com/news /in-theory/wp/2015/09/24/why-intersectionality-cant-wait/?utm_term= .f10e63715d83.

Chapter 13: Rakers and Spies

1. Mitchell D. Silber and Arvin Bhatt, *Radicalization in the West: The Homegrown Threat*, New York City Police Department, accessed January 2, 2019, p.22, https://sethgodin.typepad.com/seths_blog/files/NYPD_Report -Radicalization_in_the_West.pdf.
2. Matt Apuzzo and Adam Goldman, *Enemies Within: Inside the NYPD's Secret Spying Unit and bin Laden's Final Plot Against America* (New York: Touchstone Books, 2013), p. 127.
3. Apuzzo and Goldman, *Enemies Within*, p. 133.
4. Apuzzo and Goldman, *Enemies Within*, p. 151–152.
5. Jennifer Jenkins, "Bay Ridge Terror Case Raises Debate About Entrapment," The Brooklyn Ink, September 10, 2010, http://brooklynink .org/2010/09/10/14114-bay-ridge-terror-case-raises-debate-about -entrapment/.
6. William K. Rashbaum, "Guilty Verdict in Plot to Bomb Subway Station," *New York Times*, May 25, 2006, https://www.nytimes.com/2006/05/25 /nyregion/25herald.html.

Chapter 14: Your Fight Is My Fight

1. *Floyd v. City of New York*, 959 F. Supp. 2d 540 (2013), accessed January 2, 2019, https://ccrjustice.org/sites/default/files/assets/files/Floyd-Liability Opinion-8-12-13.pdf.
2. Dylan Matthews, "Here's What You Need to Know About Stop and Frisk—and Why the Courts Shut It Down," *Washington Post* August 13, 2013, https://www.washingtonpost.com/news/wonk/wp/2013/08/13/heres -what-you-need-to-know-about-stop-and-frisk-and-why-the-courts -shut-it-down/?utm_term=.c7a38b7d2bb2.

3. Matthews, "Here's What You Need to Know About Stop and Frisk—and Why the Courts Shut It Down."

4. Matthews, "Here's What You Need to Know About Stop and Frisk—and Why the Courts Shut It Down."

5. "The Community Safety Act," Communities United for Police Reform, accessed March 10, 2019, https://www.changethenypd.org/community -safety-act.

6. Fernanda Santos and Michael Wilson, "Police Detain Brooklyn Council-man at West Indian Parade," *New York Times*, September 5, 2011, https://www.nytimes.com/2011/09/06/nyregion/city-councilman-jumaane-d -williams-is-handcuffed-at-west-indian-day-parade.html.

7. Reuven Blau, Jennifer H. Cunningham, Lukas I. Alpert, and Bill Hutchinson, "Councilman Jumaane Williams Arrested After Alter-cation with NYPD at West Indian Day Parade: Cops," *New York Daily News*, September 5, 2011, https://www.nydailynews.com/new-york /councilman-jumaane-williams-arrested-altercation-nypd-west-indian -day-parade-cops-article-1.955030.

8. Kyle Smith, "We Were Wrong about Stop-and-Frisk," *National Review*, January 1, 2018, https://www.nationalreview.com/2018/01/new-york-city -stop-and-frisk-crime-decline-conservatives-wrong/.

Chapter 15: Social Justice Voltron

1. Chloe Reynolds, "Carmen Perez's Call to Action," *City on a Hill Press*, May 4, 2017, http://www.cityonahillpress.com/2017/05/04/carmen-perezs-call -to-action/.

2. Jim Meyers, "11 Facts About the Eric Garner Case the Media Won't Tell You," *Newsmax*, December 4, 2014, https://www.newsmax.com/newsfront /eric-garner-chokehold-grand-jury-police/2014/12/04/id/611058.

3. John M. Annese, "Seven years before his death, Eric Garner hand-wrote a civil rights lawsuit against the NYPD," SILive.com, July 22, 2014, https://www.silive.com/news/2014/07/seven_years_before_his_death_e.html.

4. "Report: N.Y. Man Put in Police Choke Hold Dies During Arrest," CBS News, July 18, 2014, https://5newsonline.com/2014/07/18/report-n-y -man-put-in-police-choke-hold-dies-during-arrest/.

5. Elahe Izadi, "Medical Examiner Rules Eric Garner's Death a Homicide, Says Police Chokehold Killed Him," *Washington Post*, August 1, 2014, https://www.washingtonpost.com/news/post-nation/wp/2014/08/01 /eric-garners-death-was-a-homicide-says-new-york-city-medical-examiner /?utm_term=.15bb18ae1729.

6. Frances Robles and Julie Bosman, "Autopsy Shows Michael Brown Was Struck at Least 6 Times," *New York Times*, August 17, 2014, https://www .nytimes.com/2014/08/18/us/michael-brown-autopsy-shows-he-was -shot-at-least-6-times.html.

Chapter 16: Nine Days in April

1. "Justice League NYC Announces 250+ Mile March from New York City to Washington, DC with Harry Belafonte and George Gresham as Honorary Co-Chairs," Arfaib, accessed March 11, 2019, http://www.arfaib.com /march-2-justice.

Chapter 17: Road Warriors

1. Victor Kappeler, "A Brief History of Slavery and the Origins of American Policing," EKU Police Studies Online, accessed December 12, 2018, https://plsonline.eku.edu/insidelook/brief-history-slavery-and-origins -american-policing.
2. Tim Prudente, "With Prosecutions Over, Six Baltimore Officers Back at Work After Death of Freddie Gray," *Baltimore Sun*, November 30, 2017, https://www.baltimoresun.com/news/maryland/crime/bs-md-ci-officers -back-to-work-20171128-story.html.
3. Alex Q. Arbuckle, "A Long Walk to Freedom," Mashable, accessed October 29, 2018, https://mashable.com/2015/06/20/a-long-walk-to-freedom /#NktOMiOC5iqP.
4. "H.R.1933 - End Racial Profiling Act of 2015," Congress.gov, accessed January 2, 2019, https://www.congress.gov/bill/114th-congress/house-bill /1933/actions; "S.1169 - Juvenile Justice and Delinquency Prevention Reauthorization Act of 2015," Congress.gov, accessed January 2, 2019, https://www.congress.gov/bill/114th-congress/senate-bill/1169/actions.
5. Jordan Fabian, "Obama Bans Some Transfers of Military Hardware to Police," *The Hill*, May 18, 2015, https://thehill.com/homenews/admin istration/242346-obama-limiting-military-hardware-to-police-depart ments.
6. Arbuckle, "A Long Walk to Freedom."

Chapter 18: Silence Will Not Protect You

1. Dean E. Murphy, "Mrs. Clinton Says She Will Return Money Raised by a Muslim Group," *New York Times*, October 26, 2000, https://www

.nytimes.com/2000/10/26/nyregion/mrs-clinton-says-she-will-return
-money-raised-by-a-muslim-group.html.

2. Kathleen Gray and Todd Spangler, "How Bernie Sanders Won Michigan," *Detroit Free Press*, March 9, 2016, https://www.freep.com/story/news /politics/2016/03/09/high-turnout-late-deciding-voters-give-bernie -sanders-michigan-primary/81527800/.

Chapter 19: The Women Who Marched

1. Eugene Scott, "White Women Helped Elect Trump. Now He's Losing Their Support," *Washington Post*, January 22, 2018, https://www.wash ingtonpost.com/news/the-fix/wp/2018/01/22/white-women-helped -elect-trump-now-hes-losing-their-support/?utm_term=.fa06f95f8eca.
2. "An Examination of the 2016 Electorate, Based on Validated Voters," Pew Research Center, accessed January 2, 2019, http://www.people-press.org/2018 /08/09/an-examination-of-the-2016-electorate-based-on-validated-voters/.
3. "Mission and Principles," Women's March, accessed November 4, 2018, https://womensmarch.com/mission-and-principles.
4. Lori Adelman, "How the Women's March Could Resurrect the Democratic Party," *New York Times*, January 20, 2017.

Chapter 20: Stand with the Dreamers

1. Oliver Holmes, "Israeli Intel Firm Spied on Palestinian-American Linda Sarsour, Report Says," *Guardian*, May 26, 2018, https://www .theguardian.com/us-news/2018/may/25/linda-sarsour-israeli-intel-firm -spied-palestinian-american.
2. Collier Meyerson, "Can You Be a Zionist Feminist? Linda Sarsour Says No," *The Nation*, March 13, 2017, https://www.thenation.com/article /can-you-be-a-zionist-feminist-linda-sarsour-says-no/.

Chapter 21: We Are Not Here to Be Bystanders

1. Madina Toure, "'She Is Us and We Are Her': Pols and Activists Rally to Support Activist Linda Sarsour's CUNY Speech," *Observer*, May 8, 2017, https://observer.com/2017/05/linda-sarsour-cuny-commencement -solidarity-rally/.
2. Eli Rosenberg, "A Muslim-American Activist's Speech Raises Ire Even Before It's Delivered," *New York Times*, May 26, 2017, https://www.nytimes .com/2017/05/26/nyregion/linda-sarsour-cuny-speech-protests.html.

3. Editorial Board, "The Fates of 700,000 'Dreamers' Hang in the Balance. This One Should Not Be Hard for Congress," *Washington Post*, November 26, 2017, https://www.washingtonpost.com/opinions/the-fates
-of-700000-dreamers-hang-in-the-balance-this-one-should-not-be-hard
-for-congress/2017/11/26/60284f62-cbd9-11e7-8321-481fd63f174d
_story.html?utm_term=.d3c9d0252bc7.

Epilogue: Love Is Not Done

1. Janie Velencia, "The 2018 Gender Gap Was Huge," FiveThirtyEight, November 9, 2018, https://fivethirtyeight.com/features/the-2018-gender
-gap-was-huge/.